The 3 Secrets of Attentional Leadership

THE 3 SECRETS OF
Attentional Leadership

How to Optimize Your Performance, Influence, and Leadership from the Inside-Out

Bruce H. Jackson

Advance Praise

"Being in the zone is what the Olympics are all about. The three secrets found within this book will help you discover and focus on that 'one thing' like an Olympian."
—Noelle Pikus-Pace, US Olympian (Skeleton)

"Dr. Bruce Jackson is an international expert in leadership and optimal performance. His new book offers effective and essential skills for improving performance. I recommend it to parents, teachers, coaches, students, and athletes. Get this book and Find Your Flow!"
—Christopher Barden, PhD, JD

"Summiting Mt. Everest with nineteen people, including the first blind man to achieve the feat, is about knowing your assets and liabilities—both inside and out. In the summit of life, you need to do the same analysis. Read and apply the tools in this book and plan for your personal summit."
—Jeff Evans, Everest Expedition Leader, speaker, physician assistant

"Going far beyond theory, this book breaks down the process of high performance into steps any dedicated person can accomplish."
—Susan K. Perry, PhD, author of *Writing in Flow*

"The 3 Secrets of Attentional Leadership is dedicated to helping you identify common factors of high performance. It's a must-read for people interested in beginning their self-development journey."
—Alan Fine, CEO/President, InsideOut Development

"No fluff. No psychobabble. Just a solid, transformational guide for life and leadership."
—Dr. Kerry Joels, International Organizational Consultant

"Having worked with the world's best performers, I can tell you that while everyone is unique, the process toward mastery is very much the same. In this book, Bruce gives you a front row seat into your own process and the steering wheel to drive toward self-mastery, higher performance, and greater influence."
—Dr. Leonard Zaichkowsky, Retired Professor Boston University. Author of *The Playmakers Advantage* and *The Playmakers Decisions: The Science of Clutch Plays, Mental Mistakes,* and *Athlete Cognition*

"The 3 Secrets to Attentional Leadership offers a road map that will benefit newcomers to self-development and seasoned leaders who are looking to coach themselves toward breakthrough."
—Rod B. Streets, MPA, CMA, CFM
Chief Financial Officer, Alterman

"The Attentional Leadership framework is straightforward and was easy for our managers to understand and apply in personal and business situations."
—Jeff Weber, VP People, Ancestry.com

"It's a treat to have an extremely important, yet complex, subject such as flow made accessible via insightful analysis. This book's practical roadmap enables anyone who is serious about performance to expand their flow."
—Dr. Jack Zenger, CEO, Zenger-Folkman, coauthor of *The Extraordinary Leader* and *The Inspiring Leader*

"Few people have gone as far and as deep studying what liberates people from mediocrity as Bruce Jackson has. Pay attention!"
—Nathaniel Zinsser, PhD, CC-AASP, former Director, Performance Enhancement Program, US Military Academy (West Point).
Author of *The Confident Mind*

"The Attentional Leadership framework extends beyond personal strategic planning. It has been fundamental in guiding our organizational strategic planning, enabling us to pinpoint our key 'WINs' as an organization."
—Linda Michels, Executive Director, American Association of Gynecologic Laparoscopists (AAGL)

To all those who seek to discover the Hero within, those willing to chip away at the rough spots, walk through the refiner's fire, iterate and evolve, and strive to discover their true greatness—the music within—all for the purpose of giving it all away—this book was written for you.

The 3 Secrets of Attentional Leadership
Copyright © 2024 Bruce H. Jackson

All rights reserved. No portion of this publication may be reproduced, stored in a retrieval system or transmitted, in any form or by any means, electronic, mechanical, recording, or otherwise, without the prior written permission of the publisher, except in the case of a reviewer who may quote brief quotations in a review online, print in a magazine or newspaper, or broadcast on radio, television or web-based streaming.

Edited by Ken Shelton
Book design by Adam Hay Studio

Hardcover 979-8-9918624-0-0
Paperback: 979-8-9918624-1-7
E-Book: 979-8-9918624-2-4

BISAC: BUS071000, BUSINESS & ECONOMICS / Leadership

Contents

Prologue	13
Foreword: The Universal Human Quest	14
Preface: Today I Am Born Anew	16
Introduction: Design and Flow of this Book	20
The Three Secrets	21
A Comprehensive Framework	22
Sizzle and Steak: A Pracademic Approach	22
Five Progressive Sections	23

Section I: Discovering Flow   25

Chapter 1: Life-Changing Moments   26
- From Mundane to Miraculous Moments — 26
- A Very Bad Day on the Court — 27
- When Elements Conspire — 28
- What Was Different? — 29
- Do You Find Flow or Does Flow Find You? — 30
- A Proxy for Life and Leadership — 31
- 788,400 Hours: That's All We Get — 32
- Placing Attention with Intention — 32
- The Wisdom of Children — 33
- Absorbed in the Moment — 34
- Racetracks and Pit Stops — 35

Chapter 2: The Nuts and Bolts of Flow   37
- Find or Fashion Your Swing? — 37
- Flow Through the Ages — 38
- Flow: A Brief History — 40
- Benefits of Flow — 40
- Positive Performance Psychology — 41
- Flowing Into Happiness — 42
- Finding Your Flow Through Attentional Leadership — 43

Chapter 3: Experiencing and Understanding Flow   45
- Moments, Arenas and Examples — 46
- Flow: A Universal Experience — 47
- So Many Arenas/So Many Strategies — 48
- Investigating Your Flow — 49
- Flow Factors: Assets or Liabilities? — 49
- Tapping into Anti-Flow Experiences — 49
- Tapping into Flow Experiences — 50
- Navigating Your Headwinds and Tailwinds — 50

Chapter 4: Dissecting Flow—Understanding the Magic Butterflies   52
    What Moments Are Made Of   53
    Flow Factors and Characteristics: The Big 9   54
    Looking Under the Hood of Your Ferrari   59
    Engaging the Adventure and Taking the Dive   60
    Believing in Principles   62
    Splitting Moments into "What" and "Who"   62
    Seeing Flow Through 3, 5, and 15 Dimensions   64

Section II: The First Secret—The One Thing that Moves the Needle on Everything   67

Chapter 5: Alignment 1—Future: From There to Here   71
    Long Future: Missions, Vision & Legacy   72
    Short Future: Goals, Planning & Time Maximation   74
Chapter 6: Alignment 2—Internal: Full Engagement   78
    Spiritual: Principles, Purpose & Virtues   79
    Philosophical: Beliefs, Values & Ethos   82
    Psychological: Thoughts, Images, & Perspectives   86
    Emotional: Awareness, Control & Generation   94
    Physical: Nutrition, Exercise & Energy   96
Chapter 7: Alignment 3—External: Place, Things & People   100
    Personal: Adequate Resources, Optimal Environment & Locus of Control   101
    Interpersonal: Optimizing Relationships   103
    Team: Synergy with Others   104
    Organization: Right Arena   105
    Community: Thriving in the Ecosystem   107
Chapter 8: Alignment 4—Historical: From Then to Now   110
    Short Past: Metrics, Analysis & Reflection   111
    Long Past: Cultivating Successes, Harvesting Failures, & Challenging Assumptions   113
Chapter 9: Alignment 5—Pulling It All Together: Eliminating Interference   121
    Focus: Where, When, and How Long? Strategic vs. Performance   122
Chapter 10: Discovering Your One Thing   127
    Less Depth Greater Light   127
    Four Phases of Self-Mastery   128
    Trading Light for Focus   128
    Leaning Into Conscious Incompetence   129
    Opening and Closing the Aperture   130
    Opening the Aperture Using the ALI 1080° Sweep Assessment   130
    Closing the Aperture Using the FOCUS Planning Process   131
    Narrowing Your WIN's   137
    Three Ways to Boost Flow   140
    Identifying Your "One Thing"   142
    Focus on Your Biggest WIN   143

Section III: The Second Secret—Failing Faster and Better   155

Chapter 11: Iterating Toward Success   156
Langley & the Wright Brothers   157
Five Important Lessons   158
Five Elements of Iteration   160
Five Types of Correlation   161
Measuring Your Progress: Doing and Getting   163
Using Scorecards   163
Identifying the Right Measures   167
Finding Flow Through Intentional Practice   168
Talent Not Required but Mindset a Must   169
Translating Values into Virtues   169

Section IV: The Third Secret—Scaling Flow and Influence Through Attentional Leadership®   175

Chapter 12: Finding Flow in Relationships, Teams, Organizations & Beyond   177
Finding Relational Flow: Winning Gold by Focusing on Others   177
Finding Team Flow: Global Elections Company. IT Leadership Team   179
Finding Organization Flow: International Surgical Society   180
Three-Dimensional Leadership   181
From Notes to Chords and the Music of Leadership   182
All the World's a Stage   183

Section V: Living Life in Flow   185

Chapter 13: Creating a Life of Flow   186
There's No Finish Line   187
One Summit After Another   188
Lifelong Learning & The Greatest Coach You'll Ever Have   190
Building a Life that Flows   191
The Hourglass of Your Life   191
Leaving Your Legacy   193
Living a Life in Crescendo   194
Exceeding God's Expectations   194

Epilogue   196
Endnotes   197
References   203
Afterword: Finding Your Music Within   208
Acknowledgements   210
Appendix A: Big Ideas to Remember   212
Appendix B: Attentional Leadership Resources   216
About the Author   216

PROLOGUE

Inspired is the person who envisions the future yet engages the moment, and does so with the end in mind.

Humble is the person who strives for truth, whose beliefs follow truth, whose thoughts follow their beliefs, whose feelings follow their thoughts, and whose actions align them all.

Immersed is the person who optimizes their arena—aligning with others in the teams, organizations and communities they serve.

Wise is the person who measures progress, analyzes outcomes, and learns from every experience—who cultivates their best, harvests their worst, and challenges every assumption along the way.

Mindful is the person who can see the forest and the tree—placing their attention with intention deliberately on their WIN—attending to that "One Thing" towards mastery.

Persistent is the person who, through struggle and strife, victory and defeat—discovers new truths, and knowledge and progresses toward the measure of their creation.

Dedicated is the person who, as a rough stone rolling, ever engaged on an upward slope—seeks to unveil their music within.

Content is the person who does these things—in the arenas and on the stages for which they have been called—in the service of others—for something larger than self—their legacy affirmed.

Foreword
Universal Human Quest

The universal human quest is to discover and realize our potential. In every arena, the human spirit seeks to identify the unique contributions that it was designed to make.

In my study of effective human behavior and relations I have discovered this: the elements of success are common to all men and women, girls and boys. There are principles and practices that, if understood, can be applied by anyone to maximize their effectiveness on the job, on the playing field, and in life.

In your life you may have experienced moments—even hours, days and weeks—where tremendous focus, meaning, enjoyment and purpose graced the stage you were performing on. You may have discovered that these were special moments where everything just came together and gave you a glimpse of what you were made of and what you were designed to accomplish. You may have recognized these moments as "peak experiences" or "moments of flow." I can attest: Our greatest growth and highest effectiveness come from our best and most profound moments—our *moments of flow*.

When I wrote *The 7 Habits of Highly Effective People*, my objective was to illuminate and simplify the key principles of individual, interpersonal and collective effectiveness. The elements that comprise this effectiveness are many and vast, and yet they are unique and personal to each person. As you read, study, and apply the methods for finding your flow within this powerful book, you will come to understand yourself and your environment more deeply.

Finding Your Flow is a book with a grand goal and purpose: to help raise your level of awareness regarding the building blocks of effectiveness, then to help you sort out these building blocks in order to identify your most important personal development plan of action. You might, therefore, think of this book as a primer for your personal development and leadership training.

The motivated reader who seeks flow to improve performance in any life arena can use this book as a starting point and framework for a lifelong pursuit of self-understanding, excellence, happiness, and for living life in crescendo!

—Stephen R. Covey, bestselling author of *The 7 Habits of Highly Effective People*

A decade ago, my father, Dr. Stephen R. Covey, reflected on the insights from Bruce's inaugural work, *Finding Your Flow*, highlighting the continuous quest for excellence in our lives and in the lives of others. In his latest book, Bruce expands and elevates these ideas with great clarity and sophistication—offering a practical framework and method for uncovering your "wins" and paying attention to what matters most.

My work in trust through the years has demonstrated the fundamental role it plays in fostering confidence and flow within ourselves and our relationships, which is pivotal across our personal and professional lives. While trust in ourselves (and in others) is the foundational factor in building personal, interpersonal, team, organizational, and even community flow—it is but the first of many factors that elevate the human condition.

In this practical book, Bruce invites you to engage in a strategic pit stop and deep dive into the multifaceted elements that significantly shape your own greatness—while simultaneously bringing out the very best in others. Enjoy this journey of self-discovery as you identify your personal brand and elevate the lives of others in the process.

— Stephen M. R. Covey, The New York Times and number-one Wall Street Journal bestselling author of *The Speed of Trust* and *Trust & Inspire*

Preface
Today I Am Born Anew

In Og Mandino's book, *The Greatest Salesman in the World*, Hafid reads Scroll One:

> Today I begin a new life. Today I shed my old skin, which hath, too long, suffered the bruises of failure and the wounds of mediocrity. Today I am born anew, and my birthplace is a vineyard where there is fruit for all. Today I will pluck grapes of wisdom from the tallest and fullest vines in the vineyard, for these were planted by the wisest of my profession who have come before me, generation upon generation. Today I will savor the taste of grapes from these vines, and verily I will swallow the seed of success buried in each, and new life will sprout within me.[1]

So, how do we shed an old skin and start a new life? By placing our attention with intention on the key dimensions that will make the greatest difference and committing to their mastery—for a long-term purpose. As you will come to discover—flow builds upon flow—and success upon success. They are self-perpetuating! Leveraging your attention to find your flow is not only about peak engagement in a chosen arena; it is a way of life—even a gateway to happiness and self-actualization.

The Eye of Horus has long stood as a symbol of protection, perception, and insight in ancient Egyptian mythology. It offers timeless wisdom about the importance of focused awareness—whether on ourselves, our relationships, or the broader world. Just as Horus used his eye to restore balance and safeguard his realm, we, too, must sharpen our focus to guide ourselves, our families, our teams, our organizations, and our communities through the challenges we face.

The Eye of Horus serves as a powerful metaphor for what it means to optimize, lead, and master ourselves—all in the service of helping others do the same. Its many meanings speak directly to what we need to do to address our modern-day challenges:

Protection and Awareness: The Eye of Horus symbolizes the watchful gaze that protects and nurtures. In leadership, this gaze represents constant awareness of our internal and external environments, and of our future in relationship to our past. By focusing on What's Important Now (WIN), we protect our energy and clarity, shielding ourselves from distractions that could sideline our growth and progress.

Balance and Restoration: Horus's eye, once lost in battle and later restored, represents the healing and balance that leaders must cultivate in themselves. As we face setbacks, we must restore our focus and help others do the same, recovering alignment and maintaining the flow needed to thrive.

Holistic Focus and the Six Senses: The Eye of Horus is divided into six parts, representing the senses—sight, hearing, taste, touch, smell, and thought. This metaphor emphasizes the need for leaders to have a holistic focus, fully engaging not just their minds but their bodies, intuitions, and surroundings. Being present in this multidimensional way allows us to lead ourselves and others with full awareness of where we've been and where we're going.

Perception and Vision: The all-seeing Eye of Horus stands for heightened perception and vision—both essential for effective leadership. Leaders, like the

Eye itself, must develop the ability to see beyond immediate challenges, leading with insight and foresight. By scanning the broad dimensions of the future, the internal and external worlds, and the past, leaders align all elements in service of the present moment and its most pressing needs.

The Eye of Horus also offers a timeless lesson in self-mastery and leadership. It teaches us to restore balance, maintain focus, and perceive with clarity as we guide ourselves and others toward greatness. In mastering our attention, we unlock the potential not only in ourselves but also in those we lead, creating a path toward thriving both personally and professionally.

We are all performers. From the athlete, pilot, salesman, engineer, retail clerk, teacher, or anyone seeking to optimize what they do, we all expend energy within our craft to engage, perform, excel, and make a difference. The only difference is the arenas we choose to engage in. While most arenas are technically unique, the principles of peak performance and flow are similar. Whatever insights you gain in one arena can be transferred to others. As you seek to extend your internal and external influence over time, you can reference your flow moments and reflect upon those Flow Factors applied at various moments and times that contributed to each experience. By doing this, you generate an evolving and sophisticated understanding of your current Personal Flow Formula—one that you will use to direct your attention and energies on your next WIN (What's Important Now).

By mastering the principles and practices in this book, you will become a high performer in any arena where you seek influence—even greatness, and by doing so, discover the joy of being at one with your purpose, your craft, and most importantly—yourself.

Your Commitment to Excellence

As I learned from the great Olympic psychologist, Dr. Terry Orlick, no great performance or outcome can occur without a commitment to excellence. No matter how much you dream and desire to become your best, achieving anything worthwhile requires clear commitments, promises, and goals. These commitments clarify your values to yourself, your loved ones, and for purposes larger than yourself. Beyond self-actualization, these relationships and purposes sustain us through our own Hero's Journey.[2]

Start your journey with the three secrets to performing, influencing, and leading from the inside out. Commit to giving your full effort and focus within your most valued arenas and relationships. Consider making a personal commitment:

I, _____, commit to:

- Completing this book.
- Doing the 1080° Sweep™ Assessment.
- Identifying my Personal Flow Formula.
- Defining my first WIN and focusing on that "One Thing" that will elevate my work and life.
- Completing the FOCUS Planning Process.

Choosing a learning path and iterating through it, knowing that this will help me improve my performance, my game, and my life, and discover the best of myself while helping others do the same.

Few have said it better than Theodore Roosevelt at The Sorbonne on April 23, 1910:

"It is not the critic who counts; not the man who points out how the strong man stumbles, or where the doer of deeds could have done them better. The credit belongs to the man who is actually in the arena, whose face is marred by dust and sweat and blood; who strives valiantly; who errs, who comes short again and again, because there is no effort without error and shortcoming; but who does actually strive to do the deeds; who knows great enthusiasms, the great devotions; who spends himself in a worthy cause; who at the best knows in the end the triumph of high achievement, and who at the worst, if he fails, at least fails while daring greatly, so that his place shall never be with those cold and timid souls who neither know victory nor defeat.[3]"

Regardless of your race, gender, age, nationality, beliefs, or how you identify, you have both the right and the opportunity to discover your unique greatness and the deep fulfillment that comes from being fully aligned with the arenas where you are meant to thrive, contribute, and serve.

Introduction
Design and Flow of this Book

Kurt Lewin, the famous organizational theorist, said, "Nothing is as practical as a good theory." And Oliver Wendell Holmes remarked, "I wouldn't give a fig for the simplicity on this side of complexity, but I would give my right arm for the simplicity on the far side of complexity." We might therefore conclude that while good theories are useful, they must be simple enough to apply in everyday life.

Flow theory is based on a straightforward idea: everyone can achieve a profound state of focus and involvement. This state is reached by reducing obstacles—what we'll call "Flow Liabilities" (typically the absence of a factor or skill such as unclear goals, poor resilience, or not learning from mistakes)—and enhancing positive factors, or "Flow Assets" (optimizing a factor or skill such as those referenced).

Whether eliminating a weakness or optimizing a strength, this requires knowing What's Important Now (WIN)—hereafter simply called WIN. This is the essence of Secret #1. But it's not enough just to become aware of the many principles and practices that inhibit or contribute to your flow, you must know how to put them into practice—that is why *Finding Your Flow*® requires the use of *Attentional Leadership*®, which is the skill you will learn throughout this book.

My journey has taken me beyond merely exploring flow theory. I had the privilege of being mentored by the master of the theory, the late Dr. Mihaly

Csikszentmihalyi and many others. I've spent years looking deep into people's experiences, from various disciplines, ages, cultures, and walks of life, to identify the principles, strategies, and practices used to attain and sustain flow in just about any work and life arena you can imagine.

The Three Secrets

After years of researching, teaching, coaching, and consulting with individuals, teams, and organizations, I have come to realize that there are *two secrets to* achieving flow, and they require placing your attention with intention on your WIN, the essence of Attentional Leadership. Yet there is a *third secret* that emerges as you master the first two, and it is this: everything you apply to yourself applies to serving and leading others. It's an inside out journey. The very skills you use to become your best self are the same for helping others become their best self.

The **first secret** requires deep self-reflection and is highly personal: it's about identifying the "One Thing" that, when improved, could significantly impact the arena you are engaging. As you might imagine, there are hundreds of things each of us could work on to improve our flow and performance, but there are a few that matter most given your current circumstances. For instance, you may lack clarity of purpose or vision and placing attention on these would move the needle on your performance the most.

The **second secret** is the willingness and discipline to fail faster and better—or to engage the iterative process on that "One Thing." This is a universal secret—one that all change and success are predicated on. There are exactly five elements to it, and five types of correlation between what you are "doing" and what you are "getting" as you seek change and mastery. When you are clearly focused on your current WIN, say it's clarifying your vision, learning and spending time to optimize it is the price to be paid for making it an embedded Flow Asset.

The **third secret** is the simple yet profound understanding that everything you can do for yourself can be applied in the service of others: that your influence is scalable from the inside out—like moving from notes to chords and chords to music—from a framework of understanding to a system for scaling excellence via influence and directed attention. This principle is equally relevant if you are working from larger scale change and moving inward toward the individual.

When you understand these three secrets your life will never be the same.

Why? Because not only will you have these three keys to optimize yourself and others—you'll also be given the framework, methods, and tools to coach and develop yourself and others for the rest of your life.

A Comprehensive Framework

The first half of this book is designed to help you understand and internalize flow, and to assess your *Flow Assets* and *Flow Liabilities*, identify your *Personal Flow Formula* (to see what's most and least important now), and discover that "One Thing." In doing so note that this book is self-reflective and self-prescriptive—designed to point the way and provide direction while giving you the steering wheel.

As you tour the fifteen dimensions and corresponding **Key Factors**, note that we have built factor-specific exercises and resources for each of them. Because this book is designed to raise your awareness of these many Flow Factors, which I often call them, it is easy to jump into the first one that seems interesting—taking you down a specific path. If that is the case, feel free to take a pit stop at any time and work through any of the Flow Tools of interest to you—or, if you want to be more strategic, wait until you've completed the 1080° Sweep™ Assessment, as it will point you to strategic tools and resources relevant to your current situation. You will find these PDF exercises and curated library of resources on the ALI website: www.attentionalleadership.com.

Sizzle and Steak: A Pracademic Approach

This book seeks to balance the "sizzle" and "steak"—a praca-demic approach, speaking directly to you with clean, simple, and actionable strategies.

Hundreds, if not thousands, of factors influence your flow and performance every day: unclear purpose, minimal feedback, lack of support, a negative self-image, unbridled negative emotions, a bad night's sleep, the weather, a rock in your shoe, uncomfortable clothing, the temperature in the room, what's on the news... The list is infinite. My focus is to help you understand flow at progressive levels of breadth and depth, with dimension and factor-specific resources and exercises to help you get started on a specific learning and practice pathway.

Five Progressive Sections

I designed this book to start you on your journey into flow through the exercise of Attentional Leadership®—a process of expanding and contracting your awareness toward the future, within yourself, within the social and physical contexts that surround you, and your past—all in the service of your present-moment focus. There are five progressive sections.

Section I explores the foundational concepts of flow, a state where you feel fully immersed and engaged in what you're doing. You'll learn how flow can transform everyday experiences and enhance performance across various aspects of life. Through practical insights and strategies, you'll discover how to cultivate flow by identifying and leveraging your personal strengths and addressing any barriers that might impede your progress. This section aims to equip you with the tools to harness flow, improving both your personal fulfillment and effectiveness.

Section II introduces "The First Secret," guiding you to identify the "One Thing" that can profoundly impact your life and work. It explores the Five Alignments—Future, Internal, External, Historical, and synthesis—to strategically refine your Focus. You'll set visions, align personal values, leverage your environment, and learn from past experiences to develop a comprehensive strategy for identifying and cultivating your "One Thing." This is supported by tools like the 1080° Sweep™ Assessment and the FOCUS Planning Process™, which help you achieve peak performance.

Section III unveils "The Second Secret: Failing Faster and Better," focusing on iterative learning to accelerate improvement. Through examples like Langley versus the Wright Brothers, it introduces the five elements of iteration and how to apply them effectively. This section covers measuring progress with tools like scorecards and emphasizes the importance of the right metrics. You'll discover how intentional practice can cultivate flow and why a growth mindset is crucial. By translating values into actionable virtues, you'll learn to turn failures into steppingstones for success.

Section IV introduces "The Third Secret: Scaling Flow Through Attentional Leadership," emphasizing how to extend flow into relationships, teams, organizations, and beyond. You will explore how Attentional Leadership across various dimensions can enhance collective achievements and effective leadership. This section highlights the transformative power of focusing on others and demonstrates leadership as an art form that harmonizes individual contributions into collective success.

Section V "Living Life In Flow," guides you through the journey of integrating flow into every aspect of your life, emphasizing that there is no final destination, but rather a series of ongoing achievements and learning opportunities. You will learn strategies for self-coaching, lifelong learning, and building a life that continually flows toward excellence. This section also explores the metaphor of life as an hourglass and encourages you to think about the legacy you want to leave, urging you to live a life in crescendo, always striving to exceed expectations and achieve greater heights.

Good luck and enjoy the journey.

Section I
Discovering Flow

Chapter 1
Life-Changing Moments

Nobody is perfect, but most of us have had a perfect moment, maybe even a few perfect moments—where there was nothing between "you" and that "moment." Such "flow" moments tend to be fleeting, few and far between. In this chapter, I will give you the insights and inspiration to recognize your own perfect moments—a foundation for the journey ahead.

From Mundane to Miraculous Moments

Most days consist of many routine moments, experiences, thoughts, and feelings. We wake up, shower, brush our teeth, pick out our clothes, eat our breakfast, kiss our loved ones, leave for work, and during the day we are sustained by other habits, rituals and routines.

Occasionally, our mundane thoughts, feelings and activities are punctuated by intrinsically motivating opportunities. These demand our full engagement.[4] These moments of deep engagement often culminate into peak performances—where we are "at one" with the moment.

These experiences stand out from the rest. They look different and feel different. They give us insights into our ability to fully engage in what we are doing, our best performances—even a glimpse of our potential.

Consider the day you gave a big presentation. Or perhaps you were playing golf, running, walking in the park, enjoying a deep conversation or engaging with your children on the playground. And everything came together just as you imagined. Time flew by. You were completely absorbed in this memorable moment, in a state of pure flow, in some *meaningful life arena* (MLA).

These times may be called optimal experiences, majestic moments, peak performances, ideal performance states, the zone, resonance…as you flow into your authentic self in relationship to the thing you are doing or the people who are part of this experience.

A Very Bad Day on the Court

My passion for flow began when I was sixteen years old; a starting point that would eventually lead to the insights in this book. I had a match at the Stillwater Open, a tennis tournament where eight schools competed. As the number one player from my school, I was paired against the number one players from eight of the best schools in the state. Our number two player played all the number twos and so on down the ladder.

Before the tournament, our team faced a small rural school, an event that set the stage for my unexpected lesson in flow. Ready for the match, I encountered my opponent, whose unassuming appearance belied his skill on the court. Yet I started the match with great confidence.

Soon, however, I began to get frustrated. I wasn't playing well, and my opponent wasn't missing much. His style was unorthodox, yet effective—every ball returned, every shot challenged. Soon I found myself on the losing side of the match, making unforced errors, and my thoughts and emotions got the best of me. No longer was I focused on the ball, a game plan, my breathing, or anything else under my control. Rather, I was consumed with frustration, fear, embarrassment and anger. In a flash the match was over, and I was left bewildered, my ego shattered. My opponent didn't win; but instead, I lost. Understanding this difference is essential.

After a cooling-off period, my coach asked me, "What happened?"

"I don't know," I said. "I just stunk it up out there today. I underestimated my opponent's persistence. I got frustrated, my thoughts and emotions were everywhere, I didn't move. I wasn't focused or engaged. I wasn't playing tennis!"

"Well, be ready for tomorrow's tournament in Stillwater. We're leaving early."

When Elements Conspire

The prospect of competing in the next day's tournament felt daunting, an unwelcome challenge following my recent defeat. But I was up early and met my teammates at the school courts. I drove one car, and Carter, our number two player, drove another, and coach a third. Despite my reservations, we embarked on the hour and a half journey to Stillwater.

About thirty miles into the trip, Carter positioned his red Buick in front of my mother's pea green station wagon. I saw some commotion in their car, followed by the rolling down of a window. At sixty-five miles an hour, suddenly, some type of projectile painted red and white, splattered across my windshield. I couldn't make it out at first. A large bug perhaps? "It's a strawberry!" someone said. "With whipped cream!" said another. "They're throwing their lunches at us." It was war! Soon another strawberry came flying, then another, two direct hits and we couldn't do anything about it. We were boxed in. The windshield wipers were working hard, and I was about out of fluid. What a mess. But in any crisis there is opportunity.

"Pull out your lunches, boys," I yelled. "It's payback time!" When I saw an opening in traffic, I took it. We flanked our teammates on the left, and then took the lead position, all windows lowered. Bologna slices were flung, along with everything else we had in the car. We made multiple direct hits, and we could see the look on their faces. Sixty more miles to go and this exchange was just getting started. In the absurdity of our impromptu highway food fight, we found an unforgettable burst of youthful hilarity. Our laughter bubbled over, tears streaming from our eyes as each ridiculous salvo outdid the last. Never had a food fight escalated to such a magnitude on the I-35W highway.

We food-fighters were the last two cars to pull into the tennis complex, and the only two parking spaces left happened to be right in front of the other teams and coaches. It was a kind of karmic payback. All the athletes were lined up and taking directions from the tournament director. Coach was beside himself with anger. Everyone stared at us, not because we were late, but because our cars were covered in food.

Our laughter soon faded under the weight of stern reprimand, yet the focus quickly shifted as the tournament awaited us. We were all assigned to our courts and paired with our opponents. It was about seventy degrees, the sun was coming out, and the day was beautiful. With laughter in our hearts, the mood was set.

As the matches progressed, one eight-game pro-set after another, I noticed something: I couldn't miss a ball. My focus was spot on. I was not only having fun, but I was moving exceptionally well. Nothing was distracting me—nothing from the inside and nothing from the outside. Yesterday was gone, and tomorrow was yet to be. Time stood still. All I saw and thought about was the ball, where it was, and where I was going to place it. Each shot was practically perfect, and before I knew it, I had won the tournament. Eight matches to zero, with less than twenty points lost the entire day! A deep sense of fulfillment surged within me as I reveled in the victory, my efforts in perfect sync with my intentions. It was the first day I was perfectly aligned with the universe—inside and out. Nothing from the past or the future entered my mind. It was just me and the ball, hit after hit—over and over again. I was in the Zone.

What Was Different?

The previous day, I had struggled against an unknown, relatively inexperienced player, and yet this day I walked off the court with a profound sense of personal excellence and control competing against the best players in the state. I sat down and tried to dissect the experience and digest what I had done differently.

Perhaps the morning's light-hearted car to car food volley generated a mood that carried over into my performance. Certainly, I felt happy and calm. It was all part of the security we feel when connecting deeply with friends and loved ones, and right sizing the importance of the game itself. This feeling of calm influenced my mood and my thoughts. No longer was I there to justify my existence or prove myself—a "winner" if I won and a "loser" if I lost. Instead, I could enjoy the moment, play the game, and simply enjoy the process of playing tennis. I didn't have to prove my value to the world through tennis. Letting go of the outcome and everything outside myself enabled me to focus on the only things that mattered: the ball, the court, and playing each point. With this attitude and focus, I was not hindered by unrealistic expectations. It was just bounce-and-hit. The winning took care of itself.

Later, I grasped other perspectives, skills, and tactics to set before stepping onto the court, allowing me to focus on each shot. Continuous technical mastery, of course, but also key internal factors like vision, specific goals, thought and emotional control, perspective, tapping into previous successes, learning from failure, persistence, and more. Whatever is your weakest link, under stress and pressure, it will break—unless you've developed what I call

"Flow Assets" and habits needed to meet those challenges and find yourself in a dance, instead of a fight.

Understanding the game's external factors was equally important: the boundaries, rules, and the strengths and weaknesses of opponents, as well as elements like weather patterns and social support. Time-based factors, such as setting goals for specific points, games, and sets, and paying attention to feedback like statistics and shot percentages, were also critical in adapting quickly.

These same factors became even more prevalent in my college years and later as I had the chance to play world-class players. Although the intensity and rigor of these games were unmatched, the principles and practices were the same—just at a different level. Each time I stepped on the court I gained new insights and used them to find my strokes, my authentic game, but most importantly my authentic self—in flow. But none of this can happen when it's time to strike the ball and your mind is attending to something other than what it should be in the moment.

Through these profound experiences, I realized there are two different types of knowledge and skill sets to master. The first type of knowledge to master was technical: the precise skills required on the court, such as executing a topspin forehand, a slice backhand, spin serve, or drop volley. The second was uniquely tied to Flow or what I call **Attentional Leadership Knowledge**, which includes knowing where, when and how long you need to spend building skills such as: setting goals, maintaining a positive attitude, emotional control, energy management, and more than a hundred others you'll find within this book. I learned that it's one thing to know the mechanics of your craft—yet another to understand the Internal, External, and Time factors required to align to those mechanics. I also learned that it takes **Strategic Focus** (time off the field working on these nontechnical skills) to demonstrate **Performance Focus** in the moment.

Do You Find Flow or Does Flow Find You?

Flow feels like finding your unique place in the world. People describe their flow experience as a peak experience, full engagement, a sense of wholeness, accomplishment, and connection to their talents, engaged with others—even to a higher power and purpose. They testify to the value that flow adds to their quality of life.[56] Flow experiences are universally seen as enjoyable and positive—a testament that we were designed and built to be in flow. It's not so much that we have to "find" our flow as much as we have to remove those things that interfere with it as well as align to those principles and practices that compel it. By nature, we are high-performance beings. When we remove the obstacles in our way and fortify those many gears and circuits that contribute to our engagement, performance, happiness, our quality of life, and our capacity to be generative and to serve are natural by-products. This is a central feature of God's and the universe's plan for each one of us. Why else are we here?

Searching for flow is the universal quest of every performer. And let's be clear: we are all performers.

Researchers, thought leaders, and practitioners from diverse disciplines have contributed significantly to the study of flow. Humanistic and positive psychologists, motivational theorists, existentialists, physiologists, health and wellness experts, neuroscientists, philosophers, spiritualists, and so on. All of them, through their own lens, speak to and look for direct and indirect influences on various systems of flow: peak experience, transcendence, self-actualization, resonance, creativity, happiness, play, and optimal functioning. Needless to say, flow is universally experienced as the simple act of focus and full engagement[7]—our natural and preferred state of being.

A Proxy for Life and Leadership

When looking at flow through a bigger lens, I started seeing the experience, not just for the elite athlete or performer, but as a proxy for life, leadership, and service. Just like flow, *leadership is an abstract idea*.[8] Few people can define it, but they know it when they see it—when they feel it.

The simplest way to understand the word *leadership* is to replace it with the word *influence*. Most people intuitively understand leadership as a form of influence. This puts every one of us in the driver's seat, moving toward something, using our agency to make a difference—however small or large. It puts us all on the field and in the game—whatever our game is. Yet at the core of influence is something even more central—directing one's *attention*[9] by knowing where to place our attention, when to place it, and how long to maintain it—keeping your WIN front and center. Whatever your current circumstances, there is typically something that needs more attention if you are to make the progress you would like to make. You may be struggling to find your purpose, have a clear vision, or to create a plan to get you to your next milestone. What's Important Now (WIN) is dependent on you and the Meaningful Life Arena (work, family, etc.) you are seeking to improve in.

Initially, as an athlete, my primary motivation for finding flow was to defeat ranked players and win tournaments. However, as time passed, experiencing flow in other arenas became a higher priority. While working with children and adults in athletic arenas, I witnessed the many benefits that my students received when knowing what needed their attention most given their current circumstances. Once I experienced flow in my own performance arenas, I began to help others find their flow. I built upon these principles and have applied them within teams and even whole organizations.

It's important to understand that finding more flow in your work and life is not reserved for elite or extreme athletes.[10,11] As you can imagine, the frequency of flow experiences varies greatly among individuals; some encounter it rarely, while others integrate it into their daily lives. Although flow moments may appear random, with increased understanding and deliberate practice through Strategic Focus, you will, over time, achieve more flow moments via enhanced Performance Focus.

788,400 Hours: That's All We Get

When looking at our lives through the lens of moments, hours often seem like a strategic unit of time. And, if modern science has us living for approximately ninety years,[12] then that number is about 788,400. While some *Moments of Performance* might be measured in milliseconds (often the difference in medaling in the Olympics), seconds (navigating a crosswind landing at Chicago O'Hare airport), or minutes (landing a sales presentation), engineering and managing our hours seems more relevant to us seeking greater focus and daily engagement.

To optimize our daily moments, becoming aware of the various Internal, External, and Time factors is the first step. Mastering Attentional Leadership® to align these factors significantly increases our ability to initiate and sustain flow as we integrate them into our everyday life. In fact, I've seen firsthand that we can find flow regularly through practice—by placing attention with intention on What's Important Now (WIN) and making improvements in the areas that are causing noise and interference, preventing our flow.

Placing Attention with Intention

"Tell me what you pay attention to and I will tell you who you are."
—José Ortega Gasset

As previously discussed a key skill in finding your flow involves intentionally focusing on what's important now—your WINs. Doing so requires both **Strategic Focus** and **Performance Focus**.

Strategic Focus is what you are doing within this book—stepping back from the field of play, work, or craft for a strategic pit stop. You are taking this time to assess the many dimensions and factors most relevant to your flow. This is what you work on when you are off the field (e.g., mental toughness, emotional resilience, personal ethos, etc.). Building capacity off the field services your **Performance Focus** so that you can stay fully engaged on the game itself. By doing this, you are better prepared to eliminate any noise or interference that obstructs your Performance Focus, ensuring nothing stands between you and your work or craft, where you are not only finding your flow, but the very best in yourself.

The Wisdom of Children

Have you ever observed young children playing and marveled at their ability to express themselves spontaneously and get so completely immersed in their activities of interest that nothing else seems to matter?[13] As they grow up, however, they start to lose this natural engagement as they become self-conscious and start over thinking their experiences. This leads to the question: Do young people have an advantage in finding flow as a natural by-product of their curiosity about the world? Or do older individuals, who have more extensive and complex patterns of thinking, experience, and wisdom possess an even greater capacity and insight for engineering their own experiences? Perhaps it's both.

The tendency to overthink is well-documented in sports and performance literature, as many describe "choking" under pressure and "over-analyzing" an experience until they are no longer able to perform (the dreaded *paralysis by analysis*).[14/15] This is similar to the story of the millipede when asked by a clever frog how its many legs could move in unison. Thinking about this, the millipede never walked again. Paradoxically, these mechanisms of self-consciousness enable us to manage thoughts, feelings, and behaviors—but sometimes they get in the way of our relationship with the moment. While intentional development may deter spontaneous and creative acts of flow, it may also be associated with greater personal insight, and better self-regulation. It's a bit of a paradox—that the ability to turn off one's mind and engage freely comes as a by-product of using your mind to remove the interference and align oneself internally and externally over time.

Again, all of this testifies to attentional *imbalance* and why knowing where, when, and how long to direct attention strategically is key to Attentional Leadership®—not only when you are performing, but also while focused on your strategic development.

Have you ever wondered what it would be like to be fully engaged and absorbed in the present moment most or all of the time? What if you could be present and focused when talking to a friend, working on a project, giving a speech, making a sale, or reading a report? What if you had a framework, process, and tools to coach yourself and find more flow in every experience, over the long term?

The premise and promise of this book is that you can develop these skills, place your attention with intention, remove noise in the system, build your capacity, and find your own personal flow. Finding your Flow requires you to broaden your awareness, then narrow your focus on your WINs—one at a time (up to three if you can swing it)—over time—as a rough stone rolling—toward ever-greater refinement and polish.

While it's important to improve your technical knowledge and skills in your game or craft (the quantitative), this book emphasizes the vastly more complex human side of the equation (the qualitative).

Absorbed in the Moment

Take a moment and recall a time when you were completely engaged in the moment—where there was nothing between you and what you were doing. Perhaps you were competing in a sport, painting a picture, on a date you never wanted to end, or taking a test where the answers just showed up. Whatever it was, it stood out—it was one of those perfect moments. Don't you wish we could trade the ordinary and average for something exceptional?

You are not average! Do you know why? Because average is not really average. You have a unique genetic code, a distinct personality, ancestral, cultural, and family heritage, education, life experiences, etc. There is nothing average about you nor anybody else. Doesn't it make sense that you were designed for something unique—that life has something in store for you that is distinctly yours? What if you could find it? Well, I attest—you can!

A friend once told me that his father was retiring and had confessed: "Son, I have worked at my company for forty-two years, and I have hated every day of it. And next week my boss is throwing me a retirement party.

And guess what? I'm not even going to show up!"

His story saddened my soul!

The following night I caught a few minutes of an old episode of the *Tonight Show*. Jay Leno was hosting and interviewing Jerry Seinfeld. They talked about their careers and how they met. Seinfeld paused, then looked up at Leno and said: "Can you believe we get paid to do this?" The two of them smiled at each other.

My soul was restored.

For the past thirty-five years, I have been driven by a single question: what principles and practices drive people to reach their full potential, to become fully inspired, engaged, and to achieve excellence in their work and personal pursuits? Through countless interviews, discussions, and engagements with individuals from diverse performance, work, and life backgrounds, including Olympic athletes, executives, artists, coaches—even mushroom hunters—and more, I have uncovered a formula for helping individuals enter their "zone" and discover what it takes to find their flow. This formula is accessible to everyone, yet few know how to unlock it and utilize it. By the end of this book, you will be able to do just that.

Unlocking your own code requires understanding two great secrets in life. The first is unique to each individual; the other is universal and applies to everyone. These two secrets are followed by a third secret that puts it all into perspective—answering these important questions: Where did I come from? Why am I here? And to what end was I born?

Perhaps my favorite quote from Mark Twain is "The two most important days in your life are the day you are born and the day you find out why." But I believe there is a third day that makes all the difference, and that day is when you learn "how" to deliver on that "why." Learning how to deliver on that "why" begins with the practice of taking strategic pit stops in order to get more strategic with your work and your life.

Racetracks and Pit Stops

As a small child I remember seeing the Indianapolis 500 on TV. The first time a car entered the pit I was certain the driver had lost because all the other cars went screaming by. My older brother helped me to realize that the car might need fuel, new tires, or some maintenance. The driver hadn't lost but was simply doing what was needed to get back in the race. Other cars also made pit stops—part of the process of staying in the race until the finish.

We are all on our own racetracks, stepping on the gas, putting on the brakes, slowing down at the corners and speeding up on the straightaways, looking left, right, behind, and forward to navigate our course—sometimes looking up for guidance. In this process, parts break, things wear out, and sometimes we need a break. But how often do we enter the pits, scan our engines, and make sure our parts are working in harmony, even making some upgrades, to stay the course, complete what we were put here to do, and to finish our own unique race? Not often, certainly "not enough." And while we get more and more focused on our jobs or the task at hand, we often fail to enter the pits long enough to ensure we cross the finish line.

So, consider this book a strategic pit stop—one designed to explore the frameworks, tools, and, more importantly, to take the time to place your attention with intention on your WINs—whatever they are right now. Consider this a three-dimensional SWOT (strengths, weaknesses, opportunities, threats) analysis that you conduct on yourself to find your "One Thing"—the most strategic and impactful thing you can do to take your game to the next level. And guess what? It's something you'll be doing for the rest of your life.

How do I know you can do this? Indulge me for sixty seconds and do exactly this:

- Close your eyes and think of a white flower with a yellow center and a green stem.
- Now think just for a moment about something you did for which you were most proud.
- Take your right thumb and wiggle it three times.
- Take your left hand and put it on top of your right hand.
- Stand up and sit back down.
- In a soft voice say, "I am ready."
- Stand up, and stretch by reaching up into the sky, then sit back down.

Congratulations! You just demonstrated personal agency—the capacity to take intentional action. All great things begin with simple actions, and you have just proven capable of taking a strategic pitstop—one designed to help you be a better mechanic and driver.

Chapter 2
The Nuts and Bolts of Flow

What is it about the exceptional skills and high performance of others that draw our attention and curiosity? What makes them tick? How do they make it look so easy? What makes them the best at what they do? This has been my quest for more than three decades of study, research, teaching, training, coaching, and consulting. In many regards, I have served as both a caddy and mentor to aspiring professionals, managers, and executives. Much like Bagger Vance in The Legend of Bagger Vance, I believe "Inside each and every one of us is one true authentic swing… Somethin' we was born with… Somethin' that's ours and ours alone… Somethin' that can't be taught to ya or learned… Somethin' that got to be remembered…" Bagger Vance encapsulates the essence of flow, advising Junah to seek it "with your soul… Your hands is wiser than your head ever gonna be…"

Find or Fashion Your Swing?

One profound idea emerging from this exchange between Bagger and Junah is the notion that we do not "construct" our swings in life—but instead align with principles that govern the situation and moment. Bagger Vance explains that achieving flow involves "put[ting] your eyes on Bobby Jones… Watch how he settle hisself right into the middle of it… There's only ONE shot that's in perfect harmony with the field... All we got to do is get ourselves out of its way, to let it choose us."[16]

In the short term, it may appear that we can make great things happen without aligning with these governing principles. However, when we humbly align ourselves with life's moments and their inherent principles, we invite the natural occurrence of flow and thus invite the muse of flow to enter, we learn how this alignment, paradoxically, is the act of identifying our own "secret sauce" for flow. We discover our best by taking none of the credit—except the exercise of meekness which opens the door to alignment, which, over time, compels greatness—enabling us to fulfill our unique potential.

When we engage in the intentional process of *letting go* in harmony with the field and alignment in the moment, we address our duties with the mindset, "I can't believe I get paid for doing what I do" while simultaneously hitting our bullseye.

Flow Through the Ages

Whether you call it flow, being in the zone, peak engagement, or some other phrase that has been applied to this desirable state of mind, the phenomenon isn't new. As early as 521 CE, Buddha embarked on a journey of self-mastery through body, mind, heart, and soul. His pursuit of enlightenment mirrors the modern quest to find flow, an essence captured by Buddhist philosophy.[17]

Over the years, many researchers have delved into the science of how such states of consciousness operate, but few have translated these models into useful tools. Since the early 1970s, most notably in Eastern Europe and Russia, Olympic athletes trained both the mind and body in order to reach peak engagement and flow. In the Olympic Games at that time, a disproportionate number of medals went to the Russians and the East Germans.[18] This was no fluke. While many claim that "doping" practices were involved, most do not realize that these Eastern Bloc athletes were actually training more holistically than the rest of the world—rightsizing the ratio between the technical and human factors.

For decades, NASA has trained its astronauts using their giant Neutral Buoyancy Laboratory pool in order to simulate movement in space while training astronauts skills of mental simulation, emotional control, stress tolerance, focus training, pre-performance and contingency planning, etc. in order to minimize risk and ensure optimal focus for everyone's role when it's time to do the real thing.[19]

Similarly, these performance technologies are used every day by professional dancers, musicians, surgeons, police and fire departments, the military, business managers, executives, and other elite performers to optimize "who" they are becoming in the pursuit of performing "what" they know.

For example, in preparation for each of Christie's auctions, Christopher Burge enters the stage with a clear goal in mind—to exceed his million dollar per minute average. Before each show, he carefully plans to ensure that each piece of art will be auctioned off at the proper time. He enters the stage with a snifter of Scotch to ease his nerves while focusing on the task at hand. He quickly seeks to exceed the reserve price on each item in order to build momentum and to exceed his sales goals. He explains that facilitating an auction contains elements of playing to a crowd in the ancient Roman coliseum: "They want blood or thrills."

During the auction, he engages the audience with expressive gestures and facial cues. He injects energy and banter to adjust the mood of the crowd and uses his skills of communication to invoke friendly competition. During transactions he works the room until everything has moved. He then exits the stage exhausted. After each show, he painstakingly reviews the auction on video, analyzing his performance, learning as he goes and preparing for the next event. Clearly, the auction arena provides the context for Burge to find his flow.[20]

In a very different arena, Viktor Frankl, the great neurologist and humanist, wrote about the mental, emotional, and even spiritual practices he and other inmates used to find meaning and endure the physical and emotional abuses of life in a Nazi concentration camp.[21] Nelson Mandela, after twenty-seven years of imprisonment at Robben Island, used that time to refine his character, emerging as South Africa's president and ending Apartheid by first doing so within himself.[22]

While such terrible events can hardly be likened to the exhilaration and joys of play or competition, they too can instruct and compel deep learning toward improvement, and forge a new character. Any Meaningful Life Arena can provide a context from which one can leverage and apply the same principles for better coping, learning, understanding—even thriving. Whether you are trying to be a better professional football player, software engineer, or parent, or sweep floors for a living—every arena gives us the opportunity to generate flow.

Motivational theorists, humanistic psychologists, neurologists, and others have contributed to our understanding of flow. Their studies of creativity, play, performance, self-actualization, and happiness form the foundation of today's Positive Psychology movement.[23]

Mihaly Csikszentmihalyi (pronounced *chick, sent, me, hi*), the father of flow theory, began his career by studying the nature of intrinsic motivation, referring to the autotelic personality (auto = self; telos = goal), describing individuals who were engaged in the activities for their own sake instead of for some external purpose.[24] After conducting and analyzing interviews with hundreds of individuals within varied life arenas, he named the concept "flow" because individuals used that word to describe the kinds of experiences they were having. And since the early 1960s the study of flow continues to demonstrate the universal and global nature of this experience.

While there are hundreds of studies on this subject, the timeline below offers a glimpse of the different arenas that have been explored.

Flow: A Brief History

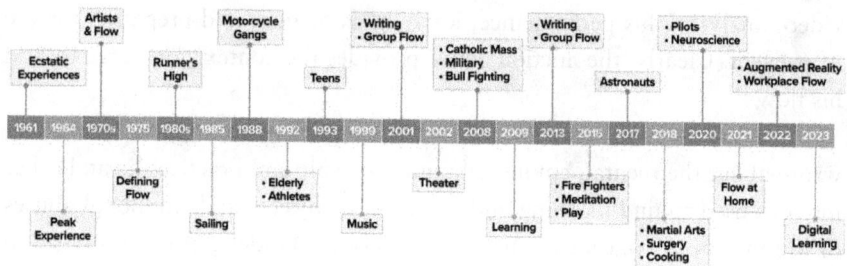

Benefits of Flow

Flow is so desirable because it is an altered state of consciousness wherein performance, satisfaction and happiness rise.[25] You become one with whatever you're doing; you feel utterly absorbed and enjoy intrinsic rewards. Your skills sharpen to meet the demands of the challenges, and everything falls into place. In essence, it is like tapping into your best self, where who you are and what you are doing fall into perfect alignment and harmony.

As many as 85 percent of individuals have experienced flow at least once. Some report attaining it daily.[26] From children and teenagers to the elderly, athletes to farmers, amid all ethnicities, flow provides a universal experience that anyone can tap into.

Commenting on the universal nature of flow, Csikszentmihalyi states:

> It is the same experience that the artist has as he works on the canvas, or the athlete during a race. It is how mountain climbers explain why they climb, how scientists describe the process of research, or surgeons whose challenging operations feel "like taking narcotics." All of these activities provide a common expanded state of consciousness that is so enjoyable that often no other reward than continuing the experience is required to keep it going.[27]

Whether your goals are to increase your Performance Focus on your job, on the golf course, increase the motivation of your teenager, facilitate greater feedback on a work-team, understand organizational dynamics and their impact on human behavior, or to channel cultural energies, flow theory provides valuable insights at every level of human engagement.

Why does flow matter so much? Csikszentmihalyi states:

> When a person's entire being is stretched in the full functioning of body and mind, whatever one does becomes worth doing for its own sake; living becomes its own justification. In the harmonious focusing on physical and psychic energy, life finally comes into its own.[28]

Positive Performance Psychology

It is important to acknowledge that while traditional therapeutic approaches in counseling, clinical psychology, and medical psychiatry, which often focus on diagnosing and treating mental illnesses as outlined in the DSM-5-TR[29] are vital, Positive Psychology offers a complementary perspective.[30] This field, encompassing theories such as flow and performance psychology, emphasizes enhancing human potential and well-being rather than solely addressing mental health issues. Positive Psychology challenges the notion that focusing predominantly on past traumas, problems, and deficits is the sole path to future success. While deficit-based and problem-centered approaches have their place, they may not always be effective or beneficial for individuals seeking a solution-oriented, behavior-driven approach to personal growth.[31]

However, it is crucial to recognize that when persistent mental or emotional health issues are present, appropriate professional treatment and support are necessary. In such instances, integrating Positive Psychology, which focuses on promoting optimal functioning, can be a highly effective complement to traditional therapeutic methods. This balanced approach allows for a holistic view of personal development, blending the alleviation of suffering with the enhancement of well-being.

Flowing into Happiness

> "Happiness is the object and design of our existence; and will be the end thereof, if we pursue the path that leads to it."
> —Joseph Smith, Jr.

Typically, we seek to find our flow in order to optimize focus and performance, perhaps without realizing that doing so consistently, over time, moves us inexorably toward fulfilling our potential. As we find our flow, happiness, joy, satisfaction and fulfillment are the natural by-products. We become one with what we are doing; we experience the intrinsic rewards of the activity; our skills are sharpened to meet the demands of the challenge, and everything falls into place. We tap into our natural gifts and talents and become our best selves when who we are and what we're doing fall into alignment and harmony.

As you become aware of the various factors that help or hinder flow, you become more adept at removing the barriers, interference, noise, and obstacles that prevent you from being fully engaged in the moment. You begin to clarify your values and develop new behaviors—even virtues—that become integral to who you are. Thus, finding your flow becomes a personal 'ode to joy,' leading to experiences and achievements that hold deep meaning for you. Your quest to find, replicate, and scale your flow often enhances personal efficacy, joy, and happiness, which radiates outward to bless and benefit others. The practices that lead to greater happiness are intrinsic to flow experiences and are rooted in making wise personal choices that align who you are with what you do.

As you identify Flow Factors and utilize strategies, tools, and practices to master them, such as clarifying your purpose, managing thoughts and emotions, optimizing your energy, and so on, happiness becomes the by-product. The connection between "doing" and "getting" becomes clear. The key is knowing which factors are most important for you to focus on now and putting them center stage so that you can integrate them into your work and life—one at a time, over time.

Finding Your Flow Through Attentional Leadership®

At its core, *leadership is influence*—it is influencing ourselves and others at multiple levels using various informed practices to achieve valued objectives. But at the core of influence is one's attention and where it is placed—internally and externally over time. As such I define Attentional Leadership as:

> *"The capacity to direct attention strategically—knowing 'where,' 'when,' and 'for how long'—to influence oneself, others, teams, organizations, and communities. It is the core of strategic change, growth, and evolution, leveraging focus and iteration to drive scalable impact."*

The concept of Attentional Leadership® encompasses **fifteen dimensions,** each focusing on specific factors of influence and engagement. The first five dimensions pertain to intrapersonal focus: Physical, Emotional, Psychological, Philosophical, and Spiritual. The second five dimensions deal with external focus: the Personal (in relation to the immediate physical environment), Interpersonal, Team, Organization, Community environments and beyond. The last five dimensions deal with time: Long Future, Short Future, Present Moment, Short Past, and Long Past.

These **Internal, External** and **Time** dimensions offer a framework for exploring influence over time and space—moment by moment—by increasing our capacity to understand where, when, and how long to place our attention on any part of this interconnected system—big or small. Attentional Leadership seeks to answer the question: "What's Important Now (WIN)?" It asserts that influence happens through physical (tangible), emotional (affect), mental (ideas/thoughts), philosophical (beliefs/values), and spiritual means (principles/truths). Where and when attention is placed with intention, influence is exercised. Our capacity to influence is transacted moment by moment, with future intent informed by past results, all influenced by many layers of physical and social contexts.

While our experiences come and go, they leave behind indelible marks—each of them informing and teaching as they refine our emerging character and personality. That is why tapping into past experiences, and consistently updating your Personal Ethos is a "Key Factor" you may find quite valuable on your journey toward flow.

As crucial as flow is for enhancing your engagement and performance, revealing insights into what drives you and increasing your influence, it also sets the stage for a deeper self-discovery. Here, atop the foundations of flow, you have the opportunity to uncover what makes you uniquely you—to discover your signature brand and the very purpose of your existence. This is the essence of Attentional Leadership—equipping you to not only identify but also effectively deliver on your life's purpose.

Chapter 3
Experiencing and Understanding Flow

At its core, life is a collection of moments… and each one of these moments are influenced by the factors that either support or inhibit your connection to it.

One moment comes, it's here, and then it's gone, just like sand through an hourglass. We are always in the here and now, experiencing one present moment at a time. Yet, our attention can wander—outside, inside, to the future, or the past. We might be looking broadly, scanning a system, or focusing narrowly on a specific thing.

For example, in The Secret Life of Walter Mitty (2013),[32] there's a scene in which Walter tracks down photographer Sean high in the Himalayas just at the moment when Sean spots a rare snow leopard—the objective of his photo shoot.

Sean: "There's a snow leopard. Right in this ridge. So we have to try to be very still. They call the snow leopard the 'ghost cat'. It never lets itself be seen. Beautiful things don't ask for attention."

Walter: "When are you gonna take it?"

Sean: "Sometimes I don't take it. If I like a moment...I don't like to have the distraction of the camera. Just want to stay in the moment. Right here. Now it's gone."

Moments, the basic units of our lives, are all we have. They are precious gifts, and understanding them is key to unlocking the experience of flow. But these moments are filled with mysterious elements, and when understood, give us keys to engage even better.

Naturally, some moments stand out more than others, particularly those where we find ourselves in flow, fully immersed and engaged. They stand out, are highly memorable, but also leave behind clues that help you optimize future moments so there is nothing between "you" and "it"—or the person or people you are with—or the moment to which you are fully engaged.

Moments, Arenas and Examples

To understand how flow manifests in different contexts, I asked my father to recount a time when he felt he was performing at his very best. Without hesitation, he said his four years serving as a PT boat commander in southern France, Italy, and Corsica during World War II. Of all the performance arenas he could have discussed with me, it was this time of his life where he discovered the best within himself.

I asked him, "what made the war so profound for you?" As he explained, for him, war was a time of great personal sacrifice, uncertainty, stress, and fear. Moreover, he felt great purpose, as his days were bound by clear roles and measurable goals. He was driven by powerful motives, and he received precise feedback on his actions. Such tasks as pursuing the enemy, managing other men, being ready for action at any time took full powers of mind and body. They pushed the limits of his mental, emotional, and physical capacity, all for a higher cause, something bigger than himself—the greater good of his country and the world. For most of those years, my father was *in the zone, in flow in a very Meaningful Life Arena (MLA)*.

For more than six decades, researchers from around the world continue to investigate the experience and structure of flow. I, among them, have interviewed or studied people engaged in such diverse activities as tennis, skiing, bullfighting, cross-stitching, sailing, computer gaming, play, flying, teaching, farming, policing, firefighting—and two of my personal favorites—wild mushroom hunting and extreme ironing, just to name a few. These, along with countless other pursuits, have been studied and analyzed again and again. And throughout the research, one powerful truth emerges: flow can be experienced in any arena of life that holds meaning for us, underscoring both its universality and the opportunity for all of us to tap into this profound experience.

Flow: A Universal Experience

While most of us do not think of cleaning hotel rooms or ironing clothes as extreme or optimal experiences,[33] *these examples reveal much about our ability to engineer our everyday environments*—that any MLA can become a time and place for the expression of personal excellence and the use of our greatest gifts or talents (*self-actualization*).

Once you've experienced flow, you may find yourself actively seeking to engineer your life to recapture those moments. Most want to tap into flow at a moment's notice, only to find that when they need it most, flow can be elusive. Still, finding your flow is possible—even probable—when you commit to certain deliberate practices that are specific to you and your circumstances.

Consider the *meaningful arenas* of your life, and ponder these questions: Are you fully engaged in the moment? Are you performing at your best? Are you getting the most out of yourself when you engage your craft and those surrounding it? Are you the high performer you are designed to be? Are you self-confident? Are you learning and growing from your experiences? Are you becoming the person you envisioned long ago? Do you have a working personal philosophy that maximizes your energy, commitment, patience, joy, and gratitude? Are you your own best coach?

When exploring the arenas where flow emerges, it should be no surprise that we can find our flow by employing specific personalized strategies that work for us in whatever arenas we engage. In our one-day training program I emphasize thirty-nine "Core Practices" yet also allude to other factors and practices—each of them relevant, at various times and places as revealed within your Personal Flow Formula, which we will talk more about in Section III.

Since flow is a dynamic and holistic experience, finding flow means engaging the whole self. No individual strategy is solely responsible for getting individuals into flow—and mastering every strategy and tactic may not guarantee a flow experience—as each situation may require a unique strategy or combination of strategies to address the challenge at hand. However, employing habitual strategies that become a part of you will increase the odds that flow can be reached more often and more consistently.

As I probed into people's flow experiences and the strategies they use to access flow regularly, I discovered that strategies are vast, varied and personal—from envisioning to time maximization, exercising faith to clarifying values, from increasing their energy to developing personal rituals.

In my interviews I ask: Where do you typically experience flow? When you seek flow, what strategies do you use, when do you use them, and for how long? Have your flow strategies changed over time? As I engage with high performers, I find that they love to talk about their flow experiences and can readily describe where they had them and what they did to replicate them.

So Many Arenas/So Many Strategies

Having interviewed people ranging from fifteen to ninety-five years of age and discovering more than **128 *different arenas*** where individuals experience flow, it was clear that I was just scratching the surface. And as I began to link age to flow, I recognized that different stages of life may require different approaches for achieving optimal outcomes. I wondered if the number and types of flow arenas or strategies used to generate flow differed based on age, education or level of psychological/hierarchical complexity (a mathematical construct that measures complexity of thought)?[34]

My conclusion: that flow occurs in just about every life arena with very similar, but highly personalized strategies to attain it. Flow appears to be a remarkably similar experience despite very unique circumstances. Irrespective of one's life journey, most people can relate to flow as a state of absorption, interest, and joy. Therefore, discovering flow isn't limited to elite athletes or performers; it is a universal experience accessible to everyone. You just need to understand its many contributing factors, discover which ones are currently working on your behalf, and then identify those that are missing to become an optimally tuned high performance machine.

Investigating Your Flow

One good way to analyze your flow experiences is through grounded theory—tapping into your experiences. Of the two great families of research: *quantitative* (things we can count) and qualitative (an essence or quality of a scientific phenomenon, something you seek to describe), the qualitative (observing) usually comes first and the quantitative (counting) comes second.

By applying grounded theory, you can tap into your flow experiences. As the investigator of your own experience, you can observe something of value and notice what emerges within the course of your experience. As you start to observe and collect data, certain themes emerge.

For example, you may notice that each time you perform poorly, you are focused on what others are thinking about you. Or, when you take time in the morning to plan your day, you're more efficient with fewer distractions. Or, whenever you have less than six hours of sleep your mood is more negative. With enough data, you can detect your Flow Liabilities and your Flow Assets.

Flow Factors: Assets or Liabilities?

As we delve into different Flow Factors and practices, we observe that each of them either contributes positively (a Flow Asset) or negatively (a Flow Liability) to our ability to achieve flow. When a specific Flow Factor is present, it works in our favor, while its absence hampers our progress.

Flow Assets act as "tailwinds," propelling us forward, while Flow Liabilities act as "headwinds," impeding our progress. It is valuable to consider both the presence and absence of these factors. Just as a ship can sail even without ideal wind patterns, understanding how to navigate the principles that invite flow allows us to navigate through various challenges.

To illustrate this, take a moment to reflect on two contrasting experiences—one where you encountered Anti-Flow and another where you experienced Pro-Flow.

Tapping Into Anti-Flow Experiences

Close your eyes and think of a time when you were overwhelmed with your work or life. You lacked interest in what you were doing, and it had little or no value to you. Time stood agonizingly still, leaving you with a sense of frustration or fear. You were not on purpose and felt a disconnect between your mind, heart, and body. You were overly self-conscious, harboring a sense of self-doubt, and impatient to do something other than what you were doing. You were stuck in a boring, routine, or uninspiring job or experienced a relationship going bad. Perhaps you froze up during an important test, speaking in front of a large audience, or stuck at a family reunion listening to the same old stories.

Do one or more experiences come to mind? Such experiences generate *Anti-Flow*.

Tapping Into Flow Experiences

Now, reflect on exceptionally positive *Pro-Flow* experiences.

Close your eyes and think of a time when your mind wasn't wandering, and you weren't thinking of something else. You were totally involved and absorbed in what you were doing, with your body, heart, mind, and spirit fully engaged. Nothing seemed to bother or get at you; you were less aware of your problems and yourself. The stars seemed to align, and everything fell into place, as if you had all the skills you needed to do the job. You were in complete control of the situation, feeling highly energized by what you were doing. You didn't see yourself as separate from the activity. Time seemed to either fly by or stand still as you and your task became one.

Where and when have you experienced such flow? Describe your observations, thoughts and feelings.

Navigating Your Headwinds and Tailwinds

Numerous factors can impede the occurrence of that incredible flow moment. These may include negative thoughts or emotions, fear, self-doubt, external elements like weather or noise, internal distractions such as memories or emotions, environmental factors like temperature or lighting, boredom, or the influence of our ego.

However, when these obstacles are eliminated or no longer demand our attention, something remarkable unfolds—flow. Flow is often associated with positive thoughts and emotions, as well as exceptional performances in areas that hold great significance to us. Naturally, we aspire to experience moments of pure flow and pure joy as frequently as possible.

Fortunately, we don't need to fully comprehend all the motivations and mechanisms of flow in order to experience it. It is akin to driving a car—you don't need to understand every intricate detail of its mechanics to operate it successfully.

Reflecting on your flow and anti-flow experiences, think about which Flow Factors contribute to or hinder these states. Ask yourself: "What conditions typically lead to anti-flow or flow experiences for me? In which arenas or environments does flow happen or not happen? What factors most commonly inhibit or encourage it?" By reflecting on your moments of flow and anti-flow, you'll uncover patterns that can guide you to strategies best suited for finding and maintaining this state.

From an elite athlete in the zone to a soldier facing high-stakes missions, flow manifests in many arenas. But flow, though universal, is uniquely experienced and deeply personal. By identifying the elements that bring you into flow or pull you out of it, you can begin to navigate your own path toward consistent peak performance.

As you look ahead to the next chapter, we'll delve deeper into the anatomy of these moments to better understand the forces at play within them. Each encounter offers a unique chance to learn, grow, and adapt, guiding you on your journey toward your best self.

Chapter 4
Dissecting Flow—Understanding The Magic Butterflies

Our moments of flow are composed of many factors that work together to support deep focus and full engagement. While we know flow when we experience it, it can be challenging to know just what we can do to generate flow more often.

With so many moving and interconnected variables influencing our moments, you might think of flow as a cloud of butterflies, each factor and variable in relation to the others, with structure and patterns unclear—yet undeniable and beautiful—especially when they align. We often struggle to define or frame flow holistically due to a lack of framework, a gap we aim to fill with the introduction of Attentional Leadership®.

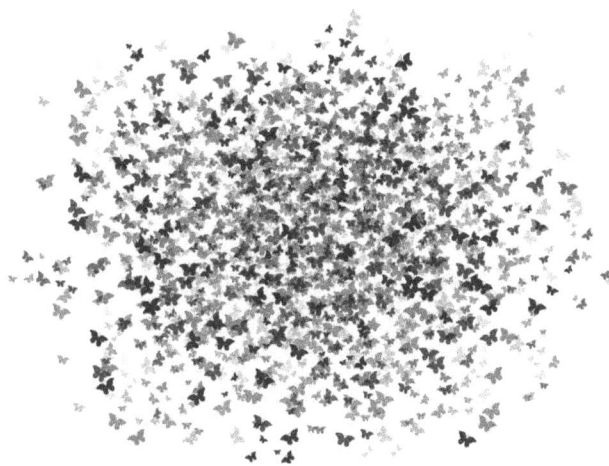

So, let's explore this framework—what I call *Attentional Leadership*®.

What Moments Are Made Of

Building on the idea that our lives are a collection of moments, let's delve deeper into the elements of these moments and what contributes to our flow experiences.

When looking at the many Flow Factors that comprise flow experiences, we recognize that all of them influence the moment, but some need more attention than others based on your current Flow Assets and Liabilities given your current circumstances.

Much like in the movie *Inside Out*,[35] where memories are visualized as colored balls, our moments of flow are similarly marked by many other influencing factors that leave a trail of clues. For example, when you have had an argument with a friend or coworker, you might remember that you were physically tired, feeling angry, thinking "this person is wrong" or clashing over core values or principles. Perhaps this argument was about something that happened a long time ago. Perhaps it took place in the break room at your office with other colleagues, with a refrigerator to your right, a sink to your left. The room may have been bright but rainy outside.

Every moment is composed of so many factors: some contributing to the experience, others distracting you from it, and many neutral factors. But they all play a role in your experience. By increasing your awareness and understanding of Flow Factors and their influence, you gain greater ability to place your attention with intention on those things to remove the noise by building greater capacity in order to direct your natural state of focus, flow and peak engagement within every *Moment of Performance*.

Flow Factors and Characteristics: The Big Nine

Nine common factors and characteristics are often used to describe and explain flow:

1. *The activity has clear goals and objectives*. When individuals describe their flow experiences, they often mention having a clear goal or blueprint of what to do. Clear goals provide boundaries that help you channel your energy and focus on the objective at hand. In the context of flow, being "mindless" refers to a state of effortless concentration and engagement, free from distracting thoughts. This duality, a combination of direction and detachment, of being in the moment, brings about flow.

Just as President John F. Kennedy declared his intent to be the first to put a man on the moon before the Russians, this mission found its way through every layer of NASA as it clarified its focus and unified the organization around this single goal. As the story goes, when Kennedy himself visited NASA and asked a janitor what he was doing. He stated, "Helping to put a man on the moon, sir!"

2. *The activity provides clear and immediate feedback*, thus creating a coherent demand for action. Feedback mechanisms, integral to both natural and man-made systems, play a crucial role in guiding us into and sustaining a state of flow by allowing us to adjust our actions in real time. They help monitor results, make adjustments, correct course, and redirect attention toward meaningful goals through measures and standards. Feedback is vital for perpetuating the flow experience and meeting the demands of the task at hand. Feedback comes in many forms—both external and internal over time. For example: an exam score, the outcome of an operation, audience applause, a change in body weight—even qualitative changes like attitude, or sense of well-being.

Feedback helps us understand how we are doing, what we need to adjust, and how we can succeed at the activity. Whether you make a poor golf shot, blow a sales call, or mess up a professional presentation, your ability to receive feedback and make adjustments is vital to maintaining your conscious attention and to moving more efficiently toward your target.

We all need to learn from, adjust to, and reengage with the many challenges that show up moment by moment. This requires constant monitoring of attention and the feedback loops that we are putting our attention in the right place, at the right time, for the right duration.

3. There is an absence of self-consciousness. Individuals in flow are fully connected to their activities. When we perform, we often pay too much attention to ourselves or to the environment. We tend to think about what happened the last time or what might happen this time, which are distractions in the moment. When focused on ourselves, we often judge ourselves negatively, since our weaknesses are more easily detected when we compare ourselves to our last performance or to the performance of others. Once free from self-consciousness, however, we feel we are our best selves; in flow we are "at one" with the experience. In contrast, people whose attention vacillates within an experience, are constantly thinking and wondering about what happened "last time," what might happen "this time." Those in flow feel as if they are in the driver's seat, reacting to every moment with relative ease—"right now." While many individuals are consciously aware of the many factors influencing their performance, those finding their flow let this go during the experience with a degree of detachment and lack of self-consciousness. Their ego takes a back seat to the moment. Neither fear of success nor fear of failure enters the experience—nor anything else for that matter. Instead, the experience is what it is, without judgment, and the performer, almost as an observer, participates in this beautiful moment uninterrupted by the frailties of their ego.

4. We feel a sense of control. Reflecting on flow experiences, people often say things like, "Everything just came together." Their actions and reactions occur almost automatically, with minimal conscious thought. They focus on their present "reality," acting spontaneously without interference. Reflecting on his flow state in a game, a college basketball player described feeling an unparalleled sense of control, with each shot feeling "like magic." "I couldn't miss. I was in the right place, and every shot felt magical. Each time I looked at the basket, I planned to make the shot. I had no doubt I would." For many, the moment seems to dominate conscious abilities, while also instilling confidence in their control over the situation.

5. Time becomes distorted. During flow, many people describe time as passing either quickly or slowly. One woman chose a seven-hundred-page book to read since her husband was away and sat down at eight thirty in the morning. She read until the book was done, eight hours later! "It didn't seem that long."

Michael Jordan once said that at the end of a game, with seconds left on the shot clock, he had what seemed like unlimited time to make the final basket—that the ball got smaller while the hoop got bigger. He felt he had all the time in the world, certain he'd make the shot. Similarly, football legend John Brodie said: "Sometimes, time seems to slow down in an uncanny way, as if everyone were moving in slow motion. I feel like I have all the time to watch the receivers run their routes, yet the defensive line is still coming at me just as fast."

In both cases, one gets deeply absorbed in an activity, where time either flies by or slows down, often during high-stakes moments—even in personal tragedies or accidents where the mind slows time down.

6. The activity is autotelic or intrinsically motivating. Flow experiences are often autotelic, meaning they are intrinsically motivating. People engage in these activities for the sheer joy and satisfaction they bring "without conventional reward" because they love what they are doing, such as a musician lost in the music, or a writer fully absorbed in the creative process. The activity is often seen as contributing to their self-realization or actualization. Autotelic activities carry few extrinsic rewards and usually no material rewards, and yet still attract participants who devote time, energy, and money to the pursuit. One female college student said, "I do not have the same desires I used to have to race while mountain biking. Now I just do it out of pure passion, for the activity itself, no other reason. I just do it because I love it."

7. We center attention with limited distractions and high concentration power. Our attention is constantly being pulled in many directions, posing a significant challenge to maintaining the focused engagement required for flow. Since many stimuli compete for our attention, our minds struggle to attend to any one subject for very long. For those who experience flow, controlling attention is a critical skill. Individuals with ADHD may face additional hurdles in achieving flow, requiring tailored strategies or specific conditions to harness their unique focus capabilities.

However, attention issues are as much about context as ability or motivation. Both the intense reader and the day-dreamer—one seemingly highly focused and the other thinking broadly and creatively—may experience opposite kinds of flow. This is one difference between narrow focus (attending to something small and fixed) vs. a broad focus (a soft focus where you see the larger environment or system).

Because of our highly focused and competitive environments, we are now seeing greater emphasis on mindfulness, which is designed to take us out of our standard narrow focus. Attentional Leadership® suggests that we must balance where, when, and how long to sustain our attention on any one dimension, and more specifically a single factor.

8. *Action and awareness merge into transcendence.* Merging action and awareness is essentially a fusion between body, heart, mind, ethos, spirit, time, and context within the moment. This fusion takes place when we are totally immersed in a task at hand and where even the tools we are using (bat, racket, piano, scalpel, computer) become part of us. The unified consciousness that results from the merging of action and awareness is a major outcome of the flow experience.[36]

D.T. Suzuki's observation about the sword master illuminates a critical aspect of flow: the merging of action and awareness, where technical skill transcends conscious thought. "If one really wishes to be master of an art, technical knowledge is not enough. One has to transcend technique so that the art grows out of the unconscious. You must let the unconscious come forward. In such cases, you cease to be your own conscious master but become an instrument in the hands of the unknown. The unknown has no ego-consciousness and consequently no thought of winning the contest. It is for this reason that the sword moves where it ought to move and makes the contest end victoriously."[37]

We don't exercise skill as much as we "align" ourselves to the physics of the moment.

9. Perceived challenges are met by perceived skills. The activity provides a context where our perceived challenges and skills meet. The flow experience represents a balance between skills and challenges, when the intra-somatic and the extra-somatic come together. Whether we are confronted with a simple or a difficult task, we are more likely to enter flow when our perceived challenges are balanced by our perceived skills—whether you are flying a fighter jet or sweeping the floor. Simple arenas often help us express complex thinking and experience flow while complex moments can reveal the simplicity of it. Think of a time when you were given a task to do that seemed boring—whether this was stacking cans in a grocery store, weeding a garden, or waiting around for someone. After a time, did boredom give way to anxiety or a desire to do something else? In contrast, think of a time when you faced an over-the-top challenge and you were not sure if you could manage it—a difficult exam perhaps, an overwhelming task, too many deadlines coming at you at once, or all the above. Didn't this also lead to anxiety?

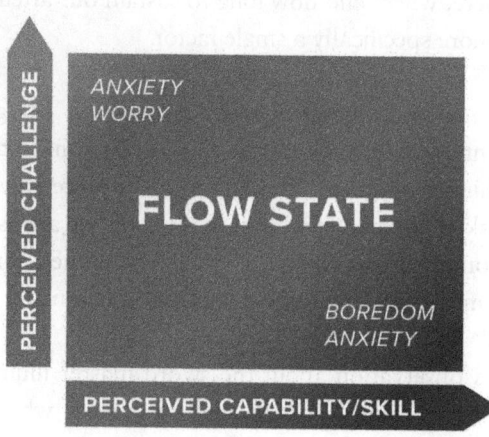

Flow occurs across various skill levels, emerging most strongly when there's a harmonious match between the challenge at hand and one's current capabilities, fostering a sense of confidence and potential for success—confident that what you know combined with your past experience means "I can do this." The challenge may be a bit higher, where you aren't sure you can achieve your goal, but you think you have a good chance to pull it off. These experiences teach you about yourself. They raise your confidence level and give you new insights into your capabilities—even your genius.

If you've watched the movie *Ford vs. Ferrari* the opening dialogue by Carroll Shelby (played by Matt Damon) says it best:

There's a point at seven thousand RPMs where everything fades. The machine becomes weightless. It disappears. All that's left, a body moving through space, and time. At seven thousand RPM—that's where you meet it[38].

Taken together these nine components give us insights into some of the foundational principles, factors, and dynamics of flow, but they do not provide a comprehensive model, map, or toolkit to generate it.

Looking Under the Hood of Your Ferrari

In the late 1920s, Henry Ford declared that the Model T had more than 4,900 parts—a very complex machine in its day. Today, however, cars have seven times that number.

Just as comprehending a complex system involves dissecting its interconnected parts, understanding flow requires us to unravel its multifaceted nature. At first, looking under the hood and taking an engine apart can be confusing and challenging. Imagine popping the hood of a Ferrari and observing all of its impressive mechanics. You may notice a large engine block, a starter, cooling fans, hoses, wires, reservoirs for fluids, nuts and bolts and other hardware.

While not everyone delves into the mechanics of how a car's components generate power, this curiosity mirrors our exploration of the intricate factors that drive flow. Most of us are happy to turn the key or press the button, step on the gas, and steer, while letting the mechanical marvel do its thing.

What parts of this vehicle are the most important? While all parts contribute to the vehicle's functioning and are used from time to time, some parts are more essential than others. We might call these Vital Factors—those that make the biggest overall difference.

Applying the 80/20 principle to flow, we find that identifying and focusing on the vital 20 percent of Flow Factors specific to our current circumstances, can significantly enhance our ability to achieve and sustain flow.[39] The trick is knowing which 20 percent—then narrowing it down even further!

How, then, can we identify the behaviors that produce the greatest results in any situation? When it comes to finding your flow, you need a systematic process of identifying your own Vital Factors that have the greatest impact on your performance. You need a framework that allows you to look under the hood, identify the parts that need your attention, and make sure they are working properly in order to add value to the system.

Through my interviews and interactions with high performers and flow seekers, I identified Flow Factors that influenced their experiences. From selecting the right context to the room temperature, from managing thoughts to generating emotions, from sleeping well to eating well, and from envisioning the future to using the past, I saw various principles and practices conspiring together. These nuanced subsystems often operate below our radar.

My study of flow aimed to identify the specific strategies and tactics people used to find it. My interviews produced over seven hundred pages of data, with a thematic analysis revealing a framework of more than 158 Flow Factors or strategies. Again, I was just scratching the surface.

To understand these factors and their interrelationship, we'll begin with the three core dimensions and five critical alignments. These are then broken down into fifteen sub-dimensions revealing the two-dimensional (2D) Attentional Leadership® Framework.

The basic fifteen-dimension model provides a more complex relationship between dimensions and corresponding Flow Factors. It also helps analyze your current Flow Assets and Liabilities in any Meaningful Life Arena, which you will explore soon. At the end of the book, I'll introduce the three-dimensional (3D) model. This model showcases the interconnection between all fifteen dimensions rendering a three-dimensional cube that will enhance your understanding even further—a significant paradigm shift. This will elevate your game and show how to scale your influence and leadership—helping you see systemically, dynamically, and holistically—beyond yourself—even in the service of others.

Engaging the Adventure and Taking the Dive

Let's look at the framework of Attentional Leadership® yet another way. Perhaps you like to take adventures from time to time. For some just deciding to see a new place is a big step. In this case, let's say you've lived your whole life in the heartland of a country and have never been to the coast, never seen a beach or an ocean, so you decide it's time to go. You make the arrangements, get on a plane, land in a coastal city you've heard so much about, rent a car, and drive to its most beautiful beach. You arrive and witness the majesty of the ocean and its beach and you are excited. What's next? Will you get out of the car and touch the sand? Probably so. Will you get in the water? According to UCLA's study on beach goers, less than one in ten get into the water.[40]

That's rather interesting.

Let's say you are a bit more adventurous and not only get in the water, but you brought a mask and a snorkel so you could see what was below the surface and maybe even catch a glimpse of some coral or fish. According to the same UCLA study 0.01 percent of those who go to the beach seek to observe its marine life—just one person in a thousand! How might these percentages compare to those who take the time and risk to look below their own surface—to explore the many dimensions and factors teeming with life and opportunity to understand it better.

To deepen our understanding of flow, let's embark on an exploratory journey, starting on the familiar shore before venturing into the depths of our consciousness and capabilities. From there we will not just use a mask and snorkel, but also a scuba vest and tank with all the gear and go below the surface, but not too deep. You see in scuba diving you have to watch your consumption of nitrogen as the deeper you go the greater the pressure and the more nitrogen you absorb. Too much is bad. That's why the deeper you dive the less time you have to explore. but it's easy to avoid by following the rules and the Navy dive tables. But interestingly, if you stay above thirty-three feet (just one atmosphere) you can dive and explore for as long as you want. For the first half of this book, we are going to stay within that first atmosphere—until you are ready for that deeper dive, which we will do in the second half.

Even at thirty-three feet—still shallow enough to swim to the surface if needed—you'll discover an entirely new world as you look around. Fish, coral, and vegetation move gracefully with the rhythms of the ocean. Taking this metaphor a step further, imagine looking down to see three expansive coral reefs, each distinctly unique and surrounded by five vibrant clusters of fish. Within those clusters, every fish stands out with its own unique features, drawing you in for a closer look—and you will.

Of the three outcroppings, let's say you focus on the middle one as you see some interesting fish, and these attract your attention. That one little fish in the fifth cluster—that's the goal for the next dive. After that who knows, as every dive offers a new opportunity to explore a new reef, cluster, and fish. Each level offers new learning and understanding.

Our journey into flow is much like this. As we explore your experience with flow and your relationship to it, we will move from the surface and start our descent, perhaps just fifteen to thirty-three feet down, to hover, scan and identify the special places that are inviting you to take a closer look—to explore and to have your own personal adventure—one that will make you a better and more complete person after each dive. And if you've ever been afraid of the water or diving underneath it, perhaps the ocean will no longer be a place filled with scary creatures like those found at the corners of old Mercator maps, but instead a welcoming place filled with new opportunities to explore and discover—each time becoming a bit wiser and more inspired to see "what else" is down there.

Believing in Principles

To truly master flow, it's essential to ground our understanding and practices in the fundamental principles that underpin all aspects of existence, from the universe at large to the minutiae of our personal experiences. The predictability and reproducibility of flow experiences, when certain conditions are met, serve as compelling evidence of the principle-driven nature of our universe. Finding flow requires the acknowledgement of principles and a healthy disregard for all things random. Success leaves clues (as does failure)—just ask Thomas Edison.

Splitting Moments into "What" and "Who"

> "Not everything that counts can be counted, and not everything that can be counted counts."
> —William Bruce Cameron

Peak performance hinges on two key domains: "What"—the technical expertise needed for a discipline, and "Who"—personal, temporal, and situational factors that influence this expertise.

Every Meaningful Life Arena (MLA) requires specific Knowledge, Skills, and Abilities (KSAs). In tennis, there are around twelve primary shots: the serve, return of serve, groundstrokes, approach shots, volleys, drop shots, and overheads on both sides. Though there are many variations, they are versions of these core shots. For a battleship XO, KSAs include advanced skills in navigation, seamanship, mechanical engineering, weapons deployment, and many more. These skills are distinct from those of a doctor, lawyer, or accountant.

While *technical skills* are unique to each discipline, the dimensions and factors of flow—purpose, vision, goals, feedback, resilience, focus, confidence, ethos, and more—are universal. Linking technical knowledge, skills, and abilities (KSAs) with flow KSAs provides an advantage over those who focus solely on the game itself. As Boris Becker, the great German tennis player who won Wimbledon as an 18-year-old qualifier, once said about five-set matches: "The fifth set is not about tennis, it's about nerves." This reflection illustrates that by the fifth set, matches transcend technical skill ("What") and become a test of mental resilience and adaptability ("Who"). At the highest levels, most performers possess similar technical competency, so mental, emotional, and other non-game-related assets become the key differentiators. After two thousand surgeries, five thousand assembled cars, or 10,000 tax returns, people gain proficiency in their craft. While the "10,000-hour rule" implies a threshold for expertise, new perspectives emphasize quality and intentionality of practice over mere hours, highlighting the interplay of "What" and "Who" in mastery. Some world-class performers achieve mastery in their teens, or even earlier, like Mozart. Studying them, it's tempting to label them geniuses, but their fast track to excellence often results from attention with intention and deliberate practice.

Beyond knowing the technicalities of the game, knowing who you need to be to find flow depends on focusing your attention on What's Important Now (WIN). This new framework, Attentional Leadership®, operationalizes your technical expertise to produce an X-Factor—where expertise meets full engagement.

What you know
Technical knowledge

Who you are
Attentional Leadership knowledge

Technical knowledge is about mastering your craft, while exercising Attentional Leadership® is about aligning who you need to be in space and time to be one with that craft. For instance, your job may require specific skills like writing, building spreadsheets, painting, wiring, or cleaning, but you're influenced by what's happening inside (beliefs, thoughts, emotions, energy, focus), outside (resources, people, context), and in time (past, present, future). All these factors shape "who" you are in relation to "what" you do.

Seeing Flow Through Three, Five and Fifteen Dimensions

There is no universal flow formula, but there is *your personal flow formula (Secret #1)*—and discovering it is an individually rigorous yet very satisfying process. Documenting hundreds of flow arenas and activities, I identified more than 150 individual flow strategies, all of which can be found within ***three primary dimensions:*** Internal, External, and Time.

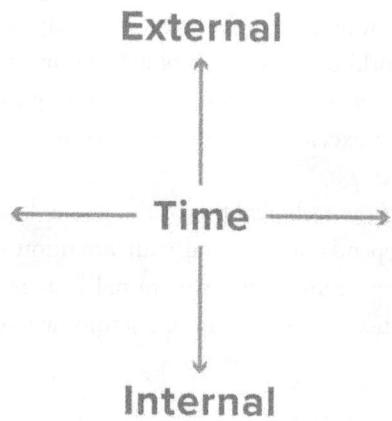

I began by recognizing flow as a series of sequentially engineered moments. Every moment arrives from the future, engages us internally and externally, and then slips into the past. The more Flow Factors we have working in our favor, the better our chances of staying engaged in flow.

Building on this, I considered how we might approach flow before, during, and after the experience. We prepare for moments through future orientation and planning; we enter them by understanding the internal and external factors that either support or hinder our engagement, and we exit them, gathering critical feedback to help us prepare for and engineer future flow experiences.

To systematically approach flow, we utilize a ***five-dimension framework*** that categorizes the key areas influencing our experiences.

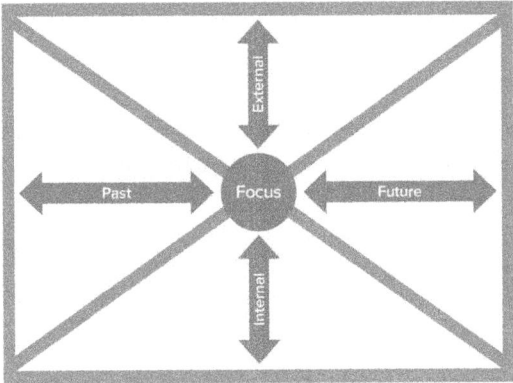

The framework has five dimensions—Future, Internal, External, and Past—that collectively enhance our Focus on any task or activity, creating a holistic alignment for present-moment focus essential to flow—hence the *Five Alignments*™.

Delving deeper into flow, I examined the Five Alignments™ and identified fifteen sub-dimensions and over a hundred Flow Factors that influence your present-moment engagement.

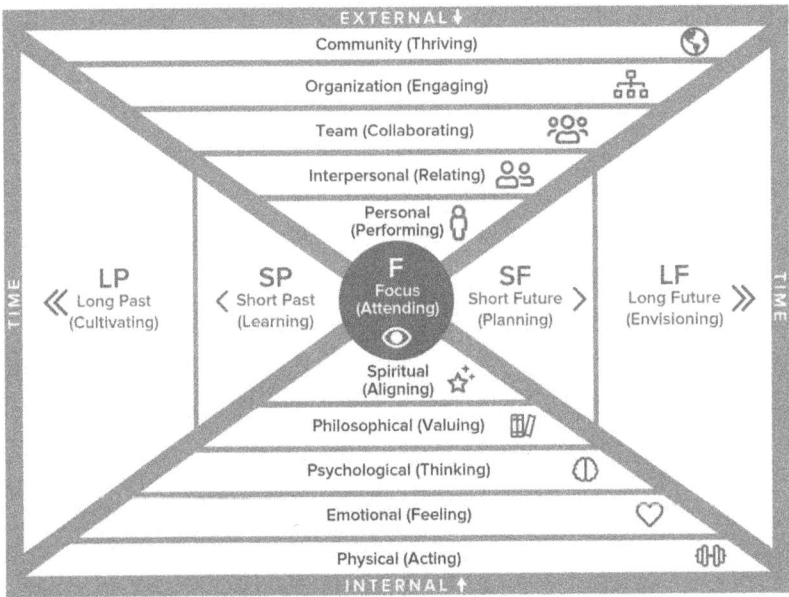

Before we dive into the fifteen dimensions and their related Flow Factors, let's take a brief tour of the fifteen-dimension model above. Both sides (right &

left) of the model comprise the core dimension of Time which includes five sub-dimensions: 1) Long Future, 2) Short Future, 3) Short Past, 4) Long Past, with the fifth, Focus, at the center.

The bottom of the model is where we find the five internal dimensions of 1) Spiritual, 2) Philosophical, 3) Psychological, 4) Emotional, and 5) Physical.

Lastly, the top of the model is where we find the external dimension that includes 1) Personal environment, 2) Interpersonal alignment, 3) Team alignment, 4) Organizational alignment, and 5) Community alignment.

These fifteen dimensions provide a detailed map for navigating our experiences and the many factors that influence them.

In the journey to master the art of flow, Attentional Leadership® helps us understand the interplay between our internal world and external environment over time. By identifying and adjusting misalignments within these dimensions, we enhance our ability to eliminate the barriers to flow by building capacities within ourselves that contribute to our focused engagement.

Section II
The First Secret: The One Thing That Moves The Needle on Everything

Applying the First Secret Through the Five Alignments

The Flow Factor that matters most to you right now (your "One Thing") is the one that will eliminate the most interference—building greater capacity through Strategic Focus in order to fully engage in the moment to optimize Performance Focus. As you'll discover in your personal ALI 1080° Sweep™ Assessment, your "One Thing" emerges by scanning more than a hundred factors down to your top twenty, then your top three, and finally to that single factor using the Focus Planning Process. I'll emphasize that finding your "One Thing" is about understanding alignments—Future, Internal, External, and Past—and identifying the dimensions and factors that need your Strategic Focus right now. This is the *1st Secret.*

These timeless principles and practices are not just theoretical; they are highly practical. Nobody is inventing them—only rediscovering and understanding them at a deeper level based on individual circumstances supported by newer research. Yet it is through the skill of Attentional Leadership® that you will learn to discover your "One Thing" amongst the many and learn to become your own best coach.

As we explore the *fifteen-dimension framework* for which to initiate our Strategic Focus, we will review multiple factors relevant in each dimension. We will take a high level look so you can see what role these factors play, how they are interconnected and influence one another (e.g., your energy on your emotional state, future vision on motivation, and social context on resilience, etc.), and how each factor (especially Key Factors) support flow (e.g., by internalizing skills that support Performance Focus). Next, we use the model as a diagnostic framework to better understand what principles and practices are currently working in your favor (*Flow Assets*) and those that may be working against you (*Flow Liabilities*).

As you explore these dimensions and factors, remember that each Flow Factor discussed has a corresponding tool or exercise (plus a curated library of free resources) to help you direct your Strategic Focus along a specific developmental path. You can find a list of these tools and resources on the website (www.attentionalleadership.com) or by visiting the book's landing page (See Appendix B).

My aim is to help you first identify your Flow Assets and Flow Liabilities to uncover your Personal Flow Formula (What's Important Now—WIN). Then, we'll narrow down the factors within your Personal Flow Formula to identify your "One Thing" that will have the most significant impact. This means focusing on one Flow Factor at a time—unless you're highly ambitious, then no more than three.

Let's start our tour of dimensions by looking at some of the Key Factors that best represent each dimension, noting that there are many other factors that influence your flow. These are included within the assessment and corresponding resources and tools, but not at this higher level. Reviewing these dimensions and Key Factors will help you better understand and prepare for taking the ALI 1080° Sweep™ Assessment.

Note to Reader

In this framework, we explore fifteen dimensions. Each dimension is typically broken down into three Key Factors, along with other factors to consider during your self-assessment. However, the Interpersonal, Team, Organization, and Community dimensions are treated distinctively.

These four dimensions are recognized as both dimensions and Key Factors due to their broader scope of influence. This approach simplifies their complex interactions by treating each as a cohesive theme. When you engage with the ALI 1080° Sweep™ Assessment, you'll encounter numerous factors within these four dimensions, providing a thorough exploration of the many factors contained within each of these external dimensions.

It's important to highlight that our comprehensive personal strategy assessment delves deeply into all dimensions, encompassing over a hundred factors. Yet within our upcoming tour we'll explore a total of thirty-nine Key Factors in greater depth to raise your awareness and get you warmed up to take the ALI 1080° Sweep™ Assessment where you will dive even deeper.

Chapter 5
Alignment One: Future—From There to Here

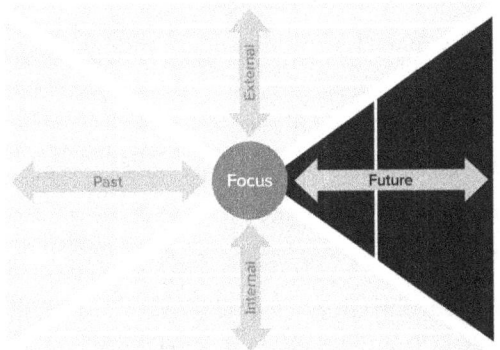

Long Future: Missions, Vision & Legacy

> "Begin with the end in mind."
> —Stephen R. Covey

Optimizing focus and flow in the present moment requires aligning current actions with your *Future* destination. This starts with clarifying your *missions*, *vision*, and desired *legacy*.

Mission(s)

> "A journey of a thousand miles begins with a single step."
> —Lao Tzu

Drafting your *Missions* represents the broad and colorful brush strokes that ultimately frame and inform the vision. It's what we seek flow for—a successful career, happy family, adventure, or service. While a singular Mission Statement provides focus, creating multiple mission statements for different areas of your life can ensure a holistic approach to achieving your aspirations. These grand objectives need to be declared in order to direct your attention toward something you want long-term. Personal missions are the "big, hairy, audacious goals" that initiate direction.[41] These might be:

- *Spiritual*: To be worthy of Heaven in the service to others.
- *Family*: To build and cultivate a happy and loving family.
- *Professional*: To become an author, speaker, trainer and coach.
- *Social*: To have a loving and supporting network of friends.
- *Physical*: To maintain a healthy body and maintain strength and energy.
- *Financial*: To be financially secure.
- *Political*: To serve in a local or state political office.
- *Philanthropic*: To give time and resources toward worthy causes.
- *Adventure*: To travel and see the world.

By offering a clear direction, each mission not only guides you toward a fulfilling life but also aligns your actions that make every task more meaningful.

Vision

> "Where there is no vision, the people perish."
> —Proverbs 29:18

After defining your grand missions, a detailed *Vision* follows. Adding detail brings forth a compelling picture. By engaging all your senses—sight, sound, touch, taste, smell, and intuition—you craft a vision that tells a story as if it's happening now. Once you have this vision, practicing *visualization* (a skill in the Psychological dimension) will boost your self-efficacy, confidence, motivation, and commitment to achieving your goal.

Consider the sights, sounds, images, smells, and feelings that make your vision tangible. Writing it in the "present tense," as if it's already real, adds clarity. Taking each mission and telling its detailed story in the present, then linking them into a compelling narrative, can ignite your motivation. For example, if your *physical mission* is to maintain health into your nineties, visualize this mission as if it's real: "I am lean and strong, with less than 15 percent body fat. My energy is exceptional; I feel terrific. People see me as the fittest person they know. I eat well, exercise daily, stretch, meditate, supplement my nutrition, and see my doctor regularly. Thanks to my health, I enjoy playing with my grandkids, swimming, and hiking."

A vision is more than a picture—it's a movie. Crafting a detailed vision can transform the quality and direction of your life, guiding you toward your desired outcomes. When the picture is clear, you can move closer to it.

A humorous example is from WWII when the US struggled to create accurate guidance systems for bombs. Psychologist B.F. Skinner proposed a creative solution: using operant conditioning (punishments and rewards) where pigeons were trained to peck at a picture of the bombsite while placed in the nose of the bomb. Pecking up to 10,000 times in forty-five seconds, a pigeon could steer the bomb to its target. Although never formally used, the system was highly accurate![42] The clearer your vision, and the more you focus on it, the greater the chance of hitting your target.

Legacy

> "Everyone must leave something behind when he dies...something his hand touched in some way."
> —Ray Bradbury

Ray Bradbury's observation on *Legacy* serves as a poignant reminder that our actions and flow states have the power to leave a lasting impact. By aligning our daily pursuit of flow with our deepest values, we shape a legacy reflecting our essence and contributions.

The ability to clearly define life missions typically separates exceptional from average performers. As Søren Kierkegaard stated: "Life can only be understood backward; but it must be lived forward." This is the stuff of personal legacy. And with your future missions and vision in place, it's time to look backward.

Reflect on this: If you could observe your own funeral, what would people say about your life and influence? Visualize yourself at your funeral, taking stock of what you became, accomplished, and contributed. What are they saying about you? What do you wish they would say?

This exercise offers a profound perspective. If it's a struggle, regard it as a wake-up call and make the necessary corrections to become the person you truly want to be.

With your missions, vision and legacy in place, you have a *three-dimensional picture*—each giving you a different vantage point for viewing and flowing toward your long future.

Short Future: Goals, Plans & Time Maximation

Let's now explore the *Short Future* practices that make your Long Future a reality. Designing your Long Future provides a clear picture of what you are seeking after, but that picture must be reverse engineered. This requires us to move toward our present moment by breaking down our Missions, Vision, and Legacy into smaller pieces. Here we define our *Goals,* specify our strategic *Plans* and optimize our use of *Time* to stay focused on what actions have the greatest value and impact.

Goals

> "Life can be pulled by goals just as surely as it can be pushed by drives."
> —Viktor E. Frankl

Finding your flow requires breaking down your long future into bite-sized *Goals*. This includes setting nested goals (long-term, intermediate, and short-term) for each mission, vision, and desired legacy.

Why are goals so important? Research shows that people with specific and challenging goals outperform those with ambiguous "do-your-best" goals, increasing performance by up to 56 percent.[43] Over 91 percent of goal-setters show positive results, boosting performance between 8.4 percent and 16 percent.[44] And, of significant importance, goal setting applies across different tasks, settings, performance criteria, and subjects.[45] At Dominican University, for example, students who had written goals performed better than those that didn't. And those who made a public commitment to their goals as well as engaged in weekly accountability, outperformed non-goal-setters by an even larger amount. This speaks to the importance of metrics and measurement (a Short Past factor).

Goal setting is an effective flow strategy across all performance arenas. Goals, whether short-term or long-term, provide structure and direct energy by turning strategic intent into focused action. Without translating good intent (missions, vision, legacy) into specific goals, consistent flow is elusive.

Your goals should align with and advance the three-dimensional perspective outlined in your long future. Use SMART criteria (Specific, Meaningful/Measurable, Aggressive yet Realistic, Time-driven) to clarify the actions needed to progress toward your long-term future.

Plans

> "A goal without a plan is just a wish."
> —Antoine de Saint-Exupéry

Beyond writing goals, building your *Plans* strategically is necessary to move from the abstract toward the concrete.

Good planning requires you to engage the *2nd Secret*, which includes:

1. Placing your goal at the center of your attention and translating larger goals into smaller SMART Goals.
2. Defining the time, energy, and resources needed to achieve your goal.
3. Clarifying the process or exactly "how" you will take action.
4. Speculating, thinking through, and observing the outcomes of your actions.
5. Knowing your available feedback loops (internal and external) to learn from every action and make adjustments until your actions produce your desired results.

While designing detailed plans transforms your intentions into actionable steps, it's important to remain flexible, allowing you to adapt and maintain flow amidst life's unpredictability. In essence, effective planning helps you clarify the resources and steps needed to achieve your goals, which, as a by-product, increases your sense of well-being.[46]

Time Maximization

"Have regular hours for work and play; make each day both useful and pleasant, and prove that you understand the worth of time by employing it well."
—Louisa May Alcott

With a well-crafted and strategic plan paving the way, knowing how to maximize your *Time* is another key factor. One effective strategy is to employ prioritization techniques such as the Eisenhower Box, which helps distinguish between urgent and important tasks, ensuring you focus on what truly matters.[47] If you've read The 7 Habits of Highly Effective People by Stephen R. Covey[48] you may remember this as Quadrant II (Not Urgent/Important)—promoting a more strategic use of time. I recommend creating a "Time Maximization" box, breaking Quadrant II into its own four quadrants, adding the principle of "Impact." This helps you stay strategic and focused on what's most important, emphasizing factors that produce the greatest results.

Whatever strategies you use, the research is clear: maximizing time reduces stress[49], increases self-efficacy,[50] job performance, achievement striving[51] and flow.[52]

Focus on what matters most—things that add the greatest value *and* impact. Clarify your WIN (What's Important Now).

Other effective time maximization strategies include designing consistent rituals and routines (fixed time), which minimize distractions and direct focus.[53] Rituals or routines are essential for high performers, readying them for daily engagement or critical moments. Early morning reflection, breathing, prepping gear, visualizing the day, etc., invite focus. One doctor I interviewed commented: "I usually get so completely absorbed in work that time flies by and I do not even give it much thought. I attribute this to a routine." In fact, most peak performers use rituals (daily or right before a performance moment) to gain consistency and elicit desired behaviors, helping them "divert attention away from negative, irrelevant information."[54]

In addition to fixed rituals, be intentional about "variable time"—clearly defining workday boundaries and allocating time blocks for high-value, high-impact activities serving your short-term goals. Both fixed and variable time help clarify values, set priorities, and focus energies, vital for finding your flow.

Aligning with our future involves mapping out a clear path from our ultimate destination back to the present moment. By defining our missions, vision, and legacy, we create a three-dimensional picture that guides us toward our purpose. Breaking down these aspirations into long-term, intermediate, and short-term goals, creating strategic plans, and maximizing our time ensures progress toward those larger ambitions. Now, let's turn inward and explore the Internal Dimension, aligning our inner world to support our pursuit of flow.

Chapter 6
Alignment Two: Internal—Full Engagement

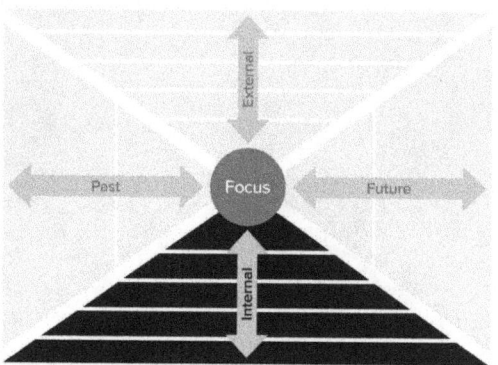

"Though he should conquer a thousand men on the battlefield a thousand times, he who can conquer himself is the noblest victor."
—Buddha

As Buddha's words remind us, the greatest battles are often internal. This principle underpins our exploration of the five *Internal Dimensions*—where conquering oneself paves the way to mastering flow.

Within the five internal dimensions—*Spiritual, Philosophical, Psychological, Emotional,* and *Physical,* our goal is to establish a clear alignment from operationalizing truths that manifest into the right actions. Essentially, we aim to eliminate any internal interference that impedes our full engagement in the present moment.

Spiritual: Principles, Purpose & Virtues

> "Science is not only compatible with spirituality; it is a profound source of spirituality."
> —Carl Sagan

Carl Sagan eloquently highlights that science and spirituality are not at odds but are complementary. Understanding the scientific principles behind our actions and aligning them with our *Spiritual* beliefs can deepen our engagement and presence in every moment, thereby enhancing our flow.

Why a spiritual dimension? Individuals who integrate their spirituality in their work reap big benefits: increased well-being, higher morale, greater commitment, less stress, greater work/life balance,[55] less burnout, higher resilience, improved self-efficacy, higher engagement,[56] a positive influence on others, higher altruism, self-esteem, self-management, conscientiousness, involvement, and ethical behaviors. They also experience less inter-role conflict and frustration.[57] Moreover, people who attend to their Spiritual dimension are usually healthier and happier[58] and believe their enterprise would benefit from an increased sense of meaning and spirituality.[59]

Finding flow—being in the moment, fully engaged, becoming our best, and performing at our peak—rests on the belief that we live in a world guided by something beyond our personal beliefs. This requires faith in **Truth** revealing **Principles** that govern everything toward your **Purpose** and **Potential**. Along the way, personal **Virtues** aid the journey, including **Faith, Hope, Charity, Humility,** and **Obedience** (or alignment) to what "is" to achieve the desired end state.

Principles

> "Every science has for its basis a system of principles as fixed and unalterable as those by which the universe is regulated and governed. Man cannot make principles; he can only discover them."
> —Thomas Paine

True *Principles* and natural laws govern everything we do.[60] We are constantly gathering more knowledge through trial-and-error experimentation, which is the essence of the scientific method. For example, we know that gravity is ever present. We know that the terminal velocity of objects is 122 MPH—at least on this planet. It doesn't matter if we believe in gravity or terminal velocity—they are realities that influence us all on earth.

Consider this: For almost two thousand years, it was believed that objects of different weights would fall at different speeds based on Aristotle's teachings. In 1654, Galileo conducted a simple experiment at the Tower of Pisa, dropping two objects of different weights simultaneously. To everyone's surprise, they hit the ground at the same time, disproving the long-standing assumption. Skeptics doubted the results, suspecting manipulation. This instant debunking raises questions and highlights the need to uncover underlying principles.

Likewise, what you believe about finding the area of a circle has nothing to do with calculating it. That is accomplished only through Pi (3.1415927…). Water boils at 212°F, scuba divers have only so much time at a particular depth based on nitrogen saturation rates. Principles with less exacting numbers but are usually consistent include the Pareto Principle—where 20 percent of efforts produce 80 percent of results—just to name a few.

Spiritual = Principles.

Since principles govern everything, we need to understand and align with the principles that govern our work and craft, and those governing flow and full engagement.

As I remind my son on the tennis court: there is a mathematical formula to hit a tennis ball from one corner of the court to the other (82.8 feet). It is exact and consistent. Your goal is to align your body and tennis racket in such a way that you can get as close to that formula as possible if hitting the ball to that corner is the goal. Finding that alignment is the objective. Yet there is an infinite number of ways that one can align with that formula. Some might strike that ball with an open stance, others with a closed stance. Whether right-handed or left-handed, using topspin or slice, leaning forward or even off balance—there is a "way" to hit that ball just right yet do it so uniquely. Consider this profound paradox as you begin to identify specific principles and practices you need to acquire to build greater capacity.

Once you seek alignment to a principle or practice to enhance your flow, "how" you go about making it work for you and your circumstances are as personal and unique as the discovery of your Personal Flow Formula. With perfect alignment comes the perfect shot—but it needs to be your shot.

Purpose

> "It is not enough to be busy. So are the ants. The question is: What are we busy about?"
> —Henry David Thoreau

Another Spiritual Key Factor is *Purpose*, which moves you toward your potential.

As previously stated, no one else has the same genetic code as you—nor do they have the same fingerprint, iris or footprint. You are unique and distinct—there never has been nor will be another you. Hence, you must seek what you were born to do.

Knowing that you are unique, and that you are living at this time and place in history, should give you a sense of purpose. Why are you here? Who might you become? The power of purpose is knowing who you are and discovering what unique contribution(s) you are here to make.

This process requires a commitment to the **2nd Secret** and the willingness to *fail faster and better* in order to align with the truth in order to discover our purpose and potential. What assists us in this process are the personal virtues we develop to see the work through.

Virtues

> "All the world is made of faith, trust, and pixie dust."
> —J.M. Barrie (Peter Pan)

This quote reminds us that embracing *Virtues* like faith and trust in ourselves and the process can lift us toward our potential, much like "pixie dust" enables flight in Peter Pan's world.

Believing in principles takes *Faith*. Faith means knowing truths exist even if you lack tangible evidence. It also requires *Hope*, which asserts that something better is ahead and that today's actions will bring you closer to a brighter tomorrow. Like Faith and other virtues, Hope is akin to a spiritual muscle. Where there's Faith, Hope often supports it. Interestingly, people with Faith and Hope perform up to 27 percent better and are up to 29 percent more satisfied with their work,[61] leading to improved outcomes.[62] Hope also fosters a sense of community, offers a greater sense of meaning, and enriches people's inner lives.[63]

Exercising faith and hope will open new doors toward flow, especially in challenging times. This often requires a "letting go" of current assumptions, previous actions and ego. This is where *Humility* enters—recognizing that we must defer to higher governing laws, which we can use to succeed if we keep what we think we know in check. Learning to let go, exercising faith, hope, and humility are all spiritual strategies. I often hear comments like "I'm letting it happen" or "freeing up" to invite flow. These have always been indicators to me that one is tapping into spiritual muscles rather than mental, emotional, or physical muscles.

To engage in any process where iterative failure is the key ingredient to future success requires the virtue of *Charity*—self charity that is. It's one thing to give someone else a break, support, or substance, when they make a mistake or need help. But how often do we give ourselves a break and support? It's this virtue that helps you manage pressure while offering greater perspective and understanding. Along the way, the virtue of *Obedience* is required to maintain your path.

Together these and other spiritual virtues play a significant role in finding your flow—especially when you recognize that life is more like a marathon than a sprint.

Philosophical: Beliefs, Values & Ethos

"My dad believed that people should have a worthwhile and productive philosophy of life if they are to amount to anything."
—John Wooden

Between principles (Spiritual) and thought processes (Psychological) resides a dimension that is ever-present but often below our conscious awareness—the *Philosophical* self. This dimension emerges as a by-product of our personal, family, and cultural history and experiences. It represents the underlying code that is our operating software. Within this dimension we explore the *Beliefs, Values, and Ethos* that inform our moment-by-moment actions.

In his essay on Nature, Ralph Waldo Emerson discussed the difference between religion and ethics. He surmised that religion and ethics were the practice ideas—the former coming from God (spiritual), and the latter coming from man (philosophical).[64] Taken together, religion and ethics powerfully affect the thoughts and actions that contribute to our virtues and character—for better or worse.

Your philosophical self functions as a foundational code, similar to a computer's permanent memory (ROM), guiding your actions automatically and persistently. In contrast, Random Access Memory (RAM) acts more like immediate thought, which takes energy.

Like ROM, the philosophical self-governs all actions, but is slightly modified after every transaction or moment—something of a software upgrade based on new information gathered after every experience.

Many great men and women have written their personal Philosophies. Some call them creeds, constitutions, maxims, tonics, rules, virtues, ethos, or codes, etc. We all have a personal philosophy—implicit or explicit—that needs to be uncovered, added to and refined through every flow experience.

Beliefs

"Whether you think you can or can't, you are right."
—Henry Ford

All you need to train fleas for a flea circus is a small cup! After hitting the top and sides of a cup, fleas "learn" to jump only as high and wide as the cup will allow. Even when you remove the cup, fleas will stay within a very tight boundary. Similarly, after a few days of being chained to a fence or a tree, a simple rope will keep elephants from wandering.[65]

We are much the same. Our **Beliefs** govern everything we see and experience. If we believe we're going to lose, we usually do. But positive beliefs (about oneself, others, and the world) are transformative. For instance, when students believe in themselves, they achieve higher academic performance.[66] And when we have positive beliefs about ourselves, our performance improves as well—by as much as 44 percent.[67] When beliefs are forged (positively or negatively), our expectations are influenced by those beliefs, so we typically stay within our conceptual and perceptual boundaries—our "comfort zone."

A few examples: when arm wrestlers were paired with opponents perceived to be stronger, they lost ten out of twelve times, even though they were objectively stronger.[68] In an interesting pain study, individuals who believed that sugar pills were morphine had a similar decrease in pain.[69] When teachers were given what they thought were "late blooming" students who were expected to show high gains in IQ and achievement, they performed as expected, even though they were chosen at random.[70] In 1954, Roger Bannister was the first person to break the four-minute mile: Within one year, more than a dozen others broke this same record. When others break seemingly impossible barriers, it's simply just a new boundary for someone else to break. And according to researchers Anders Ericsson and Robert Pool, in their over three decades of studying the world's greatest performers, they have yet to find a limit on human capacity and potential.[71]

Our beliefs and expectations can work for or against us. Believe that you have what it takes to excel, along with positive expectations, and good things start to happen.

Values

> "Education without values, as useful as it is, seems rather to make man a more clever devil."
> —C.S. Lewis

In addition to what we believe, what we *Value* directs our attention. Certain values can distract while others facilitate focus. Positive values such as honesty, dedication, empathy, and hard work all make a positive contribution. Values such as dishonesty, selfishness, and laziness produce a very different outcome.

Clarifying your values is at the core of defining your philosophical self. In his autobiography, Ben identified thirteen virtues he sought to master in life. These included: **Temperance, Silence, Order, Resolution, Frugality, Industry, Sincerity, Justice, Moderation, Cleanliness, Tranquility, Chastity, and Humility.** He was good at many but struggled with some—like the rest of us—but it was his persistent intent that supported his efforts.[72]

A clear value system can guide our daily thoughts and actions and the leadership of others, especially between team members.[73] Leaders with a clear value system "set the tone" for organizations, which offers a model and framework to help others make difficult decisions.[74]

When your values align with true principles, they inform your behavior—helping you forge a clear ethical code that informs everything you think, feel and do.

Ethos

> "When people meet their personal standards, they feel validated and fulfilled. They also feel as if they're living up to the image of who they want to be."
> —Dr. Kerry Patterson

The behavioral extension of your beliefs and values is your *Ethos*—the rules and standards that keep you "on track." Rules are like policy: they guide what you will do and not do. In 1825 Thomas Jefferson created a *Decalogue of Canons for his life*:

1. Never put off till tomorrow what you can do today.
2. Never trouble another for what you can do yourself.
3. Never spend your money before you have it.
4. Never buy what you do not want, because it is cheap.
5. Pride costs us more than hunger, thirst, and cold.
6. We have never repented of having eaten too little.
7. Nothing is troublesome that we do willingly.
8. How much pain has cost us the evils, which never happened?
9. Take things always by their smooth handle.
10. When angry, count to ten, before you speak: if very angry, a hundred.[75]

Standards take rules to a new level. Within any rule, there are degrees of adherence. George Washington had, perhaps, the most detailed and refined personal philosophy and behavioral constitution of his day. In his book, *The 110 Rules of Civility and Decent Behavior*, Washington identified specific actions and inactions that he sought to exemplify—and he kept this book with him for constant reference.[76]

At the peak of his career at Carnegie Mellon University, Dr. Randy Pausch discovered he had less than six months to live. Seeking to codify all of his life lessons and to pass them on to others before his passing he wrote his "Last Lecture" and toured the country sharing his most significant insights and values that defined his life—a testament to the power of taking time to write out your personal philosophy for the benefit of others.[77]

The standards you keep in order to find your flow can have a positive influence on others too. People who are perceived to be more ethical are seen as better citizens[78] and shown to have positive influences on organizational performance.[79]

Discovering and codifying your *Personal Ethos* enables you to keep top of mind *Who* you seek to be in relationship to the *What and Why*. Your personal ethos is like a creed or covenant that keeps you focused on what matters most, while maintaining the behaviors toward their achievement.

Psychological: Thoughts, Images & Perspectives

"The most important attribute a player must have is mental toughness."
—Mia Hamm

When your thoughts, images, and perspectives align with your beliefs, values, and ethos, and these align with true principles in the service of your purpose and potential, you are on your way toward greater internal alignment. Monitoring, managing, and mastering your thoughts, images, and perspectives are all Key Factors that contribute to your mental toughness.

Thoughts

"Change your thoughts and you change your world."
— Norman Vincent Peale

Managing your thoughts and thinking is central to self-governing, executive function, and managing focus and flow. So, let's start with your perceptions.

Perceptions. Even when we receive the same information, we all experience the world through our own unique lens. We often make attribution errors and assumptions about what we experience instead of looking at all points of view. Misperceptions wreak havoc on our thoughts and inner climate. Cognitive distortions twist our realities, influencing how we think, feel, and act in any performance arena. Recognizing and reframing these **Cognitive Distortions**, is at the center of Cognitive Behavioral Therapies.

Distortions such all-or-nothing thinking, disqualifying the positive, overgeneralization, and fortune-teller error create interference. Learning to identify, challenge, and rewrite your inner dialogue can remove that inference. Anything that we perceive that is inaccurate produces a false reality and is remedied by testing, validating or invalidating our assumptions, and getting our internal narratives back on track.[80]

It's not easy to recognize our misperceptions, but when you slow things down, you become aware of the words and language that you're using.

Like all of the other Flow Factors, thoughts can be assets or liabilities. Exceptional performers who find their flow are excellent at managing and generating positive inner language or self-talk (also known as verbal self-guidance).[81] In a study involving cyclists, the group that received assisted positive self-talk increased performance the most.[82] People who practice positive self-talk experience less anxiety, higher self-confidence, higher self-efficacy, and better performance[83]—all of which can have a powerful effect on strength and endurance.[84]

Negative thinkers struggle more with focus and flow because they're distracted by their inner voice. Nobody is immune to inner interference. Consider a recent performance and associate certain feelings with certain thoughts: "You can do it" vs. "What will happen if I screw this up?" "I was born for this moment" vs. "I've never done this before." Your inner voice is capable of playing either the advocate or the critic and can profoundly affect how well you do.

By learning to use your inner voice more effectively, you can focus more intently in the moment to facilitate flow.

Images

> "Imagination does not become great until human beings, given the courage and strength, use it to create."
> — Maria Montessori

Visualization means using the mind's eye to see, plan, practice, execute, review, and repeat excellent performances. The opposite is also the case. Yet in your mind, you can take more risks, play with various strategies, and try things you are not yet comfortable doing in real life. You can visualize the future and the past in the present moment. It is a distinct skill that separates us from all animal species.

Visualization has been used for thousands of years. As Buddhist monks trekked from India to China, they were often the victims of theft and barbarism until they learned to fight with their hands and feet, thus inventing the martial arts. Visualization allowed them to train mentally and practice at any place or time in preparation for potential attacks.

In preparing for competition, one college senior remarked: "In golf, I step back, look straight down the fairway where I want the ball to go, and then picture myself swinging the golf club and seeing the ball going straight down the middle. In shooting free throws in basketball, even before I bounce the ball, I stand and picture the shot going in before I shoot it." Another college student noted his process of visualization often includes deep breathing, progressive muscle relaxation, and other pre-visualization strategies: "When I'm really trying to focus on things, I think about my breathing patterns, in the nose, out the mouth, and picturing doing the task at hand—performing to the picture in my head. I see it all the way through, from A to Z, exactly how I want to do it or how it needs to be done."

Perspectives

> "The real voyage of discovery consists not in seeking new landscapes, but in having new eyes."
> —Marcel Proust

In Charles Dickens' *Christmas Carol,* you might remember that Scrooge chose a life of work and profit at the expense of humanity—expanding his fortune, while making bitter, the lives of those around him.[85] As the story goes, one night Scrooge is visited by three ghosts who give him three perspectives: a look at his past (positive feelings about his childhood mixed with the pain of loneliness); The present (an unfiltered view of how people really thought about him); And the future (how his current actions would negatively impact the lives of those around him—especially Tiny Tim and the Cratchit family). Each *Perspective* created a tipping point that convinced Scrooge to pivot his life course. Using intrinsic and extrinsic pain, the ghosts offered perspectives not yet seen or contemplated by Scrooge.

In my work, I find that helping people gain access to new perspectives helps remove the noise that comes through narrow and clouded thinking. As we gather experiences, we tend to put them in little boxes and define them through a narrow lens. "This was a good experience.," "Was this a bad experience?" "Why did this happen to me?" and so on.

People who go through major struggles often find that managing their perspective, or reframing their experiences, is a core strategy for coping with their challenges—even thriving through them. Using perspectives and reframing is about seeing circumstances from previously untapped angles—providing more chances to think, feel, and act in new and productive ways.

An old Hindu parable explains it best. Consider the parable of the *six blind men and the elephant:*

> Each man holds on to one part of the elephant and likens it to a familiar object. The first, holding on to its tail, says that an elephant is like a rope; the second, holding on to its leg, says it's like a tree; the third, holding on to its ear, says it's like a fan; the fourth man, holding on to its tusk, says that an elephant is like a spear; the fifth man, leaning against its side, says it is like a wall; and the sixth, holding on to its trunk, says it is like a snake. The six men argue, each sure that his information is correct. Each expresses his understanding from his own vantage point, only to recognize that he had only understood a small part of the elephant.

This parable vividly illustrates the concept of perspective, reminding us that a broader view can lead to a deeper understanding and alignment with our flow state, as we recognize the value of diverse viewpoints and experiences.

As you consider the issues in your life and performance arenas, recognize that you are only seeing through a small window with limited vision. Recognize that a new and more productive perspective—even a paradigm shift—may be available to you. In pursuing flow, you may need to access a broader perspective and awareness when your current perspective is producing excessive interference. In miserable situations, for example, some humor may be needed to shift the energy. In making sense of a difficult loss, you may choose a long-term or spiritual perspective to make better sense of it. Learning to tap into a variety of perspectives gives you much-needed flexibility when your current purview offers limited insight.

In the classic query—Is the glass half empty or half full?—perhaps neither is correct because the glass is both half empty *and half full—a third alternative. When looking at a rose bush, do you see a flower surrounded by thorns or a thorn bush that includes flowers?*

> A ***Chinese folktale*** provides another illuminating example:
> Once there was a gentleman in rural China. His only possession that really amounted to anything for him, his wife and son, who lived in a little hovel, was a gorgeous horse.

The neighbors came by often and said how lucky the farmer was to have this one beautiful horse. The wise old farmer said, "Maybe?"

One night the horse broke out of the corral and fled into the nearby mountains. All the neighbors came by and said how terrible it was that the mare was gone.

The wise old farmer said, "Maybe?"

One morning about ten days later, the horse returned to the corral bringing two beautiful wild horses with her. Now all the neighbors came by and said what wonderful luck he had: "You have these two additional horses plus your old horse. How fortunate you are!"

The wise old farmer said, "Maybe?"

The next day the farmer's son decided to break in these stallions so they could be ridden and then sold at market. One of the wild stallions threw him and broke his leg badly.

The neighbors said, "What terrible misfortune that your son has a badly broken leg."

The wise old farmer said, "Maybe?"

The next week the king sent his men throughout the land gathering troops for a war of conquest. They took all able-bodied young men as conscripts. The farmer's son was excused from serving because he had a badly broken leg. The neighbors' sons all had to go to war. The neighbors came and said, "Oh how lucky you are that your son was not taken off to war!"

The wise old farmer said, "Maybe?"

Motivation

"The only way to do great work is to love what you do."
—Steve Jobs

Understanding *Motivation*, derived from the Latin word *movere* meaning "to move," is crucial in our journey toward achieving flow, as it propels us to action and sustains our engagement. *Motive* is "the sense of need, desire, or fear that prompts a person to act" or "the direction and intensity of effort." As high performers we need to understand various motivational dimensions in order to realize our greatness.

Motivational theories abound through the centuries. From the early Greek philosophers who looked at motivation through eyes of hedonism—avoiding pain and seeking pleasure—through recent centuries, where philosophers, psychologists, sociologists, academics and gurus have discussed everything—from inner drives, satisfaction of needs and wants, methods of reinforcement and punishment, organizational engineering, identifying inner values and purpose, to actualizing full potential.[86]

Tapping into your motivation is like drilling for multiple sources of fuel. It is the "stuff" that powers everything else. That is why *intrinsic motivation* is one of the **Big Nine Flow Factors** and plays a critical role in tapping into all other dimensions to support flow.

For thirty years I've observed what motivates people to do great things, and six sources of motivation at three levels stand out: Level One contains four sources and are self-serving; Level Two moves one's focus outside of self; and Level Three links them both together.

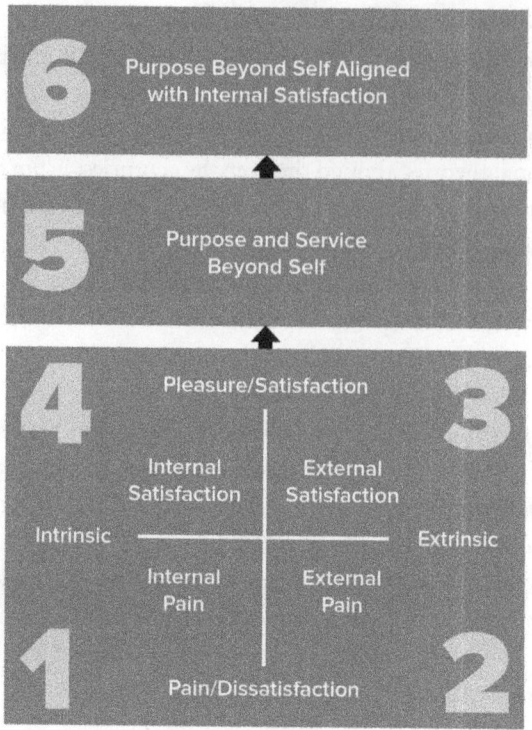

All of us have experienced Quadrant 1 motivation—the combination of Intrinsic and Pain. This motivation compels you to avoid things—like being self-critical, shame, or validating a negative self-image. These fear-based motives compel you to calculate the price of your action or inaction. When attended to in the moment, your mind is off your game.

Extrinsic and Pain (Quadrant 2) has a similar effect, such as the fear of failing in front of or disappointing others, losing money, a position, or losing face or respect. These too are powerful motivators that pull you out of your moments.

We are all quite familiar with carrots (Quadrant 3)—Extrinsic and Pleasure. Rewards such as money, food, acceptance, praise, and promotion. Most of us leap toward these sources of motivation. They spur us toward the game of "getting gain." While positive, these external sources of motivation are keenly deceptive. They sell the human experience short, yet most people rely on this motivation most of the time. Between internal and external pain and external pleasure, we are only tapping into parts of the motivation available to us.

Intrinsic Pleasure (Quadrant 4) motivation is the stuff of flow. When people speak of being in their flow or "zone," they speak of doing it "for its own sake" with no need for external reward (carrots) or for internal or external punishment (sticks). Identifying that intrinsically motivating force is a lifelong pursuit for some; others discover it early. We all experience it in brief spurts when we are doing something deeply enjoyable. It's finding joy in striking the tennis ball, teaching a complex idea to an eager class, playing the violin, climbing a challenging rock face, completing a quadruple bypass surgery, engaging with the crowd. It feels like an extension of us.

Perhaps the greatest contrast between Quadrants One to Three and Quadrant Four is the inherent nature of doing something that you love for no other reason than it energizes you to do it. Paradoxically, the inherent value of a thing—that which requires no external reward—is often the very reason for the external reward.

Whatever the situation, these four sources of internal motivation are compelling—each having their use and value. These forms of motivation primarily center on personal gains or fears. However, the most profound motivation often transcends self-interest, focusing on contributions to others or higher purposes. And as one of the best fortune cookies I've ever seen said: "A person wrapped in himself makes a very small package."

Motivation for our own sake takes us only so far. At some point, we ask: "What is bigger than me and my own self-interest?" Tapping into *purpose beyond self shifts* your focus from inside to outside, toward something of greater significance and value: raising money for a charity, visiting a family member in the hospital, serving on the school board, or running across a battlefield to retrieve a wounded brother or sister in harms way. These all speak to this fifth level of motivation.

But what if you could have both—tapping into what you love and serving at the same time? This sweet spot is *Level Six motivation*. When you tap this level of motivation you are connecting the intrinsic positive with a compelling external purpose, which answers the question: why was I born? The answer being: "For this!" When I visualize a rock n roll band playing their signature song to 100,000 fans where all the money is used for charity or a dedicated surgeon doing no-cost cleft palate surgery—we're hitting that sweet spot.

High performers who seek to be at their best know that doing what they love for a purpose that is greater than themselves is a magical combination for engaging fully in their craft.

Emotional: Awareness, Control & Generation

> "When dealing with people, remember you are not dealing with creatures of logic, but with creatures of emotion."
> —Dale Carnegie

As we all know quite well, our emotions play a keen role in our ability to focus. When we are unable to understand or manage our emotions, we are at the mercy of some unknown external or internal source. Yet when we build greater emotional capacity, we can not only manage the challenging times, but leverage our emotions to support our focus and flow.

Within the *Emotional* dimension we tap into feeling states, the bulk of which are informed and managed by our thinking. Our emotions can either help or hinder our focus and flow, but all emotions are useful barometers for self-awareness. Friedrich Nietzsche noted: "One ought to hold on to one's heart; for if one lets it go, one soon loses control of the head too."

Emotional Intelligence (or EQ) is recognizing and understanding your own emotions and the emotions of others.[87] The purpose of EQ is to translate feelings into better understanding, more effective action, and higher performance.

In a comprehensive study by TalentSmart, EQ was identified as the strongest predictor of workplace performance among thirty-three assessed skills, highlighting its importance in professional success. They also found that 90 percent of top performers scored high on EQ. In a forty-year study at UC Berkeley, researchers found EQ was 400 percent more powerful than IQ in predicting success.[88] Those with a high EQ perform better and with greater job success than those individuals with only high IQs.[89] We've all seen this—the brilliant kid who couldn't get the job or make it in the real world. Then there's our buddy who used to skip school, barely made it through math class, and is now running his or her own successful business. The difference often lies in people's EQ over IQ. As my father used to say: "Most of the A students are working for the C students."

Awareness

> "Awareness is the greatest agent for change."
> —Eckhart Tolle

Developing your EQ starts with *Emotional Awareness*, and yet only 36 percent of people can accurately identify their emotions.[90] For those who can regulate their emotions, they enjoy greater well-being, higher income, and greater socioeconomic success.[91] According to psychologist Tasha Eurich, 95 percent of people think they're self-aware, but only 10 to 15 percent actually are. And beyond individual performance, a lack of self-awareness can cut a team's success in half and lead to increased stress and decreased motivation.[92]

Control

> "You may not control all the events that happen to you, but you can decide not to be reduced by them."
> —Maya Angelou

As we are all aware, being angry in the moment gets in the way of clear thinking just as happiness and joy can engage us more deeply. That's why developing *Emotional Control* strategies are vital to removing internal interference. Stated Epictetus: "Any person capable of angering you becomes your master." And famed martial artist Bohdi Sanders confirmed, "When you react, you let others control you. When you respond, you are in control."

Without emotional control you are at the mercy of the moment—and your attention lapses. With greater emotional control you gain greater personal agency and the capacity to make rational choices—especially under stress. One positive derivative of this is the influence you have on others. Higher emotional regulation correlates with higher social competence and more socially appropriate emotions. High performers activate positive emotions while mitigating negative emotions—tapping into enthusiasm, humor and playfulness—all contributing factors to focus and flow.

Generation

> "Happiness is not something ready-made. It comes from your own actions."
> —Dalai Lama

Building on the foundation of emotional awareness and control, we arrive at the powerful practice of *Generating Positive Emotions*, where self-talk plays a crucial role in cultivating a positive mindset. As Dalai Lama XIV said,

"Happiness is not something ready-made. It comes from your own actions."

And yes, happiness significantly influences our performance. Companies with happier employees are 20 percent more productive than their competitors; happy salespeople achieve 37 percent more sales; employees who are happy at work report ten times fewer sick days; and countries with happier populations tend to experience higher productivity and economic growth.[93]

Emotional Awareness, Emotional Control, and Generating Positive Emotions helps us be more resilient and more focused, especially during stressful moments when we need flow the most.

Physical: Nutrition, Exercise & Energy

"The first wealth is health."
—Ralph Waldo Emerson

Physical = Actions. Physical strategies focus on the systems and practices that influence our ability to act, engage and flow in our many life arenas. Practices surrounding nutrition, physical fitness and energy management such as sleep, relaxation, meditation, physiological arousal, general health and well-being considerations, all enhance our physical capacity to act on the principles, values, thoughts, and emotions that service every action we take toward our goals.

Unless your physical foundation is solid (nutrition, exercise and energy management) it's difficult to perform at your best. What you eat, how much you exercise, how well you sleep, and your overall health and well-being is foundational to every other dimension.[94]

We all know these Key Factors are inherently true, but all of us struggle with the gap between "knowing" and "doing."[95]

Nutrition

"Let food be thy medicine and medicine be thy food."
—Hippocrates

Nutrition plays a crucial role in supporting focus, performance, and achieving flow states. Research indicates that a balanced diet rich in essential nutrients can significantly enhance cognitive function, reduce stress, and improve overall mental and physical performance.[96]

For instance, omega-3 fatty acids found in fatty fish like salmon and walnuts are vital for memory and learning, while antioxidants in fruits and vegetables protect brain cells from damage and enhance cognitive function. Protein-rich foods, such as skinless poultry and legumes, provide the amino acids necessary for neurotransmitter production, which affects mood, focus, and brain performance. Complex carbohydrates, found in whole grains, provide sustained energy that supports concentration and endurance throughout the day.[97]

Moreover, studies have shown that individuals who maintain healthy eating habits are less likely to experience depression and mood disorders, and they tend to handle stress more effectively. These benefits are critical for sustaining focus and achieving a flow state, where one is fully immersed and engaged in their activities (ibid.). Proper nutrition fuels both body and mind, significantly reducing productivity losses by 66 percent and allowing us to engage more fully in our tasks and passions. Interesting statistic: people who seldom eat fruits, vegetables, and other low-fat foods at work are 93 percent more likely to experience a loss in productivity.[98]

In summary, optimizing nutritional practices by incorporating a variety of nutrient-dense foods into your diet can have a profound impact on your ability to concentrate, perform, and experience flow. This highlights the importance of paying attention to what you eat as a foundational aspect of enhancing your productivity and overall well-being.

Exercise

"Those who think they have not time for bodily exercise will sooner or later have to find time for illness."
—Edward Stanley

Similar to nutrition, *Exercise* and fitness studies abound giving clear evidence of its value for supporting optimal functioning.

Studies consistently highlight the profound impact of exercise on focus and flow. Engaging in physical activity enhances cognitive health by boosting memory, attention, and problem-solving abilities. Regular exercise increases blood flow to the brain, fostering neuroplasticity and improving overall brain function, particularly in regions crucial for learning and memory.[99]

People who exercise regularly report 1.5 fewer days of poor mental health per month[100] and show improved cognitive performance, quicker information processing, and better attentional resource allocation (ibid). Furthermore, individuals engaging in aerobic fitness benefit from enhanced cognitive strategies and better task performance.[101] Regular exercisers also tend to adopt healthier lifestyles, exhibit greater productivity, smoke less, feel less stressed, and maintain better dietary habits.

Exercise provides physical release and the arousal needed to maintain alertness and generates higher alertness and the energy needed to find flow. This holistic improvement underscores the profound impact of physical fitness on focus, performance, and flow.

Net/Net: The quality of your fitness = the quality of your life.

Energy

> "Without passion, you don't have energy. Without energy, you have nothing."
> —Warren Buffett

Energy Management includes both rest and recovery. This is not just getting ample sleep each night (six to eight hours), but also taking mini breaks during the day to restore lost energy.

Sleep plays a key role in performance. "The rejuvenation provided by sleep is vital for our cardiovascular and immune systems, as well as our ability to think clearly, learn new information, and manage our emotions."[102]

In addition to prioritizing sufficient sleep and incorporating daytime rest and recovery strategies, high performers possess the ability to find their optimal level of arousal and engagement while effectively managing stress. Good stress, referred to as "eustress" by renowned psychologist Hans Selye, is viewed as beneficial and integral to achieving peak performance.[103] Successful individuals often experience a state of relaxed calmness just before entering their flow state or engaging in their chosen activity. They develop skills to navigate various arousal levels, including anxiety and depression, employing diverse techniques such as deep-breathing exercises, bathing, meditation, and yoga. These tactics enable them to regulate their bodily responses, manage arousal, and maintain control despite their circumstances.

Meditation is a common strategy used for energy management by calming down and setting the stage for flow. It relaxes and decreases arousal while prompting increased levels of awareness, higher focus, and greater personal control.[104]

A central practice of meditation is ***Deep Breathing,*** which signals your brain and body to calm down and relax.[105] Diaphragmatic breathing, a practice that includes breathing in through your nose and out through your mouth via the extension and contraction of the diaphragm, supports sustained attention, affect, and cortisol levels, which also promotes long-term health.[106] As a by-product, relaxation methods and meditation strategies often transcend the mere physical and prompt a spiritual experience that can lead to a state of flow.

By contrast, when more energy is needed, strategies like listening to high-energy music or engaging in short physical exercises, elevate arousal helping us prepare for high-stress situations. Football players often use these methods, pumping themselves up with inspiring or loud music, exchanging encouraging words, and engaging in physical interactions to increase their heart rate and energy. As one football player described it, "I listen to a hard rock song to get me going and start thinking of the game." Another player shared how he builds energy: "I put my helmet on and head-butt a certain teammate three times. That really gets the energy and adrenaline going."

In contrast to strategies that induce arousal and promote blood flow to large muscle groups, certain professions, like brain surgeons, require a different approach. Performing intricate procedures that involve precise movements in small areas call for a distinct set of techniques. In such cases, a surgeon might opt for soothing music, such as baroque or classical compositions, engage in deep-breathing exercises, and visualize the procedure before commencing a delicate incision. Whether you are preparing to deliver a presentation or working on a project that requires a boost of energy, finding your optimal level of arousal is a key factor that influences focus and aids in entering a state of flow.

As we conclude the Internal dimension, we must emphasize the interplay between the Spiritual, Philosophical, Psychological, Emotional and Physical. Each influences the other for positive or negative effects. The more you can increase your awareness of internal misalignments and build capacity where you need to, the easier you can lose yourself in the moment and be "at one" and fully engaged with your work, arena, or craft.

Chapter 7
Alignment Three: External—Place, Things and People

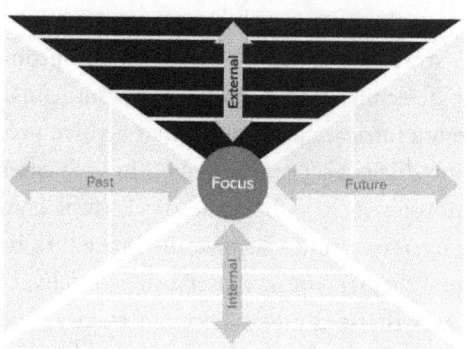

Your physical workspace, social interactions, company and community culture—collectively known as *External* dimensions—have a significant impact on your performance and ability to achieve flow. While many think of flow as an internally generated experience, external factors including place, people, and things play a critical role in either facilitating or hindering it.[107][108]

It's much easier to find your flow when you align yourself with the right people and environments. Often times this means learning how to make the best of your current relationships and circumstances. But sometimes this means finding a new ground-up ecosystem, with different people, relationships—even a new neighborhood, city, state, or even country to surround yourself with the right resources and social systems that bring out your best. It's important to remember that context is crucial when your goal is to become your best self.

Just like Future Alignment (Alignment One) and Internal Alignment (Alignment Two), similarly, these external dimensions also need your attention and alignment.

Personal: Adequate Resources, Optimal Environment & Locus of Control

> "It had long since come to my attention that people of accomplishment rarely sat back and let things happen to them. They went out and happened to things."
> —Leonardo da Vinci

The *Personal* dimension represents our relationship with our immediate physical environment—the arena itself—and things that comprise it. When we are engaged at any moment, the immediate environment influences us just as we influence it.

Among the many factors that influence your immediate environment: having *Adequate Resources, Optimizing the Environment and Controlling the Controllable* are Key Factors that help you bring your best—especially when challenge or stakes are high.

Adequate Resources

> "It is not fair to ask of others what you are not willing to do yourself. Give them the tools they need, and they will surprise you."
> —Elenor Roosevelt

To succeed in any endeavor, having the *Adequate Resources* is crucial. You can't play tennis without a racket, dig a ditch without a shovel, or craft a proposal without a computer. These tools are essential for their respective tasks. If you're aiming for optimal performance, it's important to audit your resources to identify what you have, what's missing, and what needs an upgrade.

As you consider the resources necessary for success, think of the smaller details that can make a significant impact, such as better lighting, upgraded software, or appropriate clothing. People often become disengaged when resources are lacking, yet having the right tools in place reduces stress and enables you to pursue your goals more effectively.[109]

Optimizing the Environment

"Environment is stronger than willpower."
—Paramahansa Yogananda

Learning to organize, utilize and **Optimize the Environment** is another important factor. Think of a spa and how they do it: soft music, lighting, heat, and smell. These variables, along with a good masseuse, are ready-made for focus. Or consider what makes for a solid night's rest: your favorite temperature, sheet and blanket coverage, pillow, position, darkness, silence.

Little things make all the difference. A student once explained how she prepared for reading a Harry Potter book in one sitting:

> First, I make myself comfortable and make the room comfortable by finding the right position on the couch or bed with pillows and blankets. I work from the inside out. I set the book there and light some candles or play music. When I am comfortable, I get down to business. Getting the room ready and starting to relax prepares me to read.

A divorce attorney explained how she conducted mediation sessions in her living room. When facilitating emotionally charged discussions she found it counterproductive to be in her office.

> My clients and I sit in a circle with no tables between us. When I mediate inside of a law office, I don't have flow like I do at home. I know what environment I need to lighten moods, channel communication, and focus on the issues at hand.

Do you have a certain space or place that is designed to invite flow? Is it an office, reading room, pool, gym, or car? Perhaps it is a natural space—a park, garden, or backyard. It helps to notice those environments in your work and life and then take note of the factors you can intentionally bring into these places.

Locus of Control

"Between stimulus and response there is a space. In that space is our power to choose our response. In our response lies our growth and our freedom."
—Viktor Frankl

While seeking to optimize resources and the environment, being in flow also requires **Controlling the Controllable**—learning to focus on what you can reasonably influence and ignore everything else. This sentiment, beautifully encapsulated in a well-known prayer, underscores a universal truth about focusing our efforts wisely, regardless of one's religious beliefs: *"God, grant me the Serenity to accept the things I cannot change, Courage to change the things I can, and Wisdom to know the difference."*

Seeking to control ourselves instead of others often pays the greatest dividends. For example, individuals with a higher internal locus of control are more likely to have lower stress and higher performance and satisfaction.[110] One world-class athlete and coach comments: "You need to make a clear distinction between the things that are within your control and outside your control and stay focused on what you have control over."

One of the greatest basketball coaches, John Wooden, once posed this question: "You only have a few seconds left on the shot clock. Who do you throw the ball to: The person who is thinking about winning, the person who is afraid of losing, or the person who is focused on taking the shot?" Of course, the answer is number three.

These questions reveal just how much we get caught up in the triviality of the moment and let irrelevant thoughts, feelings, and circumstances get in the way of what matters most.

Think of your most prevalent working or playing environments and consider these questions: Do you have all the resources you need? Is the place organized? Is it esthetically pleasing? Who or what is near you? Is this environment optimally designed to support your focus when it matters most?

Interpersonal: Optimizing Relationships

"The best way to find out if you can trust somebody is to trust them."
—Ernest Hemingway

As we look beyond our internal self and our work, we need to consider how other people influence our flow. *Interpersonal factors are all about exploring relational alignment* and whether others are having a positive or a negative influence on you—an assistant, copilot, stagehand, partner, colleague, family member, etc.[111][112]

One pediatric doctor explained how her staff members assisted her focus and daily flow by keeping her medical charts organized by placing them next to the door of each patient. This simple strategy enabled her to keep her mind on her patients and not on administrative tasks.

The value of connecting with others arises when people speak about interpersonal flow experiences. One female professional said: "In my flow experiences, the human connection is much more profound. I can lose myself while touching people's lives."

If we are hoping to flow in any workplace, we need to have positive relationships. A Gallup survey of US workers found that over 50 percent of respondents who have a best friend at work also feel passionate about their job and strongly connected to their organization (compared to 10 percent of workers who lack a best friend). They also found that those who are ignored by their bosses are fifteen times more likely to be disengaged.[113] "Work friendships are very important to job satisfaction," says Dr. Ho Kwan Cheung, professor of psychology at SUNY Albany. "The more relational-oriented your work is, the more your job satisfaction predicts performance. One example is creative work, or anything that involves creative problem-solving. When you're satisfied with your work and enjoy being with your coworkers, it makes you more creative and a better collaborator."[114]

Since other people play direct and indirect roles in our performance, we need to be aware of how they help or hinder our flow. Do they support you? Do you enjoy their presence? If not, they could be a distraction?

As you consider each relationship that surrounds you, you might ask? Are we both seeking principled-based truths? Am I inspired by this person? Do we share the same values or ideals? Do we think alike? Is there relational synergy? Do we share a common vision and direction and understand the roles we each play toward a common goal?

Team: Synergy with Others

> "Talent wins games, but teamwork and intelligence wins championships."
> —Michael Jordan

Flow often emerges from synergy with others, whether through collaboration with co-actors or engaging with a group or audience. If you work in a *Team* environment, consider how your team's dynamics impact your work and ability to achieve flow. In high-performing teams, collective performance exceeds the sum of its parts. In contrast, low-performing teams deliver less than the sum of their members' contributions.

Trust is fundamental to fostering open communication and seamless collaboration within teams. Safe environments promote innovation and risk-taking, both essential for achieving flow and peak performance. High trust also leads to increased performance,[115] while the absence of trust hampers collaboration. When collaboration falters, most employees (around 86 percent) attribute this to workplace failures. However, well-connected, high-performing teams (the top 20 percent) experience 59 percent less turnover, 41 percent less absenteeism, a 66 percent increase in wellness, and a 21 percent increase in productivity.[116] In contrast, low-trust and low-collaboration teams tend to struggle with conflict.

To evaluate your alignment with your team, consider the following: Does the team inspire and motivate you? Do you share common values and beliefs? Do you have similar opinions? Is the team's emotional climate conducive to flow? Are you aligned with the team's direction? Are you in the right role? Do you know what is expected of you? Do you have the resources and support needed to excel? Is there enough cooperation and coordination to support your best work? Does the team have a positive or negative influence on you? Do you like the people you work with, and do they like you? Do they help or hinder you in your role and goals? Ultimately, do the teams you engage with enhance or inhibit your flow, and do you bring high value to them?

Organization Alignment: Right Arena

"Think of yourself as a seed, and a company culture is the soil. You won't grow in just any soil. Some soil is made for you, some isn't."
—Hamza Zaouali

After exploring the role of personal environments, individual relationships, and team dynamics in fostering flow, it's important to consider how the overarching *Organizational* context and how the organization's physical, relational, and cultural systems influence you?

Early research into organizational behavior, such as the Hawthorne Studies of the 1920s and 1930s, showed that human performance is influenced not only by different work methods but also by social and physical contexts.[117]

Culture permeates every level of an organization, and today, 46 percent of job seekers consider it a very important factor when choosing where to work.[118] This underscores the significance of organizational culture in attracting talent, indicating that a culture aligned with one's values and work style can facilitate a flow state where creativity and productivity flourish.

Employees who find a strong organizational fit tend to deepen their commitment to their work, increasing the likelihood that they will feel engaged and motivated to "go the extra mile."[119] A 2019 survey by Glassdoor found that over 50 percent of respondents felt company culture was "more important than salary" for job satisfaction, and 79 percent said they examine a company's mission and purpose before even applying.[120] This highlights the importance of finding organizational alignment—a place where it feels right to work.

Organizations that prioritize psychological safety generate environments where employees feel unencumbered to experiment, take risks, and learn. Workers in such contexts tend to thrive and perform at their best. Increased psychological safety in organizations is a predictor of quality improvements, productivity, and learning.[121] For example, Google conducted an internal study several years ago to identify the factors that contributed most to its high-performing teams. The number-one factor was psychological safety. Teams and organizations with high ratings of psychological safety were more likely to implement diverse ideas, achieve higher performance, and stay at Google. As you seek to optimize your flow, get to know the cultures of the organizations you want to engage and see what others have to say about its current culture.

You might ask: Does the organization inspire you to be at your best? How do you think and feel about the organization's mission, vision, values, and goals? Do people at your organization think like you? Does its emotional climate resonate with yours? Do you have all of the resources you need to succeed? Are you in the right role or job? Is there a sense of collaboration that positively impacts your work? A large portion of job seekers (38 percent) report that they want a job that aligns with their purpose and passions; and 27 percent of employees are more likely to stay at a company when they feel that it has a purpose beyond profit margins.[122] These statistics reveal a deep-seated need for work that is not just profitable but purposeful and aligned with one's passions. Such alignment is not merely about job satisfaction—it's about creating conditions conducive to flow, where employees are more engaged, innovative, and productive. Does this resonate with you?

When you consider your work and where you thrive, you might also reflect on whether the organization's culture encourages creativity, learning, and autonomy? You might also ask: Does it align with your style and temperament? Does it feel right to work there? Does it provide you with all the resources you need to be successful? What about its pace and cadence or its politics? What about this place compels you to thrive? What about it might be interfering with your focus and flow? These are key ingredients for fostering an environment where you can consistently achieve flow and do your best work.

Community: Thriving in the Ecosystem

> "The world is so empty if one thinks only of mountains, rivers and cities; but to know someone who thinks & feels with us, & who, though distant, is close to us in spirit, this makes the earth for us an inhabited garden."
> —Goethe

Goethe's words remind us that beyond the physical landscapes of mountains, rivers, and cities, it's the connections we share with others that truly enrich our lives, emphasizing the importance of **Community Alignment** in our journey toward flow. Yet we must keep in mind that the communities we seek are often the by-product of our current beliefs and constructs about self and others:

A man goes to a Zen master and says, "I would like to move to this city. What do you think of the people here?"

And the Zen master says, "What were the people like in your old city?"

And the man says, "They were awful, mean, spiteful."

The Zen master says, "They are the same here. You shouldn't move here."

Then another person goes to the Zen master and says, "I'd like to move to your city. What do you think of the people here?"

And the Zen master says, "What were the people like in your old city?"

And the man says, "They were very nice people. Very smart. I enjoyed being around them."

And the Zen master says, "They are the same here. You will enjoy it here."

While we bring our inner selves wherever we go, and interpret these environments through our own lens, the environments that surround us significantly influence us.

Years ago, I was facilitating a workshop on flow with senior wealth managers at a large investment firm with offices in Denver, Colorado. One person shared a breakthrough she had during the session. She was a high performer—one of the best in the company. She was clear about her vision, goals, work-ethic, etc. She was well-liked, had influence, led a successful team with impressive metrics and had high self-confidence. She was fit, resilient, focused—values driven, the whole nine yards.

She loved the company and her role in it; but then said: "It wasn't until today that I realized what's been bothering me—it is the community itself." She had nothing against Denver, but she said that the environment was more casual than she was used to and this didn't fit her cadence or lifestyle. She said this awareness helped her to realize that she needed to be back in New York City—closer to the energy, speed, pace and resources she enjoyed earlier in her career. It was time to move back home.

According to Gene Theodori, one's satisfaction and attachment to their community contributes to greater well-being.[123] While four in ten Americans say they don't feel connected to their community, adults who say they know all or most of their neighbors are more than twice as likely to feel attached and connected to their community (77 percent vs. 32 percent).[124] These disparities highlight a crucial aspect of external alignment: building relationships within your community can significantly enhance your sense of belonging and support, contributing positively to your ability to find flow in your personal and professional life.

Our ability to thrive and flow is also aided heavily if we are surrounded by communities of respect—where people share common life practices that take place within families, clubs, religious groups and political parties. Such communities hold people to certain norms and accountabilities, which fosters a sense of dignity and mutual respect.[125] Communities of respect, where people engage in common practices like communal gatherings, shared rituals, or group activities, not only foster a sense of belonging but also create a supportive environment that can significantly enhance our ability to find and maintain flow.

Other factors such as trust,[126] strong networks,[127] feelings of safety, having places to meet and socialize, a sense of belonging, being involved in decision-making and having a sense of control, all contribute to one's well-being within the broader community.[128]

As you look at the larger contexts that surround your work and life, consider these questions: Does your community provide access to resources most important to you? What are the prevailing values and norms of the community, and do they align with your own? Do others in this community think like you? Does the local culture align with your style and temperament? Does it feel right to live there? Do you have positive social connections? What about local politics and policies? What about the geography, proximity to mountains, ocean, trees, parks? How's the weather? Is there a Whole Foods close by? How many sunny days do you get every year? As you consider the broader ecosystem, does it offer you a place to thrive and flow?

Chapter 8
Alignment Four: Historical—From Then to Now

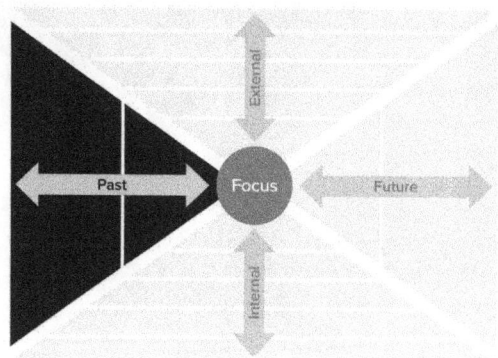

In our journey so far, we've explored Future, Internal, and External Alignments, each offering insights into the dimensions and Key Factors that influence our flow. Now, we turn to the *Historical* dimension.

By leveraging our recent past as well as reflecting on our deeper history, we can make the most of every experience and use them to support our focus on the here and now.

Short Past: Metrics, Analysis & Reflection

"To be in hell is to drift; to be in heaven is to steer."
—George Bernard Shaw

By analyzing performance moments just completed—your *Short Past*—we can identify immediate areas for improvement and strengths to build upon. Here is where you capture metrics, analyze what happened, and internalize key lessons to inform future action. Here is where the iterative process is informed with new information—each experience giving you greater insight into principles and lessons for aligning better to the moment the next time.

Metrics

"When it is obvious that the goals cannot be reached, don't adjust the goals, adjust the action steps."
—Confucius 551–479 BC

Processing any *Moment of Performance requires data collection or* **Metrics**—either quantitative (something you can count) or qualitative (something you can rate by intentional reflection or external judgment). This gives you the feedback you need to compare your efforts to your outcomes and to modify your approach for ongoing refinement and improvement.

Feedback is a key element in every system. Knowing where you are on any learning or performance path requires you to capture what you are doing and compare it with what you did—whether you are measuring weight loss, a test score, a competition, or a performance review. Whatever the arena, measurement brings intention to any action.

With clear and consistent feedback, your focus is informed, and you are often compelled to reengage, to try again—this time taking fresh action with greater knowledge. Receiving both positive recognition and constructive criticism as forms of feedback is crucial, as each play unique roles in sustaining motivation and guiding us toward flow. Case in point: when receiving feedback, especially when recognized for work well done, 69 percent of employees say they would work harder and 78 percent of those recognized would be more motivated to do their job.[129]

Whatever your circumstance—giving a speech, conducting a heart transplant, landing on an aircraft carrier, or baking your first cake—learning from the immediate past and gathering objective data are requisites for better aligning to the moment and flow.

Analysis

> "The ultimate authority must always rest with the individual's own reason and critical analysis."
> —Dalai Lama

Through in-depth *analysis*, captured metrics transform into actionable insights, guiding us to refine strategies and practices that align with achieving flow. Metrics without analysis are just numbers. Transforming analysis into actionable steps, such as setting specific goals or adjusting techniques, directly impacts our ability to find and maintain flow. People who use analytical tools, like rubrics, report better strategies, higher performance, and higher accuracy. When awareness is increased via analytics, clear gaps appear, and greater improvement is possible. That is why *After Action Reviews* (AARs) are a central practice for our armed forces. Every Moment of Performance enables us to recognize and capitalize on teachable moments in real time, enhancing our journey toward flow by learning from each experience. It's why pilots and surgeons have both pre-and post-flight operations checklists and why scuba divers have dive logs. Formal and informal analytical frameworks help people refine inputs and processes to close gaps in performance outcomes.

Reflection

> "I love those who can smile in trouble, who can gather strength from distress, and grow brave by reflection. 'Tis the business of little minds to shrink, but they whose heart is firm, and whose conscience approves their conduct, will pursue their principles unto death."
> —Leonardo da Vinci

Reflection suggests internalizing new information and insight for future use.

Through reflection, we internalize experiences, turning them into profound personal insights that fuel growth and significantly enhance our capacity for flow. ***It's always better to bear a frustration once than to make the same mistake twice!***

Integrating reflection with flow-enhancing strategies, such as setting clear intentions and practicing gratitude, deepens our learning and embeds critical lessons for future use. When people reflect on their learning, performance increases by as much as 23 percent. And when you share your learning with others, this number increases even higher.[130]

Of the many factors that influence flow, capturing metrics and feedback, analyzing the experience, reflecting upon and internalizing insights compels individuals, teams, and organizations to learn, adapt, and to thrive in ever-changing and challenging circumstances. This is the essence of learning agility—the capacity to learn at or faster than the pace of change.

Consider this: In the most important arenas in your life, do you get consistent, objective, and clear feedback or just receive others subjective opinions? What are your sources? Do you get feedback that is highly quantitative and or qualitative? What is your attitude about this feedback? Are you reactive and cautious about receiving it or are you proactive in seeking it out? Do you use measurement tools like scorecards to define inputs, processes, outcomes, and feedback loops? When you get feedback, do you take time to analyze it? Do you ask: What's working? What's not? How might I adjust my efforts? Do you have a rubric, take notes, keep a journal, or engage in a reflective process to get the most from every experience?

While finding your flow is a distinctly unique and personal process—the process of identifying that "One Thing" (The 1st Secret)—can only be accomplished by measuring results, getting feedback, analyzing it critically, and reflecting on it to close gaps in understanding and alignment (The 2nd Secret). By using your Short Past well, you will systematically move toward your flow—one principle and practice at a time, especially when you learn to Fail Faster and Better.

Long Past: Cultivating Successes, Harvesting Failures, and Challenging Assumptions

> "Those who cannot remember the past are condemned to repeat it."
> —George Santayana

The *Long Past* dimension is the collection of all of your moments and experiences beyond recent memory. It is where previous lessons have been internalized and wisdom acquired (or not). It's where your current self-image has been forged, beliefs formed, and old stories reside.

Your past can be one of your greatest assets for achieving flow if you take time to cultivate your best experiences; but it can also be a grand liability if you ruminate on your failures, do not learn from your past mistakes, or if you fail to challenge previously held beliefs that limit understanding about yourself, others and the world.

Historical moments are snapshots in time that tell a story, perhaps one of success, failure, or old ways of thinking. Think back for a moment. Do you remember a time where something happened, or a comment was made that changed your life for good or for ill? Maybe it was a coach or a teacher who said you weren't good or smart enough—a single mistake so vivid that in a moment you solidified a negative belief about yourself. Perhaps that memory has been the barrier that keeps you from a much-needed breakthrough!

Three distinct Key Factors stand out in the Long Past: Cultivating Success, Harvesting Failure, and Challenging Assumptions. Each, working together, can help you remember the best parts of yourself, learn from times that you'd rather forget, and shatter the paper dragons that have been holding you back.

Cultivating Successes

> "Success is not final; failure is not fatal: it is the courage to continue that counts."
> —Winston Churchill

When was the last time you spent five minutes reflecting upon a successful moment and unpacking it to understand what contributed to the experience? Where did it take place? What were you doing? Can you describe the environment? Who was present? What were you thinking? How did it feel? What took place?

Reflecting on your Successes—spending even a few minutes tapping into one of them (the aced exam, a completed project, getting acknowledged by your teammates, being accepted into a friend group, a great one-liner at a party)—builds greater self-efficacy and confidence. Whatever your ratio of time spent making the most of your personal history, research shows us that it is time well spent. In one study those who were asked to reflect upon their past successes, or failures (with respect to mathematical ability), improved their performance by as much as 10 percent.[131] What you think most about yourself is most likely what you will begin to believe and achieve.[132] When your dominant thoughts and images are those of successful experiences, situational self-confidence or self-efficacy naturally improves.[133]

Whether mastering a sport, excelling in a creative pursuit, or navigating social interactions, domain-specific self-efficacy empowers us to achieve flow by instilling confidence in our capabilities. The concept of self-confidence is often over-generalized—as if you could meet every challenge with all the right stuff. Albert Bandura, the famed Stanford psychologist, taught us that self-confidence is situational. For example, Will Smith is one of the greatest hip-hop artists and movie icons of our time, yet he's terrified of swimming. When George Washington found himself in discussions with John Adams and Thomas Jefferson, he sometimes felt intellectually inferior. At the same time however, Jefferson was a reluctant public speaker, and Adams was known to be emotionally unstable—each with their own unique genius and flaws. Both Lady Gaga and Barbara Streisand struggled with their physical image, yet both transformed arenas with their unique voices, personalities and brand. Nobody is perfect, but that doesn't keep them from being great in areas they have developed their skills and self-confidence.

Most people have self-confidence in something—it just requires tapping into it and building that confidence over time. Flow experiences not only require self-efficacy but also serve to enhance it, creating a positive feedback loop where each flow state builds confidence for the next. In that moment you feel confident that you can execute whatever task you're determined to do, and do so repeatedly. Self-efficacy is an acquired state—one that comes over the long-term, after many moments and positive transactions—where you learn to *confide in yourself*.

Harvesting Failures

"It is better to fail in originality than to succeed in imitation."
—Herman Melville

Let's consider your Long Past again by tapping into one of your worst moments. In the Introduction, I told the story of my best and worst game of tennis and how both took place less than twenty-four hours from one another. How could this be? I was the same person on both days.

During my anti-flow match, I had more confidence than I deserved. I underestimated my opponent, not from a talent perspective, but from his sheer will to fight for every ball. First big lesson: talent and technique rarely win matches by themselves—it's often the things you can't see that make the difference. During the anti-flow match, my mind was focused on the crowd and not on the ball. My ego was under attack. Thought distortions were everywhere, and my self-talk was destructive, triggering negative emotions and eliciting flight/flee responses. Instead of hitting the ball, my attention was racing from dimension to dimension looking for a place to address my biggest concerns—but it was not in the here and now, on the ball or present moment. Upon further reflection, I failed to exercise faith and was afraid to "let go" of the outcome. In this case it was a multi-system failure—the official "meltdown." Maybe you've had one of these—where your attention is everywhere except where it should be—where your dashboard has multiple red lights flashing. That's why analyzing and understanding these moments are just as important as the study of your successes.

Being haunted by past experiences is yet another form of interference—a Flow Liability that wrecks confidence. Can you remember a time where you were trying to do something, and your mind was pulling out stories or playing "tapes" from long ago? I just did as I rewrote this paragraph. Those moments are as clear to me as they were more than three decades ago. A blessing or a curse based on how you use them.

Whether you were taking a test, giving a speech, hitting a golf ball or having a difficult conversation—you can reflect back on previous mistakes, how you felt, struggles you experienced, and your many failed attempts. When your mind goes to these places, you are not focused on the here and now because you haven't learned from these past experiences nor internalized their lessons. If the experience is an unprocessed failure, you can easily find yourself on failure-cruise control. If, however, you truly learn from the experience, then what you "can" do in the moment becomes more prevalent than what you "should have" done.

When you **Harvest Failure**, every experience can be exploited for maximum learning and personal benefit. For those who look closely, these anti-flow experiences can give you a high Return On Investment (ROI).

Challenging Assumptions

> "Your assumptions are your windows on the world. Scrub them off every once in a while, or the light won't come in."
> —Isaac Asimov

The concept of *Learned Helplessness* was coined by Dr. Martin Seligman after the discovery that dogs, after getting randomized shocks while in a cage, came to accept their fate and stopped trying to avoid them. We humans do much the same thing. In essence, we learn from our past experiences, form beliefs about ourselves, others, and the world around us, then tap into those memories and act in accordance with our previously held beliefs—whether they be correct or false. Remember what happens to confined fleas or chained elephants.

Most of us are poor scientists until we learn to think critically about our experiences. This means that we need to consistently **Challenge our Assumptions**—what we think we know about ourselves, others, and the world vs. what's true. This requires gathering data with a neutral mindset.

I once took my mother on a beautiful drive through the stunning American Fork canyon in Utah. We were in a convertible taking in the diverse rock formations, trees, and streams. It was a beautiful day, but when I looked over at my mother, she was covering her head with both arms—burying herself in her lap. I thought this a rather irrational reaction. When I asked why she was doing this, she said that in 1953—the last time she rode in a convertible—she got a bad cold and so she was afraid of getting another one, despite it being eighty-five degrees and sunny. Even though her first experience was more than fifty years ago, it continued to shape her belief about convertibles.

Maybe it's time to challenge your beliefs because who you are and what you are capable of have yet to be fully discovered. Self-limiting beliefs put you in an emotional and mental cage, until the box is reopened, the paper dragon slayed, and you are liberated!

In 1953, the same year my mother caught that cold, Roger Bannister, unlike so many runners of his day, had the audacious belief that the four-minute mile could be broken. While most people believed no human was capable of such a feat, he, a medical student, broke through that belief. In a small oval at Oxford University, he became the first man to pierce that limit, clocking in at 3:59.4. As astonishing as this was, even more intriguing were the number of others who broke that same barrier within that same year. It seems his breaking of that barrier changed the beliefs in others. Monkey see monkey do.[134]

This is now commonplace. Every year, old records are broken, and new possibilities emerge—resulting in a paradigm shift regarding what is possible. So aptly said by Morgan Housel who wrote The Psychology of Money: "Things that have never happened before happen every day."[135]

If I may, there are a few memorable stories of my own that have inspired my passion for giving adequate attention to the Long Past and leveraging old memories to optimize my confidence in the present.

From Private to Public School

As a curious, hyperactive youth, I was politely escorted from an elite private grade school at the tender age of ten into the local public school, making the grand assumption that school perhaps wasn't my thing. Holding this belief prompted me to play the role of the struggling student for several years, until it didn't.

Once I discovered my passion, my focus narrowed and my energies were directed and it was time to get to work. This was similar to Scott Kelly's early miseries with school.[136] He too floundered until he decided he wanted to become a fighter pilot and later an astronaut. Just like that—motivation spurred by a clear and present vision! Once you know what you want, the best question you can ask yourself is: What's the next most important thing I can do to get started?

As for me, after graduating in the lower half of my high school class (distracted by tennis and dating), I shifted my summit. I went from being a B and C student to an A and B student. Undergraduate studies led to course work at Oxford, and then Georgetown. My academic chops grew. This led to four master's degrees and a PhD, completing my final degree at Harvard. I went from being a C/B student in high school to an A student at Harvard—a total reversal in self-image and what I believed was possible. Do I consider myself a world-class student? No. It wasn't an easy path. But I learned that it was possible, even probable, primarily by the application of the *2nd Secret*, that most of what you believe about yourself can be rewritten if you put your attention with intention toward something you value and iterate through it until you're transformed. This insight made all the difference—opening up new worlds and opportunities.

One More Story of Satisfied Failure

Another story of failure occurred at an all-boys summer camp in 1977. Ah, yes, the much-anticipated end of Summer dance with the girl's camp.

The day came, the girls arrived, and the dance began.

Being a bit of a chubby kid, confidence in speaking with the opposite sex was rather low. During the dance I tried to muster the courage to ask a girl to dance, watching closely as other boys just went for it. Song after song, I couldn't find the courage, and no girls asked me to dance either—so the feedback cycle wasn't in my favor. I counted down the minutes, knowing my window of opportunity was closing. When the final song ended (just three minutes on the shot clock), I still found myself without a dance partner. The buzzer sounded, and the dance was over. How depressing—knowing I should have asked at least one girl to dance. Ah, regret—a personal defeat I lamented for years. The experience solidified itself like a fortress—one I couldn't penetrate at the time. And although I was one of the best competitive shooters in the country, I lacked confidence in the girl department.

As the years went by, I grew up, leaned up, became an athlete, and had a beautiful and brilliant girlfriend (way out of my league). But that previous self-image still lingered—until the summer of 1993. I was fortunate to spend part of it in the south of France with my best friend from Sweden and two of his buddies—both blonde-haired, blue-eyed tennis players. Let's just say, *not* ugly. They were fantastic guys, and we did everything together. But the contrast between us reminded me of summer camp sixteen years earlier. So much had changed, but at the same time, it seemed like nothing had. I decided it was time to break the belief barrier.

That afternoon, we were all on the beach at Cannes, and I decided to go for a long run. The rich and beautiful were everywhere, the perfect environment to feel inadequate. Seizing the opportunity, I challenged myself to find a beautiful girl and ask her to dinner. I knew it was foolish. But I wanted the most awkward moment I could find to sink or swim. I had no interest in succeeding in my quest. That wasn't the point. It was the ask itself—challenging the fear of the unknown, the judgment, the potential embarrassment. I wanted the inner victory.

I fixed my eye on a beautiful brunette; she was lean and fit, wearing sunglasses, and reading a fashion magazine. I walked up, introduced myself, and went right for the ask. She looked at me, understood my request, and in a quaint French accent, said something like "No thank you" and went back to her magazine. And that was it—just a paper dragon. In that moment, I didn't care about the outcome, only the personal triumph of overcoming FEAR (False Evidence Assumed Real). I walked away so empowered and excited that I held on to that feeling for weeks and years; in fact, I can still tap into it!

Through that experience, I realized that a single moment could affect you for years, interfering with similar moments and challenges. Needless to say, being stuck in the past can consume your focus and deny you the flow you seek.

During graduate school, I encountered similar moments and still felt fear, but it was less powerful. I drew power from my first personal victory and kept at it until the fear of rejection was resized—no longer a barrier between me and going for it. In my studies of psychology, I learned about theoretical and therapeutic methods. From Freud to Jung, Adler to Allport, I came to appreciate the many clinical perspectives used to understand neurosis and mental health. But truth be told, pulling out a dusty old memory, exploring a different approach or choice, and then compelling myself to do it differently is about as transformative as it gets. You don't need years of therapy to explain the origins of many fears and anxieties. Gradual exposure to fears, reframing negative thoughts, and seeking evidence to counter irrational beliefs are effective ways to dismantle the "paper dragons" that obstruct our focus in any moment of performance. And if all that doesn't work, just going for it at least proves that most of our deepest fears are unwarranted.

So, what is true about you and your potential? If you want something badly enough, you can find the courage, energy, and focus to deconstruct many, if not all, of the self-limiting beliefs that hold you back. It's in this place of deep history where you can challenge your assumptions about yourself, others, and the world, and retool your beliefs so that when the time comes to perform, nothing from your past will derail you from what you want to accomplish in the present.

To capture everything you've learned from your successes, failures, and assumptions, building a *personal lifeline* is a great way to explore the key experiences that have defined you as a person. Divide the lifeline into two parts: the journey you have taken professionally and personally, marking high moments (big wins, great moments, personal transformation, major learnings) and low moments (big losses, memorable mistakes, major challenges). Taking in the highs, the lows, and neutral moments where important values, lessons, and principles were discovered is a powerful process for creating greater historical alignment.

By cultivating your successes, learning from your failures, and challenging your assumptions, you can take greater control and eliminate the noise that gets between you and present-moment flow.

Chapter 9
Alignment Five: Pulling It All Together— Eliminating Interference

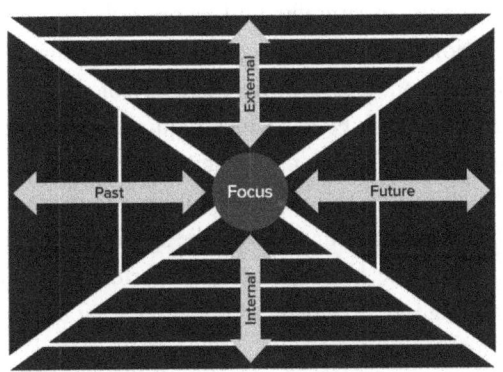

"To be successful in the new world of work, we need to create a structure for capturing and organizing all of the forces that assail us; and to ensure time and space for thinking, reflecting, and decision-making."
—David Allen

Focus: Where, When, and How Long? Strategic vs. Performance

Present-Moment Focus

In reviewing the previous fourteen dimensions and key underlying factors, we've been exploring what influences your *Focus* and flow. Like gears and circuits, each component has its own function and purpose, all designed to work in harmony so that you, a complex machine, can be optimized to fulfill your purpose and potential.

By examining these alignments and their impact—internally, externally, and over time—your awareness will increase. However, we're just getting started.

There are countless ways to improve yourself. As you take your ALI 1080° Sweep™ Assessment, we'll identify which gears and circuits are in working order (Flow Assets) and which require critical attention (Flow Liabilities). Flow Liabilities are like missing, broken, or rusted gears that slow your system down. Once repaired or replaced, however, things begin to run more smoothly—more flow-like.

Maintaining deep, present-moment focus requires constant self-monitoring—internally, externally, and temporally. This process involves identifying distractions and interferences while developing new capabilities to eliminate the obstacles that hinder your focus. Achieving **Performance Focus** demands mastering **Strategic Focus**, which requires you to take a pit stop from time to time to scan your current circumstances, realign and recalibrate. This reveals a crucial skill related to focus—the ability to broaden your perspective systemically and to narrow your focus to the specifics. The former represents Strategic Focus, while the latter pertains to Performance Focus—and both require understanding where, when, and for how long to focus on your WIN ("What's Important Now").

Let's explore the three Key Factors that define Focus through Attentional Leadership, whether in strategic preparation or during the performance itself.

Strategic Focus

Broad Focus at the strategic level involves taking a deliberate pause to assess What's Important Now (WIN). It enables you to scan multiple dimensions and evaluate both technical and human factors that require attention. By looking systemically and scanning the Future, Internal, External, and Past factors, Broad Focus helps identify the issues needing attention. This allows you to narrow your focus on the single most critical factor that will have the greatest impact on your overall performance.

Each person faces unique situations, challenges, and needs at any given time. One colleague might struggle with a lack of purpose, another with low energy, and another with maintaining a positive attitude. Using Broad Focus to assess these individual needs or gaps allows us to apply Narrow Focus to effectively address and close them.

Additionally, we must consider the time investment required to maintain our focus on strategic issues. This process enables us to build capacity off the field, ultimately serving and optimizing our Performance Focus when it's time to be fully engaged.

This is the essence of Strategic Focus—consistently working on your WINs, building capacity off the field, and finding your flow when it's time to perform.

Performance Focus

When you consistently build new capacities through Strategic Focus, you lay the groundwork needed to optimize your Performance Focus. These skills are universally applicable—whether applied to large social systems over time or by individuals engaging in daily work.

During any activity or performance, **Broad Focus** takes a holistic view of your situation, such as scanning the chessboard, observing who's in the meeting, or checking in on your own physical state. **Narrow Focus**, on the other hand, zeroes in on specific, immediate demands: calming a frustrated client, managing crosswinds during a plane landing, applying a clamp on a bleeding artery, or making a key point during a presentation.

The primary difference between **Strategic Focus** and **Performance Focus** is scope and timing. Strategic Focus is about concentrating on that "One Thing" and building capacity off the field. In contrast, Performance Focus is about paying attention to that "One Thing" in real time, adapting your focus to enhance your immediate performance and address the challenges at hand.

Leveraging the framework and process of Attentional Leadership®—knowing where, when, and how long to focus attention both strategically and tactically—is the meta-skill for influencing self, others, and larger social and physical systems.

Below are a variety of factors that can interfere and create noise when you are trying to stay focused on the task at hand. Consider these and assess which skills you currently possess (or might need) to reconnect to the moment.

Nine Internal Barriers to Focus

Here are nine common internal barriers to present-moment focus and flow: 1) *win/lose mentality*—by paying attention to the outcome, you compromise attention on the present moment; 2) *choking under pressure*—this comes from pondering "what-if" scenarios and trying to control the outcome, thus not placing attention on your Moments of Performance; 3) *distorted evaluation of the present*—you may be overly negative or overly positive, ignoring your mistakes or paying too much attention to them, thus not accurately seeing and performing well in the present moment; 4) *negative self-talk and worry*—this involves distortion and destructive language that impacts your thoughts, emotions and ultimately your physiology; 5) *inability to manage emotions*—emotions that are not understood—even too negative or too positive—become distractions, produce interference and compromise present-moment focus and flow; 6) *overanalyzing mechanics*—this results from paying attention to external variables during moments of performance; 7) *too many techniques*—when you have many tools, models and advice, you struggle to stay focused in the moment; 8) *tension/stress*—you may have runaway thoughts, emotions and physical arousal or exertion that block present-moment focus; 9) *fatigue*—a lack of energy, strength, fitness, endurance or resiliency can disrupt present-moment focus and flow.

Five Time Barriers to Focus

Here are five time-based barriers to present-moment focus and flow: 1) *focusing on the future*—visualizing the end game (standing on the podium victorious with medal in hand) while you are still in the game only disrupts present-moment focus; 2) *too focused on the goal*—less far reaching then distant future but just as distracting is attending to the goal of the performance moment instead of the moment itself; 3) *fear*—you are focused in the future—often due to accessing past failures at the expense of faith and focus in the present moment; 4). *looking backward* or attending to what just happened instead of learning quickly and moving on and saving analysis for after the game; 5) *self-doubt*—this is often the result of replaying past failures and allowing the past to dictate the present.

Three External Barriers to Focus

Three external barriers to present-moment focus and flow: 1) *visual distractions*—anything that draws your attention away from your aim like moving objects, people in close proximity, or disorganized, cluttered, or dirty spaces; 2) *auditory distractions*—various noises can also distract your present-moment focus: ticking clocks, construction equipment, lawnmowers, or dialogue; 3) *environment distractions*—poor lighting, temperature, and general aesthetics.

Do any of these sound familiar? As you learn to control your Present-Moment Focus by maintaining alignments, you gain a greater awareness of where your attention is compared to where it ought to be. There is a time and place for every dimension and factor in between performances. Knowing where, when, and how long to place your attention to optimize dimensional alignments in the moment is the exercise of Attentional Leadership®. Whatever the interference or noise, we'll provide tools and resources to help you improve your capacity off the field so you can be at your very best on the field.

The Center of the Center

When you are at the very center of the model, you are entirely at one with the moment. You are not thinking about the future or the past. You aren't looking broadly or narrowly. Everything you experience is entirely focused on the here and now, on your craft or task at hand. Dr. Terry Orlick, a renowned performance psychologist, emphasized the importance of this total connection to performance despite changing demands. He comments: "The ideal focus is total connection to your performance in spite of the constantly changing demands. Often, focusing means tuning in to your body or remaining connected to your task. Focusing practice involves learning to stay connected to what you are doing; discovering the feelings that free you to perform flawlessly; not letting irrelevant or distracting thoughts interfere with the natural performance program in your mind and body; trusting your body to do what it's been trained to do without forcing; and directing your mind or body when it begins to tire or deviate from an efficient performance program."[137]

Back to the Game Itself

As you begin to utilize Attentional Leadership® to identify your WINs both on and off the field, you will find yourself fully engaged, in "the Zone," and experiencing flow more frequently. As you continuously remove the interference that has been hindering your focus and flow by building greater skill and capacity, you will become more deeply connected to the here and now. **Enter the fifth alignment**—back to the craft itself, striking the ball! This is the moment when your entire being, through space and time, aligns with the "What"—allowing you to fully immerse yourself and achieve a profound unity with your work or craft.

It's now time to transition from exploring the framework of Attentional Leadership to actively applying it. As we discussed earlier, we aim to leverage your Strategic Focus to support your Performance Focus by first scanning broadly—this we'll do using the ALI 1080° Sweep™ Assessment. We will then guide you through five progressive stages (using the **FOCUS Planning Process**) to help you identify your "One Thing" and then get to work on it.

After you go through this process for the first time, you'll soon realize that this is a journey of continuous self-improvement—both technically and personally—and will become a lifelong pursuit designed to help you coach yourself, to evolve, and to grow as both a performer and a person, and elevating others along the way.

Chapter 10
Discovering Your One Thing

The photographic concept of *depth of field* offers the best metaphor I can think of to explain the relationship between Strategic Focus and Performance Focus.

Less Depth Greater Light

When a camera lens is sharply focused with a small aperture (e.g., F22), it allows less light to enter but provides a greater depth of field, resulting in clarity both near and far. On the other hand, when the aperture is wide open (e.g., F1.6), more light enters the lens but sacrifices focal depth, leading to a clearer image up close but blurriness in the distance. This tradeoff between light and focal depth is crucial. In low-light conditions or at night, or when you are clueless about your blind spots, it is necessary to open up the aperture to allow more light in. More light equates to greater options for seeing and optimizing the picture. But what happens when you have too much light? It can overwhelm the picture and wash out the image. Conversely, in bright environments or during sunny days, closing down the aperture reduces the amount of light so you can optimize your depth of field.

Just as more light offers increased options regarding focal depth, greater knowledge about yourself or the challenges at hand give you more options for choosing what, how deep, and how long your attention is required, strategically and during a performance, to succeed at the task at hand. In both cases, having more light (similar to information or knowledge) is beneficial as it provides more options and possibilities.

Like a camera lens, when we are in the dark and unaware of factors affecting our work and lives, we need light, feedback and data to see, to make adjustments, learn and change. As we gain new insights, light and knowledge, we narrow our focus and execute until more insights are needed. In essence, we are constantly opening and closing our own apertures whether we are on the balcony or on the dance floor.

Four Phases of Self-Mastery

As we journey toward greater flow, we pass through *four phases of development:* 1) **Unconscious Incompetence**—not knowing what we don't know, a gap in self-awareness or understanding; 2) **Conscious Incompetence**—knowing what we don't know, becoming self-aware and able to choose, or not, to make a change; 3) **Conscious Competence**—developing the skills to perform at a new level (like clarifying our vision, eating better or increasing emotional awareness). Once practiced and embedded, these skills are then integrated into our being (muscle memory), generating habit patterns that evolve into 4) **Unconscious Competence**—enabling us to demonstrate new behaviors with little conscious effort.

At the beginning of any transformational process, we start off *Unconsciously Incompetent.* We may be surrounded by something that is so much a part of us that we can no longer perceive it. That's why self-awareness is the first step toward change, growth and self-mastery.

Trading Light for Focus

Given our habitual tendencies, all of us lack self-awareness to some degree—or at least fail to utilize it on a proactive and consistent basis. There are things about us that we can't see as we engage in our focused and ritualized day-to-day activities. Therefore, we may need to gain self-awareness via various awareness and feedback mechanisms.

Gathering new insights and understanding about our strengths and weaknesses and what's getting in the way of our focus and engagement requires us to examine the many factors that influence us. If we don't do this, we start losing momentum. We then need to learn and embrace new knowledge. For instance, even at the peak of his career, Tiger Woods exemplified the importance of continual improvement by making adjustments to his grip, demonstrating the need for constant evolution to stay ahead of the competition. He had to keep evolving and modifying his approach to the game to stay ahead of the curve.

To maintain our competitive edge, it's essential to embrace this continuous learning and improvement, adapting our strategies as needed—not just to improve our craft, but who we must become in our relationship with it. That is the purpose of the fifteen dimensions and corresponding Flow Factors. They all influence the "who" in order for you to engage more effectively with the "what."

To identify what's interfering with your flow is the purpose of the ALI 1080° Sweep™ Assessment. It was designed to give you a comprehensive look at the key Internal, External, and Time factors that contribute to or inhibit your focus and flow.

By widening the aperture and expanding your awareness, you begin to see the many systems that surround, comprise, and influence you; so you can place needed attention within various dimensions in order to grow your Flow Assets and eliminate your Flow Liabilities. To engage in this process brings you to the place of *Conscious Incompetence*—that beautiful place where unawareness meets awareness, and you gain insight into what to do about it.

Leaning Into Conscious Incompetence

Without self-awareness, change, growth and flow have little chance. Thus, cultivating self-awareness through reflection and feedback is essential for enabling change, growth, and the attainment of flow. Deciding to enter *Conscious Incompetence* means seeing the gap between where you are today and where you want to be tomorrow. Developing awareness and seeing the gaps that need closing or skills that need elevating means making a conscious choice to learn, apply and grow.

Recognizing your flow assets empowers you to capitalize on your strengths, while addressing liabilities often requires only small adjustments for significant improvements, or failing a little bit less. Often the difference between winning a medal at the Olympics is less than one-tenth or even one-hundredth of a second. Again, little things can have a profound effect. As you capture new insights, apply what you learn in small ways, this begins the journey toward greater *Conscious Competence*.

Through *Conscious Competence* you demonstrate higher levels of effectiveness and performance based upon the acquisition of new knowledge, skills, and capacity. Flow begins with awareness, is strengthened through learning and practice, and ends in developing **Unconscious Competence** where you are now in sync with your new skill. You do it automatically—without thinking. It has moved from a simple intention to a lasting virtue or impact. In Shakespeare's play, *As You Like It*, my favorite line says it all: "Twas I but tis not I." This elegantly conveys our capacity for change—even transformation—through intentional efforts.

Opening and Closing the Aperture

To enhance your self-awareness, we will employ the ALI 1080° Sweep™ Assessment. This tool will pinpoint your current Flow Assets and Flow Liabilities, unveiling your Personal Flow Formula and your key WINs—focusing particularly on the "One Thing" that should be at the heart of your Strategic Focus.

To translate your assessment results from abstract to concrete, we'll apply the **FOCUS Planning Process** to develop a robust action plan. This process includes five steps that transition from a broad to a narrow focus, starting with identifying your "One Thing" (1st Secret). Subsequent steps will guide you in crafting measurable strategies and tactics.

By consistently and deliberately practicing your "One Thing," you will accelerate through cycles of rapid improvement (Failing Faster and Better), advancing from Conscious Competence to Unconscious Competence (the 2nd Secret). This journey will enhance your mastery of specific skills or capacities, facilitating a shift toward greater alignment.

Opening the Aperture Using the ALI 1080° Sweep™ Assessment

This assessment was derived by interviewing performers from diverse backgrounds, disciplines, and arenas and validating with the research and practice literatures. Each question maps to one of the fifteen dimensions found in the Attentional Leadership® framework. Consider this a three-dimensional SWOT (strengths, weaknesses, opportunities, and threats) analysis designed to help you optimize flow in any MLA.

Your focus will progress through several dimensions: Future (Alignment One), then Internal (Alignment Two), External (Alignment Three), Past (Alignment Four), and then at the center, Present-Moment Focus (Alignment Five).

When you complete your online assessment, you will receive a complete report, including a color-coded "heat map" of your aggregated scores, stack-ranked Flow Assets and Flow Liabilities, your Personal Flow Formula, and detailed information for each of the fifteen dimensions with suggestions for improvement.

As a purchaser of this book, you are entitled to a complimentary assessment. Go to: bit.ly/3UJUymu and use the code: **ALI10802025.**

After taking the assessment, have it on your computer screen or print it out so that you can refer to your own assessment as we take you through a detailed example of how to read it and utilize the FOCUS Planning Process to identify that "One Thing" and get to work on it.

Closing the Aperture Using the FOCUS Planning Process

The FOCUS Planning Process begins by examining your current circumstances to provide a comprehensive overview of what's happening generally and within each dimension of your assessment. This process narrows your focus from a broad awareness of your situation, guided by your Personal Flow Formula, to identifying your WINs and ultimately your "One Thing." As you specify your area for development, you'll construct a detailed and strategic plan complete with tactics and measurable metrics to ensure continual improvement.

To illustrate the FOCUS Planning Process, let's consider Merritt, a mid-level data analyst on a well-regarded finance team within a global Fortune 500 company. Although Merritt is a high performer, she encounters certain interferences that hinder her ability to consistently deliver her best work.

In this example, we'll explore portions of Merritt's assessment. The report uses a color-coded heat map to represent scores across the fifteen dimensions, with progressively darker shades of red indicating negative scores (-5 = dark red to -1 = light red) and blue indicating positive scores (+5 = dark blue to +1 = light blue).

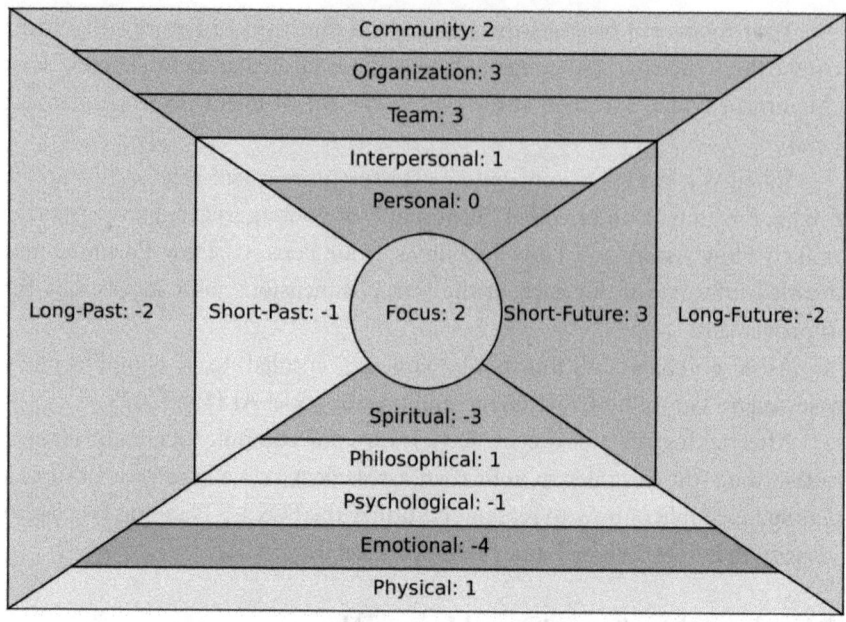

At the dimension level, we scan broadly to identify general themes, which reveals the current circumstances or tells the person's current story pertaining to the arena being assessed.

The report also includes a list of Merritt's top five highest and lowest ranked scores—her most relevant Flow Assets and Flow Liabilities.

Flow Assets

- Goals & Plans — Dimension: Short-Future — 5
- Time Maximization — Dimension: Short-Future — 4
- Team Direction — Dimension: Team — 4
- Technical Expertise — Dimension: Psychological — 4
- Community Culture — Dimension: Community — 4

Flow Liabilities

- Emotional Awareness — Dimension: Emotional — -5
- Emotional Control — Dimension: Emotional — -4
- Faith — Dimension: Spiritual — -5
- Resilience — Dimension: Emotional — -5
- Purpose Driven — Dimension: Spiritual — -4

If you look closely, you will notice a Flow Liability rated at -4 in a higher position than two of the -5 scores. That is because when using the online assessment, after completing your rankings, you can drag and drop your Flow

Factors (up or down) if you think that they deserve to be positioned differently (more or less relevant) after further consideration.

The report also includes Merritt's *Personal Flow Formula*, which separates her highest ranked Flow Assets and Flow Liabilities internally and externally:

YOUR PERSONAL FLOW FORMULA

INTERNAL ASSETS	EXTERNAL ASSETS
Goals & Plans +5	Team Direction +4
Time Maximization +4	Community Culture +4
Technical Expertise +4	Organization Direction +4
Exercise +3	Organization Role +4
Rules & Standards (Ethics) +2	Interpersonal Inspiration +3
INTERNAL LIABILITIES	**EXTERNAL LIABILITIES**
Emotional Awareness -5	Interpersonal Feedback -3
Emotional Control -4	Interpersonal Climate -2
Faith -5	Community Climate -1
Resilience -5	Team Climate -1
Purpose Driven -4	

Also, the report gives Merritt an overall score:

In Merritt's case her score is 0. This means that when taking all of the Flow Factors and their rankings into consideration, Merritt is in a neutral zone—with as many Flow Assets working for her as well as Flow Liabilities working against her. This isn't a bad place to be. Many people are working with negative scores and desire just to get to 0. The objective now is to decrease Flow Liabilities and increase Flow Assets and start moving into + territory.

Your goal is to either remove the largest Flow Liability, acting as a headwind, or enhance a Flow Asset, serving as a tailwind, based on what best fits your circumstances.

As I take Merritt's example through the FOCUS Planning Process, I invite you to take your own factor scores and follow along so you can observe as well as go through your own process. The FOCUS Planning Process includes five steps and twenty questions—each designed to shift your attention from broad to narrow as you progress from high level themes toward more granular strategies and tactics for taking action.

Let's now use Merritt's assessment so you can see the FOCUS Planning Process in action.

Step One:
Find Your Flow Assets & Liabilities

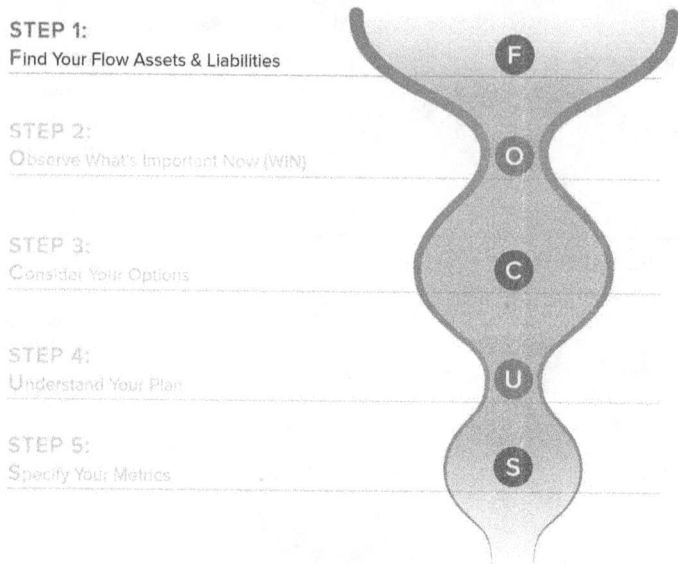

STEP 1:
Find Your Flow Assets & Liabilities

STEP 2:
Observe What's Important Now (WIN)

STEP 3:
Consider Your Options

STEP 4:
Understand Your Plan

STEP 5:
Specify Your Metrics

Start by critically reviewing your performance dimensions to identify standout areas or underlying themes that shape your current narrative.

As you look over Merritt's dimensional scores above, you'll see there are several - scores and several + scores.

If you were having a coaching conversation with Merritt she might interpret her current situation this way:

In my organization, my short-term goals are clear because quarterly metrics demand that I constantly keep my eye on the financial ball. And frankly, my consistent achievement of quarterly targets and positive feedback from peers and supervisors affirm my proficiency in my job. I'm not sure what my next role or job will be, or what my next professional move will be over the next few years, so I'm not sure where my career is going at this moment.

My long-term vision and focus on my potential may have taken a back seat to short-term high performance. I'm not clear if I'm moving toward my true calling so sometimes it feels like my faith is being tested. However, I pride myself on my values and ethics. This grounds me.

I often worry and struggle with my emotions at work, which can find its way into my personal life. Too often I think my emotions are getting the best of me—sometimes to the detriment of a few key work relationships. Emotional challenges notwithstanding, I try to keep my body in shape so that I can maintain my energy but I'm not as resilient as I used to be.

Looking externally, I work with great people, have a job that I'm good at, and feel strongly that our team is well aligned with where the company is going. Regarding the context of my life and work, I live and enjoy the city and the neighborhood where I live, but things are changing so there are some unknowns—including politics—both inside and outside of my company and work.

I could use more feedback from my team. My focus on performing my own work sometimes compromises my relationships with team members. I might spend time reflecting on where I've been and what I've learned during more satisfying times in my life and career.

Let's look into Merritt's current story and take this question by question:

QUESTION ONE:
Scanning your overall results, what Flow dimension(s) stand out as most relevant or important at this time?

In this case the Emotional dimension is Merritt's lowest dimension score at -4, as she struggles to control her emotions. What also stands out are the Spiritual (-3), Long Future (-2) and Long Past (-2) dimensions. Her higher dimension scores reside in Short Future (+3), Team (+3) and Organization (+3). Merritt's narrative for this question might read something like this:

"From a Flow Asset perspective, Short Future, Team, and Organization are my higher dimension scores, while my Emotional and Spiritual are my lowest dimension scores. Emotional dimension is lowest."

Now review your own dimension scores and identify those that stand out as most relevant for you.

This next question has you shifting your attention from dimensions to more specific Flow Factors. Based on how you ranked each question you identified each item as either a Flow Asset (if ranked +) or Flow Liability (if ranked -). Or you may have ranked a question "0" to make it neutral—a non-factor.

And remember, while these questions have been designed to capture common Flow Factors, there may be other Flow Factors that are personal to you that only you can identify. If you identify something outside of these assessment questions, by all means, rank it appropriately and place it (or they) where it/they belong within your Flow Assets or Flow Liabilities lists, then within your Personal Flow Formula if it makes the cut.

As you review your most relevant Flow Factors, first scan your top five lists to see what made it to the top of each, and then scan your Personal Flow Formula, which gives you a broader, more nuanced perspective. When doing this look back at your dimension scores once again for context.

To better understand your current circumstances, alternate between examining the broad scope of your career and the detailed aspects of daily tasks. For example, consider your overall career goals and then zoom in on the specific skills you need to develop to achieve them.

Let's begin by looking at Merritt's Flow Assets.

QUESTION TWO:
What are your current Flow Assets (at the factor level) and how are they helping you?

Review Merritt's answer to this question and then capture your own highest ranked (+) Flow Asset(s) that stand out as most positive and influential.

"I'm good at delivering results and achieving short-term goals, and stay focused on what matters most. I'm good at my job, and am well aligned with my team and organization. I maintain the right physical energy and my core values keep me fully engaged in doing my best work. I'm in a positive working environment and enjoy where I live."

QUESTION THREE:
What are your current Flow Liabilities (at the factor level) and how are they hindering you?

We'll take a similar approach to Flow Liabilities (most notably -5s and -4s)—those Flow Factors that hinder Merritt the most.

"I'm experiencing a fair amount of stress at work and it can be a problem, showing up as negative emotions I struggle to control. While I'm productive, I can lose sight of my long game—even become ungrounded and lose faith in the "why" and "purpose" of my work."

Take some time to reflect and write your own answer to this question.

QUESTION FOUR:
In a sentence or two, what story is being told by your most prominent dimension, Flow Assets and Flow Liabilities scores?

In this fourth question, we seek to understand the overall story told by the assessment.

"I'm a high achiever who is goal directed—working with a high-performing team and organization. My long game is not yet clear. I think there is an opportunity to work on my emotional skills so I can decrease my stress and be more resilient. Clarifying my long-term vision and faith, perhaps by taking some time to process my past experiences, could make a positive impact."

Now do the same. Scan broadly and look narrowly to capture the essence of your assessment.

Narrowing Your WIN

Now narrow your focus on the most relevant Flow Factors or WIN until you identify your "One Thing."

While every Flow Factor plays a part in your experiences, most Flow Factors do not need your attention at this moment—only a few *vital factors* matter, with your "One Thing" mattering the most. Since only a few of your efforts produce most of your results (the *80/20 Pareto principle*), you need to identify where your attention is needed and then place your time, energy and resources on what's most important. There is power in knowing where, when, and how long to focus your time, energy, and other resources in order to leverage your Strategic Focus and to change something, so choose wisely.

Placing your energies on the right few things—even the "One Thing"—for the right amount of time is the central premise of Attentional Leadership. Investing resources on too many less relevant things may seem well-intended, but yields minimal return on investment (ROI).

Step Two:
Observe What's Important Now (WIN)

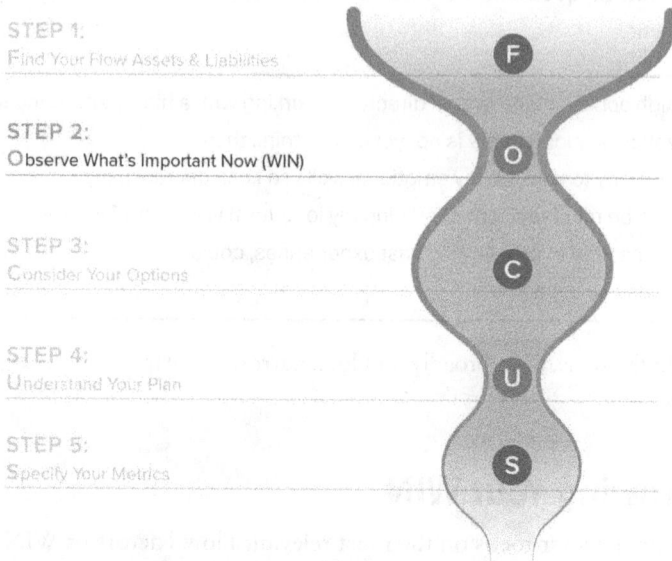

F. Scott Fitzgerald observed: "The test of a first-rate intelligence is the ability to hold two opposed ideas in mind at the same time and still retain the ability to function." While many factors might help or hinder flow, you should focus on those few key Flow Factors to gain competitive advantage. This requires seeing the forest while focusing on just a few trees.

QUESTION ONE:
Which three factors (Flow Assets & Flow Liabilities) do you think placing your attention with intention would give you the most return on invested time, energy, and resources?

As you become more intentional about "what" you place your attention on, you begin to get more value and impact from your time, energy, and attentional resources. From Merritt's report, these three Flow Factors may stand out:

1st: Emotional Awareness
2nd: Faith
3rd: Purpose Driven

In Merritt's example "Emotional Awareness" stands out as the lowest internal Flow Factor with "Emotional Control" and "Resilience" as close companions. Both "Faith" and "Purpose Driven" stand out as important factors as well. Seeing that Merritt's Spiritual dimension score is in the negative, "Faith" and "Purpose" might deserve some attention as well.

As you do your own assessment, consider the three Flow Factors (any combination of Flow Assets or Flow Liabilities) that stand out for you regardless of how you originally ranked them. What matters most is choosing wisely. Drawing some important connections will help you choose the most relevant Flow Factors to work on. By identifying the three most important Flow Factors, you give yourself permission to put everything else to the side and narrow your focus in order to give your full attention to your WIN.

QUESTION TWO:
What are the benefits of making progress in each area of development?

You can start tapping into the motivations behind the changes you want to make by using both carrots and sticks. Using carrots, Merritt's might read something like this:

1st: I will gain greater awareness and control over my emotions. This will help my self-confidence and relationships.
2nd: Increased faith would help me let go of outcomes.
3rd: Greater purpose would increase my motivation and help me find meaning.

What are the benefits of making progress in your three areas of development?

QUESTION THREE:
What might be the consequences if you ignore these areas of development?

While it is motivational to identify the rewards of investing your time, attention, and resources toward greater rewards, tapping into the consequences of inaction can also be a motivating force. In Merritt's case:

1st: I will continue to lose control if my emotional triggers disrupt my flow and compromise my relationships.
2nd: If my faith decreases it could negatively impact my attitude and sense of grounding.
3rd: If my purpose remains unclear, I may keep spinning my wheels professionally.

Now, identify the consequences of ignoring your own areas of development.

QUESTION FOUR:
If you made improvements in each of these areas, what outcomes would you expect?

1st: Greater self-awareness, control and confidence—especially under stressful situations.
2nd: Improved attitude, higher energy, and less stress, and knowing things will work out for the best.
3rd: I will move more confidently toward my goals and dreams, becoming even more resilient as I seek to achieve them.

Now identify your potential positive outcomes. Tap into the possibilities and the energy that comes from seeing what is in store for you.

Three Ways to Boost Flow

Here are the three best ways to boost flow: 1) grow a Flow Asset, 2) decrease a Flow Liability, or 3) convert a Flow Liability into a Flow Asset.

Historically, we have focused on fixing problems and flaws, but over the past twenty years we've moved toward a "strengths-based" culture with "Appreciative" modes of inquiry and positive psychology. This is the approach we are taking by identifying factors relevant to your flow experience.

1. Strengthen a current Flow Asset. For instance, if one of your *Flow Assets* is high physical energy, then you might build additional routines to fortify this strength. This may include getting ample sleep each night, eating small meals multiple times a day, or taking short breaks every sixty to ninety minutes to optimize your energy. If a high internal Flow Asset is your intrinsic motivation, then you may choose to reflect on the purpose of your work from time to time to reinforce those positive feelings and tap into even deeper forms of energy. When working with Flow Assets, your goal is to identify where and when you can use them and to strengthen them. If your current Meaningful Life Arena isn't giving you much opportunity to use these assets, then look for—or even ask for—new opportunities to tap into your personal gifts.

2. Decrease a Flow Liability. If a current *Flow Liability* is holding you back, you might seek ways to decrease this interference, such as closing an office door, turning off your phone, arranging your work schedule to minimize distractions, and so on. If you struggle to manage your time and are late for appointments, you might use a planning system to analyze your daily actions while holding yourself accountable for each segment of the day.

Some of the changes we need to make are less about getting better and more about doing something less poorly! There is little difference between getting better and screwing up less." You can then start aiming for higher goals and standards. Decreasing a flow liability can be even more valuable than strengthening a flow asset.

3. Turn a Flow Liability into a Flow Asset. This is often the most powerful way to increase your flow. For example: consider the strategy of improving *inner dialogue or self-talk*. Perhaps you find yourself in situations where your attitude is self-defeating. Your critical self-talk squanders your focus and contributes to performance problems. As you become aware of this habit and wish to modify your beliefs and attitudes by working on your self-defeating language, start noticing when such thoughts begin and use more positive language to describe the situation. Through this change, your attitude, emotional climate, demeanor, and confidence increase. You start seeing yourself as a more positive thinker and adopting a positive paradigm of perceiving, feeling and behaving. Such changes are possible if you make a concerted effort to convert liabilities into assets.

Consider the case of a highly stressed stockbroker who becomes a master at deep relaxation when the markets are volatile, an attorney who skillfully manages negative emotions during a trial, a nervous firefighter who learns to stay focused longer during a complex fire, a teenager who develops intrinsic motivation (finding passion in a subject instead of focusing on grades), or a doctor who develops a new system of organization that creates greater efficiency in the operating room.

Since most Flow Factors are highly learnable and not simply inherited talents, we have practically unlimited capacities to change and evolve in ways that are most important to us.

Let's look at the math. Let's assume that we have twice the number of Flow Assets as we have Liabilities. Let's see how manipulating the numerator or denominator changes the outcome:

Strategy 1: Increasing a strength by twenty units

Strategy 2: Decreasing a weakness by twenty units

Strategy 3: Decreasing a weakness by twenty units, turning it into twenty units of strength

Any of the three actions contributes to the result but turning a liability into a strength has the greatest impact on performance because decreasing the denominator and adding to the numerator at the same time produces an exponential effect. This is a nice reward for removing the interference and putting in place a new factor, practice, or habit that stops working against you and starts working for you. Investing your time and resources anywhere will positively contribute to your flow but turning a Flow Liability into a Flow Asset has a multiplier effect.

Identifying Your "One Thing"

In the 1991 movie **City Slickers**, Billy Crystal, Daniel Stern, and Bruno Kirby portray three mid-career professionals seeking to become more adventurous by participating in a real cattle drive led by an intimidating cowboy named Curley. During their adventure, these "city slickers" notice something special about Curley—his philosophy of life. They come to believe that this rather crude and intimidating man has the answers they are looking for. During a deep discussion about the meaning of life, Curley explains his simple yet profound mantra—that life is all about *"One Thing."* The character played by Billy Crystal inquires, "What is the one thing?" The old cowboy says: "You've got to figure that out for yourself."

Yes, there is a formula for finding your flow, but that formula is specific to you...and only you can discover it. So, to find flow more often, follow Curley's advice—keep your attention on your "One Thing" until the next most important "One Thing" requires your attention.

In his autobiography where **Ben Franklin** detailed his thirteen virtues, he also shared his approach to working on them. Recognizing that he could not work on them all at once, he wrote: "...to acquire the habitude of all these virtues, I judged it would be well not to distract my attention by attempting the whole at once, but to *fix it on one of them at a time*; and when I should be master of that, then to proceed to another; and so on till I should have gone through the thirteen."

While many factors comprise your Personal Flow Formula, consider that *"One Thing"* for which you would like to place your attention with intention.

Which Flow Factor will be the focus of your development plan? Think: nose and wings. The nose leads the airplane, and the wings are right behind.

From the three Flow Factors you identified in Step Two, choose **the one factor** that, if you could make progress with it, would move the needle on everything.

If you've identified your "*One Thing*," you've unlocked the **1st Secret**. If not, take time to reflect and explore—it's a discovery process worth pursuing. All other factors now take a back seat because this one area of focus requires you to explore it broadly and deeply.

Focus on Your Biggest WIN

To further narrow your focus, ask yourself which area, if improved, would have the most profound impact on your performance and satisfaction. In Merritt's example improving **Emotional Awareness** will be her focus. Remember, these Flow Factors are not prescriptive elements, but instead are topical areas or personal strategic initiatives for which deeper exploration is in order—whether you are coaching yourself or working with someone who is supporting you. Think of each factor as a doorway to a topical area that you are eager to explore—that single fish swiming amongst a cluster atop that specific reef.

Step Three:
Consider Your Options

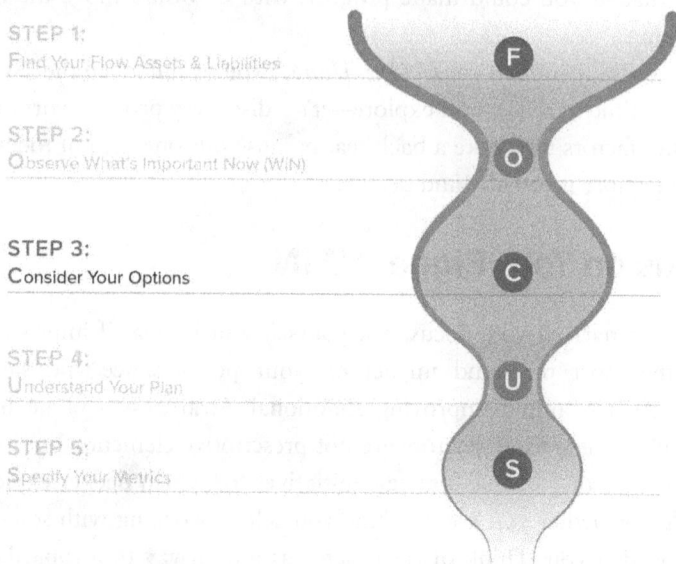

QUESTION ONE:
Based on the Flow Factor you've chosen to focus on, are your change efforts more about expanding your Awareness, increasing your Knowledge, or developing new Behaviors? Explain.

Sometimes getting started requires more awareness—getting additional feedback from others, more self-reflection, or some deeper assessment work. At other times you may already be aware of what needs attention, but more knowledge and training are needed. And sometimes (more often than not) you may already be aware of a particular developmental area, even have the knowledge and skills to do something about it, but have yet to design a plan or find the motivation or purpose for taking action.

Thinking through these three lenses, Merritt's answer might read like this:

"Emotional Awareness is critical for me right now so increasing my awareness is my highest priority. I will do this, however, by getting feedback and seeking new knowledge. I will then start to put what I learn into daily practice toward new behaviors."

As you review your own report, which type of development is best for you: to increase awareness, new knowledge, new behaviors, or more than one of them?

QUESTION TWO:

Brainstorm all the things you could do to improve this Flow Factor. Identify several strategies or approaches you could take over the next thirty to ninety days.

While brainstorming this by yourself can be a useful and productive process, having a partner or coach to work with can be exponentially helpful. Here's what Merritt came up with:

To improve emotional control, I might:

- Write each time I lose control of my emotions.
- List my typical emotional triggers.
- Ask three colleagues to let me know when they see that my emotions get the best of me.
- Find a few emotions lists. Choose one and get to know about the nuances of different emotions.
- Check off which emotions show up most often.
- Track each time I keep my cool.
- Ask three people I respect and trust how they maintain emotional awareness and control under stress.
- Study strategies for improving emotional control.
- Find the top three books on the subject and read fifteen minutes daily.

Brainstorm your list or do this with a trusted colleague, family member, or friend. More is better

QUESTION THREE:

From your best ideas, which ones make the most sense to take action on right now?

After Merritt expanded her thinking and captured several possible options, she focused on three Strategy/Approaches that she felt would give her the most traction:

Strategy/Approach One: Learn more about different emotions, what they do, and how they affect me.

Strategy/Approach Two: Monitor and track my emotions when triggered. Note the situations that triggered them.

Strategy/Approach Three: Talk to colleagues about how they maintain awareness and control of their emotions.

As you review your own report, which three strategies/approaches make the most sense for you?

QUESTION FOUR:
What resources, tools, people, are available to support you?

Merritt has many resources to support her. She explains:

- I have access to the curated library of articles, videos, and books offered on the Attentional Leadership website and other subscriptions my work offers.

- My spouse and boss will support me.

- I have a few colleagues who are good at this. I'm going to tap into them for advice.

What resources are available to support you?

Step Four:
Understand Your Plan

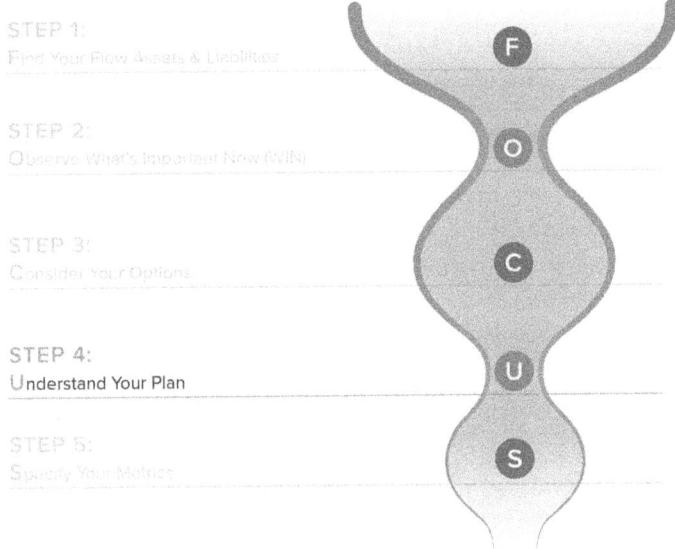

Clarify, customize, and personalize your plan to suit your life and circumstances. How you approach any new behavior must be tailored by you and for you. You may have found your developmental focus, but there are many ways to approach and engage it. You must figure out what works for you—just like working in a pair of new leather boots. While I encourage you to capture best practices from others, remember that how they approach their improvement may differ from your custom approach even when you work on the same Flow Factor.

Merritt sees the value in taking action on all three approaches as each compliments the other. She wants to learn more about different emotions and how they affect her, track those emotions when they occur, and tap into a few colleagues and discuss their best practices.

Now choose which approaches/strategies might give you the most return on invested time, energy, and resources.

QUESTION ONE:
What outcome do you want to achieve by taking the strategies/approaches you listed above? Be as detailed as you can.

This question prompts Merritt to visualize what success would look like when she engages her strategic approaches for improving her emotional awareness and control.

I want this outcome:

- I want to remain calm and collected under even the most challenging circumstances. Rather than let my emotions get the best of me, I want greater emotional control and self-mastery. Doing this will decrease my stress, improve my self-confidence, and improve my working relationships.

Answer this question for yourself. Get specific on what actions you will take in order to achieve your desired outcome.

QUESTION TWO:
What specific actions will you take daily/weekly to achieve this outcome?

Generate The SMART Goal

Once you've identified your "One Thing," brain-stormed ideas and options and identified your strategies/approaches, you are progressively moving toward specifying what you are going to do and how you are going to do it. Now you are ready to set a goal that is **SMART**: Specific, Measurable and Meaningful, Aggressive but Realistic and Time-Bound with a clear plan of action. Setting your SMART goal focuses on your actions (inputs) more than the outcome of those actions.

For example, if your greatest challenge is managing your time, your SMART goal might be this: *Over the next sixty days I will spend fifteen minutes planning and preparing my calendar each day.* This goal is specific and meaningful because it's your "One Thing," it's measurable (planning fifteen minutes each day), it's aggressive yet realistic (it pushes your limits but does not thwart your resolve to complete it), and it's time-sensitive (to be completed within sixty days). It's also within your control. By making your goals SMART, you greatly increase your odds of success by defining clear standards of action that will ultimately lead to your desired outcome.

Merritt must clarify "exactly" what she is going to do to engage new behaviors that will produce the results she wants.

I will achieve this outcome by doing what:

- Take ten to fifteen minutes twice a week to learn about emotions and how to control them.

- Create a list of emotions and keep track of which ones I'm experiencing and under what circumstances.

- Set appointments with three of my colleagues within the next two weeks and ask them for advice and best practices.

After writing your action-oriented goals, assess how well it meets the SMART criteria. To test how SMART your goal is, ask yourself or an accountability partner: How specific is my goal? How meaningful is my goal? How measurable is my goal? How challenging is my goal? How realistic is my goal? And when will I complete this goal in order to identify my next one?

With your SMART goal, or goals in place, you need to commit to change by having a tangible written contract (paper or electronic) with yourself—one that you keep with you every day and review often to keep your vision and goals top of mind.

QUESTION THREE:
What might get in the way of your plan? How will you remove those obstacles?

Perhaps you have heard this quote: "If you want to make God laugh, just tell Him your plans." As we all know things do get in the way of well-designed and thoughtful plans, so it's best if you have put some thought into what countermeasures you might take when obstacles arise.

Potential obstacles and countermeasures:

- Time is always a challenge, so I won't over-commit and try to do too much.

- I will set up a repeating time block on my calendar (ten to fifteen minutes twice a week) so I can make learning a new habit.

- Continuing to socialize my goal and getting continued support will be helpful.

Reflect on how you will eliminate any obstacles getting in your way.

QUESTION FOUR:
What is the simplest and easiest next step you can take to get started?

This question sets Merritt up for a quick and early win.

"I will set up the repeating time block on my calendar by the end of the day."

Think of something you can do by the end of the day that takes less than a minute to get things rolling.

Step Five: Measure Your Progress

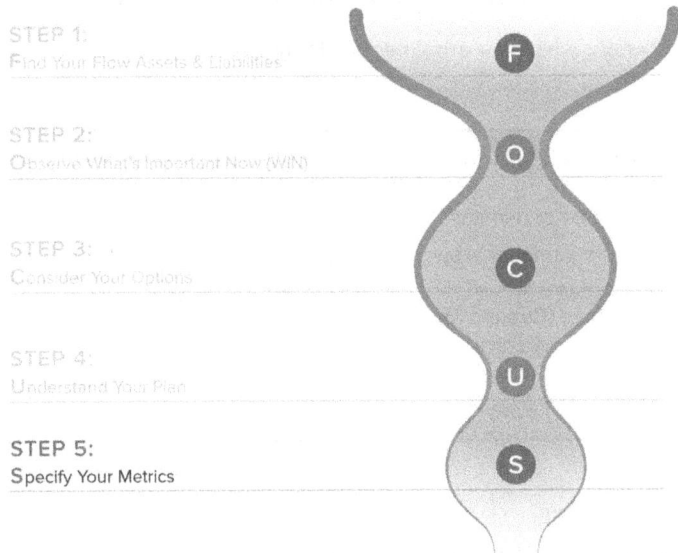

STEP 1:
Find Your Flow Assets & Liabilities

STEP 2:
Observe What's Important Now (WIN)

STEP 3:
Consider Your Options

STEP 4:
Understand Your Plan

STEP 5:
Specify Your Metrics

It's time to get specific about your actions and desired outcomes, to translate good intent into specific actions that lead to specific results. Doing this requires some measurement on both the Input and Outcome, but also includes observation of your Process and your Feedback loops.

QUESTION ONE:
Describe what success looks like after your goal is already achieved. Be as detailed as you can.

This short-term vision or mini legacy enables you to see yourself as a different person after doing the work and making the changes you want to make. It can be difficult to make a change that you cannot see, so visualize it as if it's already complete!

"When I'm at work and in social situations I can see myself surrounded by challenges and people who no longer trigger my emotions. Instead of making knee-jerk reactions, I see myself taking a strategic pause and choosing how I want to react. I will be taking my game to a whole new level and my life and relationships will be better for it."

QUESTION TWO:
How would you measure/track what you are Doing (Input Measure)? How will you measure/track what you are Getting (Outcome/Results Measure)?

Specify exactly what you are going to do and what outcomes those actions are having.

Doing (Input Measure):

- "Number of minutes I spend learning new strategies and techniques for building emotional awareness. I plan to study thirty minutes each week."

Getting (Outcome/Results Measure):

- "Number of times each week that I successfully manage my emotions. I will rate myself every day."

QUESTION THREE:
How will you know if you are making progress?

Based on your goal, identify whether your own observations are all that is needed or whether you need to get external feedback from various sources. You need to get all relevant feedback to know if what you are doing is getting you the outcome and results you desire. In Merritt's words:

I will know I am making progress by:

- "How much I am learning through my weekly study of emotional control strategies."

- "Reviewing my trends and correlation pattern."

External feedback sources:

- "I'll ask a few of my trusted colleagues to give me their feedback once a week for the next few weeks for external validation and additional feedback."

QUESTION FOUR:

How often will you assess your progress (daily, weekly, monthly)?

Specify the frequency and method of your measurement:

- "I will track my inputs (reading) daily."

- "I will track my personal outcomes daily (via the 1080°Sweep App) and request feedback from my colleagues weekly."

Well done. I'm hopeful that as you read through Merritt's FOCUS Planning Process that you were able to follow along using your own assessment to see firsthand how each of the five steps and twenty questions help you move progressively toward your own strategic initiatives, goals, strategies, tactics, and even metrics.

Remember, within your account you not only have the assessment, but also a goal-tracking system to track your actions and results. After completing the FOCUS Planning Process, you can transfer the information into your own scorecard and track the critical actions you are taking (Doing) and the outcomes that follow (Getting). This is how you master the **2nd Secret**.

Section III
The Second Secret: Failing Faster and Better

Applying the Second Secret Through the Five Elements of Iteration

The 2nd Secret—failing faster and better, operationalizes the 1st Secret, helping you to remove the noise and interference surrounding your focus and aligning yourself with the principles and practices that build your capacity to over time.

Chapter 11
Iterating Toward Success

> "The most splendid achievement of all is the constant striving to surpass yourself and to be worthy of your own approval."
> —Dennis Waitley

As Dennis Waitley's words remind us, the journey toward excellence is marked by a constant effort to surpass our previous selves, embracing both successes and failures as milestones of growth.

Before we explore how the 2nd Secret operationalizes our efforts, let's briefly recap: The 1st Secret entails identifying that singular focus—the "One Thing"—that can significantly enhance our flow. Reflecting on the discovery process, you began by experiencing your best and worst moments, tapping into both your Flow and Anti-Flow experiences. You journeyed through fifteen dimensions and evaluated over a hundred Factors that influence your present-moment focus in the service of your work or craft. After sorting through your Flow Assets and Liabilities and identifying your highest and lowest scores, you differentiated between Internal and External factors while constructing your Personal Flow Formula. You narrowed your focus to three developmental areas, ultimately selecting one as your primary focus, guided by the FOCUS Planning Process.

Now, it's time to elevate your performance by concentrating, with intention, on your "One Thing" in a manner that is uniquely personal and specific to you. Enter the *2nd Secret*.

Langley & the Wright Brothers

After over five hundred years of efforts by numerous scientists, inventors, and entrepreneurs, how did the Wright Brothers, despite having no formal education and minimal resources beyond a bike shop, manage to unlock the secrets of sustained air travel?

The key to their success: embracing failure as a rapid learning tool, thereby failing faster and more effectively than their predecessors—a principle we identify as the *2nd Secret.*

Others were chasing the same goal of sustained flight, including Samuel Langley, the third secretary of the Smithsonian Institute. With all of the resources of the US government behind him, including a $70,000 budget to support his experiments, Langley built his "Aerodrome" to compete with the Wright Brothers' "Flyer." In stark contrast to the Wright Brothers' iterative experimentation, Langley, with the support of the US government and a substantial budget, conducted his flying machine experiments with great pomp and circumstance, only to face public failure. And with eager onlookers, he launched it—only to have it plunge into the river to the great amusement of the press and other onlookers. After doing this twice (October 7 and December 8, 1903) he then scrapped the experiment.

In contrast to Langley's costly, largely theoretical experiments, the Wright Brothers understood that success was less about financial investment and more about navigating the learning curve. With an unyielding commitment to discovery, they viewed each failure as a step closer to success, exemplifying the resilience and mindset required for groundbreaking innovation. They not only constructed their own wind tunnel, but also chose Kitty Hawk, a coastal region in North Carolina's Outer Banks, where the rolling sandy hills and constant winds provided ideal conditions for their tests. Day after day, month after month, the Wright Brothers repeatedly launched their "Flyer," meticulously recording observations and making adjustments after each failure. In a workshop behind their bike shop, they tirelessly iterated through hundreds of micro-experiments, collecting data that would eventually enable them to synchronize all the necessary elements for sustained flight.

On December 14, 1903, they conducted four trial flights: the first two flights lasted twelve seconds each, the third fifteen seconds, and the fourth an impressive fifty-nine seconds, covering distances of 120, 175, 200, and finally 852 feet at altitudes ranging from eight to fourteen feet. A gust of wind after launch severely damaged their Flyer, ending its brief 138-second career in the skies. Nonetheless, the Wright Brothers had achieved their goal—they had deciphered the fundamental principle of wind displacement and immediately set to work on rebuilding and refining new prototypes, where the duration of flight was now only limited by fuel capacity. Observers were astounded to see a machine powered by humans achieve flight. However, akin to reaching the summit of Mount Everest, they found that mastering the descent was often more perilous than the ascent. The brothers faced several learning curves and injuries as they learned to land safely, but through meticulous data analysis, leveraging successes, learning from failures, and challenging prevailing assumptions, they persisted with a clear vision, ready to shatter old paradigms and produce unprecedented results.

Encouraged by friends and colleagues to secure patent protection, the Wright Brothers were in no rush; they recognized the extent of their progress on the learning curve compared to others. Ultimately, while Langley had spent over $70,000 on his unsuccessful attempts, the Wright Brothers, after countless micro-experiments, had spent less than $500. Their approach was the epitome of a lean start-up.

Five Important Lessons

The Wright Brothers' story offers profound insights into the nature of innovation that applies to personal and professional growth. Let's explore five lessons that we can apply to our own journey toward mastering the art of failing faster and better.

First, it required someone motivated to declare the mission—even have the vision to think that it was possible to achieve it. This mission and vision had to be converted into smaller goals and plans to achieve those goals. Being intentional about daily tasks and actions compelled the strategic use of time and daily preparation (Alignment One).

Second, Achieving the first sustained flight wasn't about authority or financial resources. Instead, it was accessible to anyone who could align with the governing principles of flight. It required them to observe, theorize, challenge current beliefs and theories, and the humility to modify their beliefs based on new information. Visualizing new possibilities, seeing problems from new angles, staying positive and seeing the possible, managing thoughts and emotions during success and failure, and taking repeated actions demanded full engagement, commitment, and the willingness to take their lumps (Alignment Two).

Third, the experiments required the right resources and tools—organized workspaces, navigating what was under their control, effort, commitment, and the acceptance of things outside their control. In the case of the Wright Brothers, it also required alignment between the two brothers: trust, communication, feedback, challenging and accepting each other's perspectives and ideas. They were surrounded by family, friends, competitors, organizations, and governments, most notably the French and British governments—all having their external influence. They also looked for the optimal geographic and weather conditions to test their "Flyer" (Kittyhawk) and conduct more dynamic experiments (Alignment Three).

Fourth, there is no greater teacher than history. Through each experiment, even those lasting just a few seconds at first, the Wright Brothers embodied the essence of iterative learning—collecting data, learning from each attempt, and progressively refining their approach. Experiment after experiment, each taking place over a series of moments. Refinements of materials, size and power of the engine, strengths of struts, tweaks to wing design, steering capacity, modified controls to address pitch, yaw, speed, etc. Persistent experimentation meant taking notes, avoiding the same mistakes twice, and internalizing lessons from each experiment. Along the way, they cultivated previous successes, harvested every failure, and constantly challenged their assumptions about what they "believed" or "thought" was a correct principle or practice. This required radical humility—the capacity to quickly discard what was not true for the purpose of discovering what was true, day after day, experiment after experiment (like Thomas Edison and his thousands of "successful failures"). Hundreds of variables had to be mastered, until the mission and vision could be fulfilled (Alignment Four).

Fifth, everything requires focus. Focus is the foundation of all progress. It takes focus to envision and plan for the future, to discover principles, refine one's beliefs, manage thinking, control emotions, and to keep your body healthy. It takes focus to organize, optimize your environment, build relationships, coordinate with others, understand and navigate the influential forces of our organizations and communities. And it takes focus to gather feedback, analyze experiences, internalize lessons, and make the most of past experiences. And yet all of this ultimately services the present moment, the "now"—helping you give your full and complete attention to the game, arena, craft, or work that is before you. (Alignment Five).

The **2nd secret** will ensure that you can make the improvements you need to set and achieve any goal. Whether your attention is required for just a few moments to address a factor relevant to your flow (Performance Focus) or whether your attention is needed on a particular theme over a more extended period of time (Strategic Focus)—it is all driven by your ability to know where your attention is needed, when it is needed, and how long it is needed—to influence your current WIN.

Five Elements of Iteration

To elevate performance, you must first identify the critical factor or factors that matter most. This must be the center of your *Focus* and commitment for as long as it takes to align yourself with the principles that govern a particular factor toward its mastery. The second element requires you to identify the *Inputs* you are willing to invest (time, energy & resources, etc.). The third element requires you to define the *Process*, or exactly how you are going to begin to engage any change effort.

With your focus centered, inputs clear, and process defined, you begin taking action with intention. This remains an ongoing experiment as you observe and examine what is happening (fourth element)—the *Outcomes* showing up from your efforts. Taking note of what is happening, you assess how well aligned you are with your combined resources and processes by getting *Feedback* (internal and/or external) which you use to make adjustments to any one or more of these elements, until you have iterated yourself through the mastery of that factor.

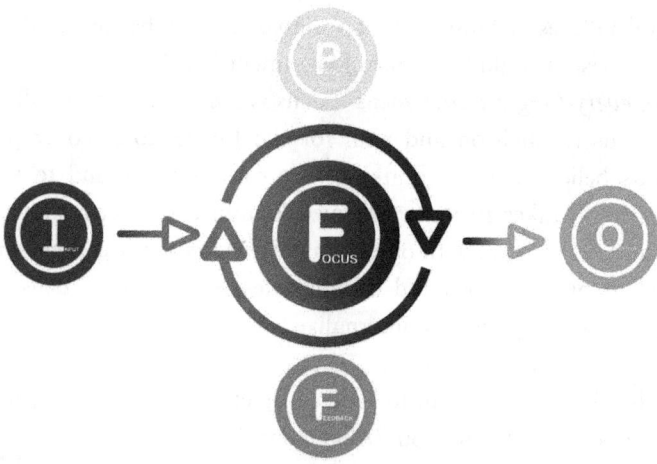

Tweaks and refinements typically involve adjusting your inputs or process.

Sometimes, it's about refining the outcomes you're observing or seeking different feedback sources. It may be that you need to identify other types of feedback (from a more credible or reliable source). Sometimes, the very thing you are focused on needs to be reconsidered and you need to reset your attention on a different goal or objective. In short—every element of iteration requires iteration.

Five Types of Correlation

As you engage in most experiments where there is an action and an outcome, you'll begin to see a correlation between what you are "doing" and what you are "getting." Understanding five basic types of correlation can unlock insights into how your actions influence your outcomes.

The first is simply doing something to get anything. You may be doing more of something (e.g., learning a new skill at work), then observing what's happening. Perhaps your performance is improving, perhaps not. Or perhaps it is getting worse. You are starting to make sense of the connection between actions and results.

The second is doing more to get something more. As you acquire a new skill and put it to good use you hope your performance improves. You may see improvement, for example, by making more refined sales calls and closing more deals. Or, perhaps you find that spending more time preparing for your day increases your productivity.

The third is doing more to get something less. You might be intent on getting more sleep each night to be less exhausted during the day or paying more attention to your past successes to decrease your fear of making errors.

The fourth is doing something less to get something more. Perhaps you find that micro-managing people less increases their performance and your credibility with your own boss. Or, by watching less news you increase your sense of inner peace!

The fifth is doing something less to get something less. Perhaps drinking less caffeine decreases your anxiety. Or, thinking less negatively about what you are doing decreases the amount of chocolate you consume to combat bad moods.

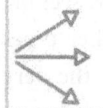   

Whatever you are trying to change, drawing a connection between what you are doing and what you are getting, makes what you are doing highly motivational. You will no longer just "do things" to see what happens (or at least not for long); instead you will take action and experiment with intent, notice what is happening, refine one or more of the 5 elements of iteration (over and over again as needed) until you find the proper alignment between your actions and results—Doing and Getting.

Transitioning from passive experimentation to intentional action and observation marks a critical shift, empowering you to actively shape your journey toward mastery. There are few performance secrets as simple yet profound as thia. It's where the real work and results take place. This 2nd Secret is a universal secret, and no individual, relationship, team, organization, or society has ever evolved or succeeded without understanding and engaging in this process—whether they are aware of it or not.

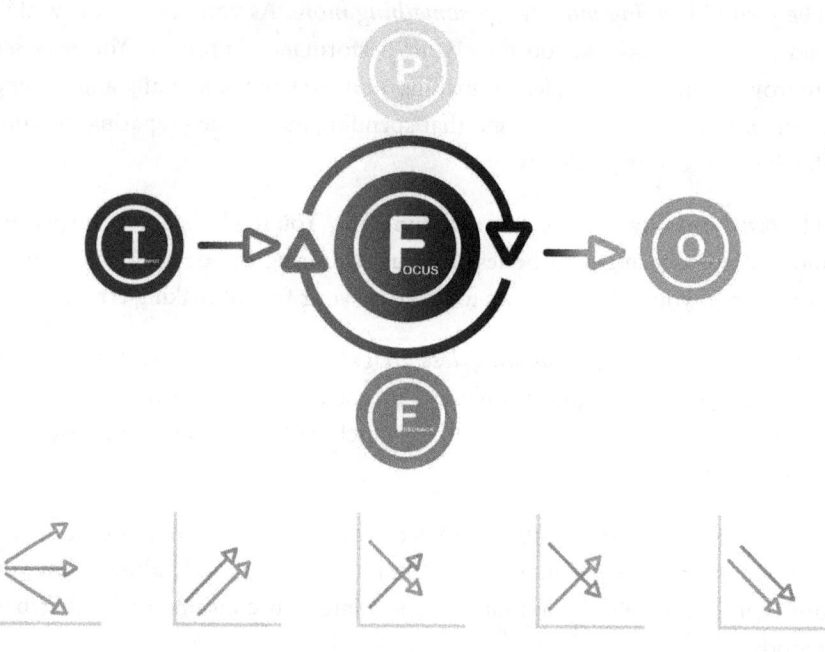

Measuring Your Progress: Doing and Getting

After setting your SMART Goals, the next critical step is to bring them to life through the creation of a scorecard for active measurement and tracking. This enables you to monitor progress and make adjustments as needed.

By adopting an Attentional Scorecard, you gain a powerful tool to meticulously track your daily progress—holding you *accountable* while giving you the feedback you need to modify the experiment, stay the course, and to achieve the goal at hand.

All great performers are masters of accountability and feedback, gathering as much accurate information as possible on their actions and making adjustments while moving closer toward their goals. Every system requires feedback to course correct. Moreover, all great performers use scorecarding (informally or formally) to monitor their progress. Here's what happens when they don't...

The story of *Florence Chaddick*, the first woman to swim the English Channel both ways, exemplifies the critical role of having measurable indicators of progress. In 1952 she set a goal to swim to Catalina Island off the coast of California. With her goal clearly set, she had everything in place to meet her objective, including a support team—even shooters to keep the sharks away in the frigid waters. A dense fog rolled in and made it nearly impossible to see, having no perspective and no way of measuring her progress, she ultimately asked to be pulled from the water—but she was only a half-mile from the shoreline! Her first attempt was thwarted by an inability to measure herself against her end goal. Ultimately, however, she achieved her goal, beating the men's record by more than two hours! Just as the fog obscured Chaddick's view of her goal, the lack of a clear measurement system can cloud our progress toward our objectives.

No objective is ever achieved by simply declaring the mission and then drafting the SMART goal. Goals must be operationalized by clear and measurable plans of action. It is difficult to manage our body, thoughts and emotions without charting our progress toward the end goal.

Remember: what gets measured gets done.

Using Scorecards

To see the difference that scorecarding can make in tracking goals, let's look at three examples.

Example One: Sleep. Suppose that you decide to work on your Flow Liability of being tired during the day. After going through the FOCUS Planning Process, you select the strategy of getting your optimal amount of sleep at night and taking a twenty-minute nap in the afternoon. You convert your current five-hour sleep habit into a seven-hour habit, and you build a simple chart or scorecard to hold yourself accountable.

While traditional methods like paper and spreadsheets work, utilizing the specialized assessment and tracking tool in the 1080° Sweep App offers tailored features that enhance your ability to monitor and adjust your progress. If your goal is to get at least seven hours of sleep each night over thirty days in order to feel more energy during the day, you are now clear on both the input (sleep) and outcome (energy). Incorporating this activity into your daily routine by scheduling a specific time not only organizes your day but also reinforces the habit, making success more attainable.

To arrive at an input number, simply write how many hours and minutes you slept the night before. The *outcome measure* relies on your judgment (or a good sleep app). You might rate how you feel at the end of each day, using a 1 to 10 scale. Each day for thirty days, record how many hours you sleep and how much energy you felt during the day. Over thirty days you might just see a positive correlation between how much you sleep and your energy throughout the day.

SMART Goal: To increase personal energy by sleeping over seven hours five to seven days a week.

This SMART Goal of enhancing personal energy through adequate sleep is a foundational step toward achieving a consistent state of flow, where productivity and well-being intersect.

Date:	Input	Outcome	Notes:
6/1	6.5	6	More than expected. Not enough.
6/2	7.0	8	Better sleep/higher energy today.
6/3	7.5	9	Modified schedule a bit. Even better energy.
—	—	—	"..."

A personal scorecard system will help clarify your SMART Goal, identify preliminary tasks, set milestones, and boost your flow. Here is a slightly more detailed process:

Example Two: Deep breathing and pre-visualizing your day. Begin by identifying a key area of your life for improvement—perhaps the Psychological dimension. Next, using the SMART criteria, state your strategic actions in the form of a goal: To breathe deeply and pre-visualize my day for up to twenty minutes each morning for the next thirty days.

To clarify why you want to achieve this goal, list the expected benefits, such as a smoother flowing day, getting more done with less stress. Visualizing your day helps you develop a clearer picture of what needs to be accomplished.

Next, identify several strategic action steps, such as creating a space at home, setting your alarm, and getting up fifteen minutes earlier each morning—a daily ritual to put into your daily calendar.

With your pre-steps in place, identify the input and outcome measure that will help you track your progress. For instance, after each visualization session, quickly jot down a score on how clear and actionable your day's plan feels, using a 1 to 5 or 1 to 10 scale. Emojis can work just as well—whatever helps you draw a connection between your actions and your results.

This immediate reflection can help refine your approach to assess your daily clarity/flow. In the example below (a sample of what you will see when using the goal-tracking app), both your input measure and outcome measure are charted daily—each measured vertically with time represented horizontally. Both are quantitative (the process goal measured in minutes and outcome goal measured on a scale). This type of scorecard system is more visual so you can actually see your progress and correlation pattern.

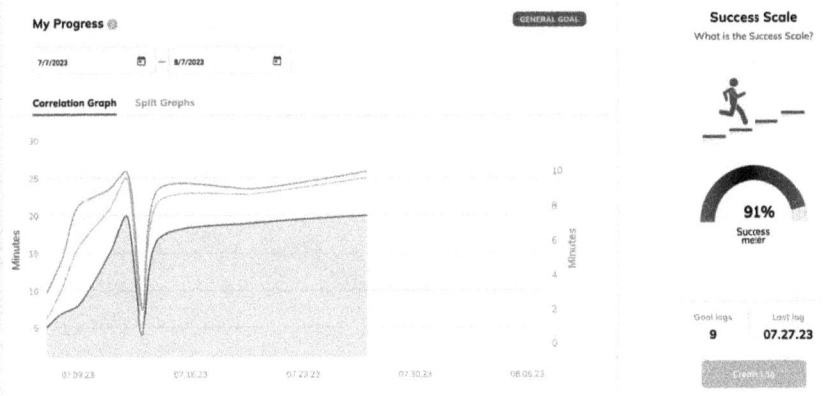

Iterating Toward Success   165

For every goal, you want to see a correlation between what you are doing and what you are getting—or Inputs and Outcomes. If you are not seeing the connection between your actions and your results, reconsider what you are doing and measuring until you find a practice that delivers the outcome you want. Once you are moving in the right direction (seeing the appropriate correlation—noting the five correlation types above), you can then set milestones and mini victories along the way toward goal completion. You might set three mini-goals, or milestones, with three distinct rewards to drive motivation: 1) perhaps after the *first ten days of action*, you take an hour off work to do something fun; 2) the *second ten days* may prompt the purchase of an audio book; and the *third ten days* perhaps you can take a night off with friends or see a movie. Your rewards (in this case external) can supply added motivation for you.

Unlock the full potential of your goal setting by visiting https://attentionalleadership.com/attentional-leadership-1080-sweep-app/ to use our exclusive Attentional Scorecard template, designed to streamline your progress tracking.

Example Three: Losing weight. Again, first identify the life arena or dimension, *Physical*. Next, using the SMART criteria, state your goal: "Lose ten pounds in sixty days." To clarify why you want to proceed, write the expected benefits: gaining a sense of self-control, improving the fit of clothes, better stamina, enhanced appearance, lower cholesterol, etc. Listing meaningful benefits help keep you motivated.

Next, determine the strategic action steps, such as purchasing a gym membership and getting up an hour earlier.

Now identify the *input measure* and *outcome measure*. For example, you might count calories, minutes of exercise, total weights lifted in a workout, steps taken per day, etc. In this example, aerobic minutes per day are counted with the expectation that this will lead to losing weight and facilitating flow.

Measuring your input and outcome enables you to see your progress graphically with trend lines.

In the case of losing weight, you may be **doing something** more to get **something less**, and you might expect to see an input trendline increasing (amount of exercise) while the outcome trendline decreases (weight loss). Your scorecard might look something like this:

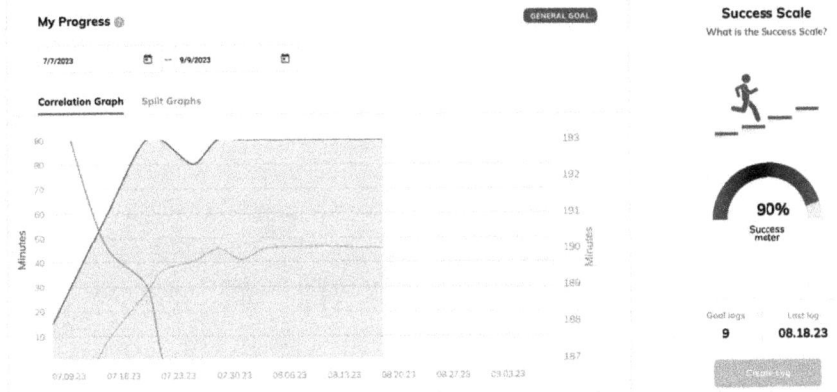

When seeking to find more flow by placing your attention with intention on specific factors and by setting and measuring SMART goals, you need to draw a clear connection between doing and getting, and types of correlations in order to get the outcomes you want. Your FOCUS Planning Process will take you through all of the key steps and questions, but the scorecarding process will give you a visual and compelling graph to see your progress.

Identifying the Right Measures

There is one more catch: *making sure you are measuring the right things!* With regard to weight loss, you might set a goal to lose ten or more pounds. Achieving this goal requires balanced and complementary strategies that encompass both dietary management and innovative exercise methods, including both aerobic (rapid heart rate) exercises and resistance training (lifting weights), and ensuring a comprehensive approach to health and wellness. If these strategies are part of your regimen and you measure your aerobic minutes daily, you may be disappointed, because your measuring system may not be giving you the whole story. You may be losing fat and excess weight, but because of your resistance training (which actually does more to burn fat) you may be gaining muscle weight. This is a good thing, yet your outcome number may not be going in the desired direction and giving you the wrong message.

The solution: *change what you measure.* In this case, your real goal may be to lose body fat, with the added benefit of gaining a stronger, more toned body. In this case you may still count your input as the number of aerobic minutes per day (or you can add those minutes with the minutes you engage in resistance training): however, instead of measuring weight loss, you could now measure the decrease in body fat percentage—a measure that more accurately measures progress toward your real goal.

Some metrics are simple and straightforward. For example, the number of compliments given per day (outcome: to find more flow in relationships), number of smiles per day (outcome: to increase happy feelings), number of minutes organizing your day (outcome: to remove immediate distractions). Yet, with more complex change, think about what measures tell the real story of change.

Finding Flow Through Intentional Practice

Becoming consciously competent means developing new patterns of behavior that you own. Once you identify and craft a specific training objective that will produce the desired outcome, you must be intentional about developing it through applied practice toward a new and sustainable habit pattern. There are no short-cuts to skill-building and habit-formation. Finding flow involves repetition and building muscle memory, not just in physical activities but through intentional practice using specific methods to master a particular flow factor or skill—the 2nd Secret.

While some people believe there is a magical threshold of 10,000-hours to acquire expertise, others become experts in their craft much faster because they: 1) align with the governing principles, models and processes, 2) are intentional about their practice, getting feedback on how they are doing, and iterate through failure until they master a competency; and 3) have the fortitude to break through old patterns of behavior faster. By engaging in highly intentional, focused and consistent practice, they significantly decrease the time needed to acquire and master a new skill.

For any change, you have to ask yourself: "Do I really want this?" Then, you must determine if you are fully committed to doing the work. Relatively few people stick with the program. Instead, they push hard for a short time and slip back into old patterns of behavior. Most of us have setbacks when we seek personal change. This is natural. Regardless of these setbacks, your strong desire for change and your capacity to iterate toward success will prevail, if you have ample motives to sustain your discipline, and the tools and methods to support you along the way.

Progress with a partner. As you ponder any new goal or goals, consider finding a partner to support you. Choose a partner who is equally committed to making a change. Develop a *buddy system* for holding each other accountable. This social process may inspire you and your partner to "go the distance" together.

Talent Not Required But Mindset a Must

After three decades of research on developing expertise, Andres Ericsson and Robert Pool conclude that it's not innate talent that produces greatness, but instead the steady acquisition of discrete and attainable practices internalized toward ever-higher levels of performance. And yet we often assume that natural ability (IQ, strength, traits, etc.) is what makes people great.[138]

Hence the phrase "practice makes perfect" is woefully inaccurate: only "perfect practice makes perfect." Going through the motions of any action rarely leads to greater improvement. *We are either getting better at our craft or getting worse.* If we are not intentional in our efforts, we're probably getting worse.

Yes, even highly accomplished people have their weaknesses and struggles—in fact it's often the reason they succeed. What sets them apart is their willingness to identify the most important thing they need to change, the *1st Secret*, and then commit to mastering the knowledge, skills, and behaviors needed to excel at it—*the 2nd Secret*.

Translating Values into Virtues

A myriad of *case histories* of people finding their flow prove that putting our attention with intention on What's Important Now pays dividends. Each situation is different, and each person's "One Thing" and process for influencing it is unique to their current circumstances. Once they discover that *1st Secret*, they can build a plan to align, iterate, and master it, the *2nd Secret*. By becoming more aware of our own interference and identifying the dimension(s) and Flow Factor(s) that need attention, we will find greater alignment while drawing a clear connection between what we are doing and what we are getting. A few client cases stand out:

Case One: Kathy.
Dimension: Physical (doing something less to get something less)
This middle-aged woman was interested in improving her health and decided to lower her cholesterol level. After meeting with her doctor, Kathy discovered

that her cholesterol was so high (around 220) that it was a potential Flow Liability (Physical dimension). While it didn't hinder her ability to excel in many of her life arenas, it weighed on her mind as she knew it had long-term consequences. Kathy decided to replace certain daily food items such as chips, cookies, and French fries with healthier foods. Her SMART Goal was to get her number under 180 within ninety days. She met with a nutritionist and identified several food items to start consuming, including, of course, more fruits, vegetables, and water. She hoped that this new pattern of behavior would take her out of the red zone. She measured the number of servings of fruit or vegetables daily for ninety days, kept a daily food and hydration log, and saw her cholesterol number drop. Having a personal plan with a clear process and outcome metrics ensured this outcome.

Case Two: Gina.
Dimension: Spiritual (doing something more to get something more)
Gina wanted to give more attention to her spiritual dimension. As you can imagine, growing spiritually can be somewhat abstract. We discussed what growing spiritually might look and feel like and what actions she might take to make this happen. She felt strongly that daily scripture reading would be the input to help her feel more spiritually attuned. We explored different ideas for measurement: minutes of scripture reading per day, number of paragraphs or pages read, number of principles comprehended, etc. Measuring the number of principles comprehended seemed to her the best measure, as the other measures were too easy to cheat on or too easy to focus on time or pages without comprehending what was read.

Her SMART goal was to read and apply three principles each day. Her reading may take only a few minutes or up to an hour, a few paragraphs or several pages. With this *input measure* in place, we identified an outcome measure that would satisfy her desire to become "more spiritual." Again, the goal of becoming more spiritual can only be assessed based on a self-rating scale. A *qualitative outcome measure* might include how confident, happy, altruistic, or content you are. Gina created a *spirituality index* and rated herself on a scale of 1 to 100 at the end of each day. This rating pushed her to reflect and consider how her actions influenced her sense of being. With this system, Gina could hold herself accountable while seeing progress on her path to greater spirituality.

Case Three: Carson.
Dimension: Personal (doing something less to get something more)

Social media can be a strong detractor from building relationships and excelling at work. On the job Carson found himself jumping onto his phone between projects and becoming more isolated. Wanting to change, he began to measure his screen time during the day and decided that he wanted to lower it so he could focus on building relationships with his shop-mates. In this case he was doing something less to get something more. He decided to lower his input measure from four to two hours a day and intentionally connect with others. He rated his outcome measure with either a smiley face emoji, neutral face, or frowny face. This allowed him to see a correlation between decreased use of social media and increased relationship, job and life satisfaction.

Case Four: Neal.
Dimension: Personal (doing something more to get something more)

This mortgage broker knew that one area of weakness was a sloppy desk. He discovered that his lack of organization caused him to look for papers that he needed to close a particular deal. To find more flow, Neal decided it was time to get more organized and employ strategies to get his work done more efficiently. Recognizing that a more advanced filing system might do the trick, Neal read two books on filing and organizing strategies and decided to purchase a desk-top system where he could separate his clients by closing date. This was to accompany his general reference filing which was often left to chance. He committed to organize his files and his desk for fifteen minutes each day. This included purchasing a label maker and making his files more presentable. His outcome measure was a simple "flow index" (1 to 5) for rating how smoothly his day went, as he could now find what he was looking for and stay on track with each of his clients. In addition, Neal asked his assistant to rate his flow from her perspective. This additional feedback loop, shared each week, was a helpful reinforcement and accountability process. This simple strategy directly impacted his daily and hourly focus.

Case Five: Britta.
Dimension: Interpersonal (doing something more to get something more)

This student rarely smiled, and her "blank stare" affected her emotional state and that of her associates (her interpersonal flow). She felt that if she could smile more intentionally she would have a happier disposition and be more approachable. Britta set a realistic goal to smile each time she came into direct contact with a friend or loved one. She counted how many times she smiled each day and tracked her progress. Her outcome measure was a scale of 1 to 100, indicating her level of connection and interpersonal flow.

Over ninety days Britta used the scorecard to chart her progress. Steadily the number of her smiles grew and smiling at people became easier. Each day she rated her level of connection, and her score increased each week. By making this simple change, she initiated more intimate conversations, developed deeper connections and felt much happier.

Case Six: Jesse.
Dimension: Team (doing something less to get something more)
This man was a workaholic, a hyperactive perfectionist with a passion for his work. Examining his family life (his chosen arena) showed him that finding his flow depended on building a solid foundation with his family, especially his children. He recognized that *no success at the office could compensate for failure at home*, and he wondered what he could do to let his family know how much he cared and wished to serve them.

After deep reflection, Jesse recognized that in addition to spending at least two hours with his family each night after work that he could be more connected with his kids at breakfast. Typically, his wife made breakfast while the kids got ready and while Jesse was tucked away in his office. He set a SMART goal to make breakfast for his family five days a week, which meant carving out thirty minutes of each morning. A simple *input measure* was either a "yes" or a "no" (he did it or he didn't). Jesse then created an *outcome measure* he called "family unity" on a 1 to 10 scale. This simple accountability process made a big difference toward greater interpersonal flow. It was also a rating he could ask his wife to score at the end of each week (an external feedback loop).

As you begin to remove your own Flow Liabilities and grow your Flow Assets, you'll become a different person—one principle and practice at a time. Your capacities will expand. Each iteration of awareness, decision-making, action-taking, and habit-forming rearranges your life. If you do this well, principles will govern your values, your values will govern your thinking, your thinking will govern your emotions, and your emotions will drive your actions—repeated actions, which form permanent habits, which change your inner and outer reality.

Thanks to the science of **neuroplasticity**, we now know that the brain and body change over time—not just in twenty or thirty generations, but within our own lifetime! We become what we are intentionally practicing. And then there is the science of **Epigenetics**, which shows how the actions we take influence others, often unconsciously, by our own example and behaviors.

Ralph Waldo Emerson wrote: "Sow a thought and you reap an action; sow an act and you reap a habit; sow a habit and you reap a character; sow a character and you reap a destiny."

Once embedded within our daily norms, new behaviors and habits become virtues, part of our character. In some small way we add to what we are given at birth—we become something more, evolving into something better.

Through our personal evolution we get closer to finding our flow toward our purpose and potential.

When we are in flow we experience integrity in the moment. We project something that is authentic, not an illusion of something that we are trying to be. Our moments of flow become self-confirming. At this point we move beyond simply valuing this change. We *are the change.*

Section IV
The Third Secret: Scaling Flow Through Attentional Leadership®

Applying the Third Secret Through the Five Dimensions of Influence

The exercise of Attentional Leadership® may begin as an inward journey, but ultimately extends itself through everything and everybody that surrounds us—each being a collective yet singular body with interconnected parts—like a *fractal—a self-repeating structure in nature.*

Just as fractals reveal repeating patterns from the microscopic to the macroscopic, they metaphorically illustrate how principles of flow and leadership can scale across different domains. Fractals are easily recognizable when you look at snowflakes, crystals, flowers, coastline patterns, even entire galaxies, etc. Discovering your first fractal is just the beginning, much like recognizing the foundational patterns in leadership and organizational dynamics opens a world of insight. For example, look at a sprig of broccoli and compare it to that of cauliflower, then compare these to the branching alveoli of the human lung. When you look at a forest you see the same thing—a collection of smaller objects representing a collective body. Much like these natural patterns, Attentional Leadership® reveals how individual growth can reflect and influence larger organizational or community structures.

Look at the magnificent pictures made by the Hubble and Webb telescopes where you can observe billions of years of self-repeating structures—solar systems and galaxies; then compare these to orbiting relationships at the atomic level. These ubiquitous principles of the universe find practical expression in the fundamentals of Attentional Leadership®, guiding our interactions and decisions on every scale—from the smallest to the largest physical structures and spaces. This also holds true for the structure of humanity—for you as an individual, within the relationships that surround you—from self to society. *At every level and scale, principles prevail.* We might consider this a *3rd Secret: that every principle, strategy and skill that you utilize to find your own flow are relevant when seeking to influence the external world*—to influence and lead others, teams, organizations, communities, even nations.

All dimensions are equally relevant to you as they are to others. While personal development, performance, and discovering one's full potential are crucial, the journey doesn't end with the self; it naturally extends to influencing and uplifting those around us to discover their potential. From individual relationships to teams, extending to organizations and encompassing entire communities, our quest for alignment and flow amplifies the impact of Attentional Leadership ®.

Chapter 12
Finding Flow in Relationships, Teams, Organizations & Beyond

> "Neither shall they say, Lo here! Or, lo there! Behold, the kingdom of God is within you."
> —Luke 17:21

Finding Relational Flow: Winning Gold by Focusing on Others

In many Meaningful Life Arenas (MLAs), we find ourselves as individual actors among a sea of competitors and colleagues. We engage with family, work with others in teams or within broader organization and community contexts. And in the quest to be our best, we must ask: *how much of our time should we spend focusing on our own flow vs. serving others toward theirs?*

Paradoxically, by serving others, we are elevated; by the giving of ourselves, we receive; by helping others to find their flow, we find more of our own.

I once worked with a colleague who won Gold at the 2004 Olympics in Athens, Greece. At six foot, four inches, Lucas (not his real name) was built to row. After years of training and experiencing the ups and downs that compel most athletes to hang it up, he continued to apply the 1st Secret (identifying his "One Thing") and iterating through it via the 2nd Secret—continuing the challenge of moving forward and upward—was ultimately invited to train with the national team, the precursor of making the Olympic team.

Within this elite group of thirty rowers, it was anyone's seat—but only twelve would be chosen. During the final stages of the selection process, his winning principle took shape. He realized that success wasn't just about his own efforts but about lifting others alongside him. What he needed was a way to turn what he had done inside out.

Admittedly, Lucas was not the clear favorite. Others had more strength and experience, but he had a distinct strategy that eluded the others. He described the "paired matrix" vetting process where every rower was paired with every other rower to determine which two-person teams would clock the fastest times and ultimately reveal the best rowers. He noted that a team can choose *three mindsets* when rowing: 1) row your best and hope your teammate does the same; 2) seek to bring out the best in your teammate with your own performance taking a secondary focus; and 3) both rowers focus on bringing out the best in each other to maximize synergy.

Aware of the rarity of the second and third mindsets, Lucas saw an opportunity to distinguish himself by fostering unmatched synergy with his partners. Especially when everything is on the line, Lucas knew that if he could bring out the best in every member he rowed with, that he might elicit this synergy. So, while not the fastest or strongest, he made up for it with strategy. He studied the strengths, weaknesses and personalities of everyone on the list and developed unique strategies to tap into their deepest motivation and energy to bring out the best in each rowing partner. This philosophy landed him, and whomever he was paired with, the best times in every heat. With his name amid almost every winning pair, *he made the Olympic team—and ultimately won gold in Athens—not because he focused on performing at his best, but because he was focused on bringing out the best flow in others.*

In his personal and professional life, he retains this winning philosophy, recognizing that achieving greatness does not come solely from physical and technical gifts and training, but through the other-focused mindset that raises the bar, and performance, of every team he serves.

In a world where "selfie" is now a registered word, this secret principle puts much-needed attention on the value of bringing out the best in others as we seek to win our own gold medal!

As we conclude this story on enhancing interpersonal synergy, it's important to recognize that these same principles apply on a larger scale. The following cases will illustrate how optimizing personal flow can serve as a foundation for fostering alignment and flow within teams and organizations.

Finding Team Flow: Global Elections Company. IT Leadership Team

Working with one of the world's premier elections firms redesigning, updating, and supporting one of our largest US cities during one of our most contested national elections, was a fascinating experience. "Help these senior IT directors work together as a team" was the mandate. Since they were all brilliant, Ivy League graduates, experienced, and independently minded—building cohesion was a tall order. Yet, like any team, there was noise and we were there to find it.

While the mission and vision were clear and exact, each member of this team had their own WIN. One was measured on hardware development, another software development. One was over physical and cyber security and another over local county executives who were constantly moving the goal post. Each was incentivized to succeed in their respective area, and many were more focused on their own vs. the collective win. Noise and interference came in the form of operational meetings filled with updates and talking but little consideration to team function and outcome. In fact, there was no time set aside to improve team process. The result was a disconnected group of geniuses without a coherent team strategy.

By taking just a few minutes during team meetings to work through mutual understanding and team process, greater appreciation and support began to rise. While there were many factors to consider, the main objective was to decrease self-focus in order to increase team synergy. By doing this, a collective focus emerged by allotting time for team process, increasing communications and feedback. There was still interference, but slowly we began eliminating noise and redirecting focus on those things that mattered most and letting go of things that mattered least. Exploring historical wins, losses, and challenging previous assumptions, all while monitoring continually shifting external factors, required this team to keep their eye on the ball while placing their attention with intention on their current and collective WIN.

Finding Organization Flow: International Surgical Society

Designing and executing a strategic planning process for a well-established international surgical society was another fascinating arena to apply Attentional Leadership and the principles of flow.

Conducting a strategic planning process takes months of preparation, including significant data gathering—looking externally at socio-demographic, technological, environmental, economic, political, and industry trends. Internally there is an analysis of Strengths and Weaknesses, Opportunities and Threats in relationship to the external environment gathered from member segments, internal staff, the board of directors, and other stakeholders. Along the way it's important to study the organization's recent history, its financials, wins, losses, recent challenges, etc. Drawing from its long past and understanding the principles and values from which the organization was founded also provides valuable insight into where it has been in relation to where it wants to go.

We identified the WIN—three strategic priorities that would add the greatest value. The team then translated these broad themes into concrete actions—moving from strategic issues statements to goals, followed by outcomes/objectives, and then into key metrics and critical success factors. This required the team's members to do the same thing, so that their focus and attention aligned with that of the organization.

As we consider the many factors of flow, the inevitable question is: What's Important Now (WIN)? And the answer always is: "Whatever it is that you, the team, or the organization should be working on to eliminate the interference that thrwarts daily focus"—the *1st Secret*. As you do this over and over again and master each WIN via the *2nd Secret*, failing faster and better (iteration), you come to know that for each new Flow Asset you acquire or Flow Liability you purge, each is additive, working in concert with the others—building a broader repertoire of assets and skills that enable you to influence yourself and others (*3rd Secret*) by knowing where, when, and for how long to place your attention on What's Important Now (WIN) at every level and dimension of the system you are engaged in.

Three-Dimensional Leadership

It's one thing to understand these principles and practices at a higher scale, but it's entirely different to see them as part of an interconnected system—one that tells a much more compelling story.

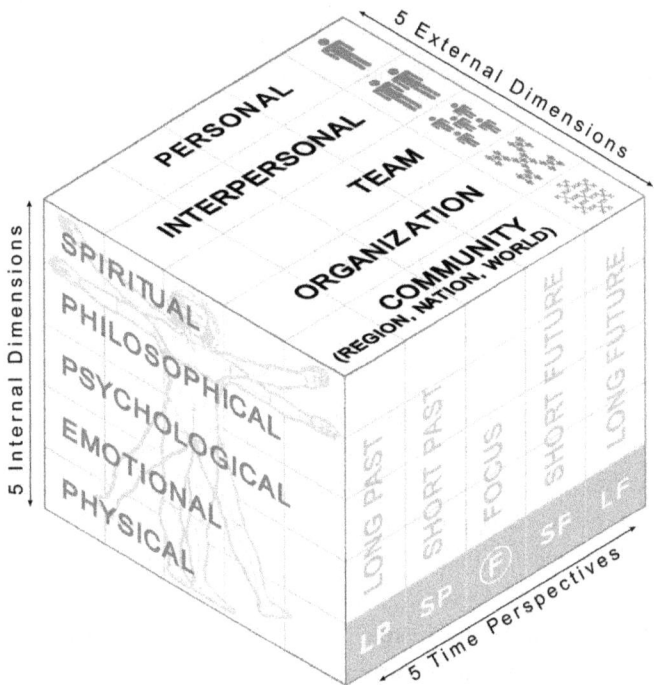

This 3D model introduces a new paradigm for understanding influence and leadership, placing greater emphasis on how we allocate time, attention, and resources as we begin to see the many systems we impact. Whether it's at the level of yourself, a relationship, a work team, a division within an organization, or an entire community, each level involves Physical, Emotional, Psychological, Philosophical, and Spiritual factors, relevant to the Long-Future, Short-Future, present moment Focus, Short-Past, and Long-Past. Navigating your attention within this 3D space is where leadership becomes more like a dance—fluid, adaptive, and interconnected—rather than just a collection of self-applied skills.

From Notes to Chords and The Music of Leadership

When children begin to play a musical instrument, they start by learning notes. On a piano after learning where middle C is they learn about octaves and then different keys in sequence to play simple songs. After Chopsticks and Happy Birthday, simple chords are introduced. As they engage more than one key simultaneously with another, new sounds and tones emerge—not so elegant at first but moving toward the emergence of real music.

Just as transitioning from playing single notes to creating harmonious music represents a paradigm shift, evolving from individual competencies to orchestrating a comprehensive leadership approach marks a profound transformation in one's ability to influence and lead effectively. You might begin by creating a vision and setting specific goals. Next you focus on designing plans, maximizing time, optimizing sleep, eating well, taking care of your body, managing thoughts and emotions, or clarifying your values.

Seeking greater alignment with others, you might focus on building trust, communicating better, and learning how to manage conflict. Soon you may learn how to form and optimize a team, or engineer an organization's culture. You become proficient in measuring performance, analyzing effectiveness, and internalizing key lessons. You revisit previous experiences, recalling your greatest moments, harvesting past failures, and challenging previous assumptions in relationship to current realities.

Yet in our complex world, circumstances require us to exercise our influence based on multiple demands in the moment—hence the importance of internalizing new concepts and skills, much like adding new notes to your musical score. *This requires us to make the shift from single skill, factor or dimension thinking to exercising multiple skills, factors, and dimensions simultaneously and harmoniously.* These are the chords of Attentional Leadership®—seeing the connection and alignment among such things as rest and energy, thoughts and emotions, building trust and collaboration with others, co-visioning with them, looking at the past emotional climate of a team, or the previous values and beliefs of an organization.

Today, *leaders must draw upon a multitude of leadership skill sets on demand by moving quickly within and between various factors and dimensions.* Instead of thinking about single competency-development (or single note thinking), today's leaders must address complex circumstances and see their leadership as a symphony of skills required to address the unique challenges of the moment.

All The World's a Stage

Whether you command an elite team, lead a small family, or are just trying to figure out what's next for your life, understanding the flow dimensions, factors, and their relationship to each other via the Attentional Leadership® Framework will help you better identify what's in alignment, where the noise is, and what you might do to remove it by building greater capacity—over time.

Each person, relationship, team, organization, or community has their own unique and distinctive set of circumstances. Some lack purpose, vision or goals. Others may struggle with physical challenges, thoughts and emotions that impede progress. Still others struggle knowing what's important, what they value, or why they are even here.

We are all influenced by our history—our successes and failures, our beliefs about ourselves and others. We all have challenges when aligning, working, and collaborating with others. Our lives aren't perfect. Political, cultural, and environmental factors pull our strings and produce uncertainty. The world is an imperfect place with plenty of strife and struggle.

And yet you have agency—the capacity to make choices, to engage with yourself and others in any arena of your choosing, and to see the outcomes of your actions.

Whatever your age, you have already experienced moments of focus and flow as well as interference and distractions that have impeded your progress. Through it all you've been learning and refining your relationship with yourself, the world and everything/everyone in it—a rough stone rolling and getting ever more refined as you continue your journey.

Remember this: you are an actor on a stage, at this period of time—an amalgamation of all your ancestors who have come before you. Their genes, experiences, and life stories are part of you. It's now you on the stage. The lights are on, the stage is set, and there is one question left to ask: ***What is the "One Thing" that if you could change it now, would move the needle on everything—including your ability to flow when it matters most?***

Section V
Living Life in Flow

Chapter 13
Creating a Life of Flow

Striving to live what I teach, my last 1080° Sweep™ Assessment pointed me in the direction of my Short Future and my "One Thing" was the development of Rituals and Routines. As I dug into this factor I realized that I had been neglecting my writing, meditation, morning study (scriptures and science), and spending quality time with my family, so I decided to start a new behavioral ritual and hoped it might impact my life, increase my flow and add value to others. Using the FOCUS Planning Process I got to work.

I set a specific goal to rise at 4:45 a.m., understanding that a disciplined morning routine could significantly enhance my daily flow. I began my day with one hour of writing, followed by twenty minutes of meditation, then thirty minutes of aerobic activity while reading scriptures and books, followed by making breakfast for everyone.

As is common with the adoption of any new habit, I faced significant challenges initially, mirroring the universal struggle to integrate meaningful change, but the idea was compelling. I knew what each new activity would do for me personally, professionally, spiritually, and for my family. What was initially a difficult pattern to weave eventually became second nature. Through this new pattern and rituals of morning activity, I have become more productive and centered. Getting my body active early in the day, turning away from various media and being more present, has made an appreciable difference.

Although I have made this my morning ritual, I confess that there are days when I miss the mark, so it's crucial to forgive myself and persist, understanding that perfection isn't the goal—progress is. Early morning flights and late-night meetings sometimes get in the way, but I'm about 90 percent on target—and it works. Placing my attention with intention on this series of rituals serves many of my core values: my health, profession, spiritual growth, and my wife and kids. My life runs more smoothly (more flow-like) throughout the day and my relationships continue to grow and evolve. I'm more in flow because I am paying more attention to those things that are the most valuable and critical—leaving the extraneous and low-value activities out of the picture.

It is through our specific journey through self-mastery that we refine ourselves—one principle, skill, and practice at a time. And while you continually do this for yourself perhaps it's clear that the pursuit of our own refinements helps us to apply that influence in the service of others, the *3rd Secret*. Does it ever stop? Only you can make that decision. The simple answer: NO. And would you want to?

There's No Finish Line

One of my students called me eight years after his graduation. Having started a summer sales company, and after many cycles of applying Secrets 1, 2, and 3, he went from broke student to having a net worth of more than ten million dollars. In light of his success, he sought to instill resilience in his team, drawing inspiration from the demanding training regimen of Navy SEALs. One drill involved having each member carry forty pounds of sand while soaked in water and march to the top of a large hill. Just when team members thought that the summit was near, the course was changed and a new summit identified. This went on for more than three hours as the group became more and more exhausted. Dogged determination turned into despair. Members were supporting one another as their emotions and tensions were running high. Hour after hour they persevered and continued on their trek.

One person finally asked: "When will this be over?" This question sparked a crucial realization about personal agency—a key component in mastering our journey toward flow.

The instructors on the mountain said that it would be over whenever they wanted it to be over. Shocked at this answer, they decided to keep going—this time on their own accord, recognizing that they, at any moment, could stop the journey and call it a night. The team members, seeing the power of their agency pushed on further until they collectively decided that they had had enough. They were exhausted, spent, but proud of their degree of accomplishment, but even more of their ownership.

One Summit After Another

In 2005, fourteen of us decided to hike Mt. Kilimanjaro (summit 19,341 feet). It was a twenty-one-day expedition with seven days to summit and return to base. We had many experiences along the way, starting in arid conditions and climbing up through five climates and ecosystems. After six days, we entered the "Death Zone" where people become ill from altitude sickness, complications with Malaria medications, fatigue and injury. But we worked together, adjusted our efforts and approach, and made it through sections of glacial ice to summit around six o'clock in the morning. Exhausted, we spent twenty minutes at the top, took a few pictures, then started the descent.

On the descent, new problems arose. For example, one member had an ACL tear, and another threw out his back and had to be carted down the mountain. But we made it to the bottom and spent the next several days enjoying the magic of Tanzania. Our Kilimanjaro expedition, with its myriad challenges and triumphs, served as a profound metaphor for the journey of finding flow through persistence and adaptability.

During our time together we talked about climbing other mountains together—bigger mountains: Denali in Alaska (20,322), Aconcagua in Argentina (22,837), Everest in Nepal (29,029) and completing the "seven summits"—the biggest peaks in the world. That seemed like a significant accomplishment. But when I arrived home at the airport, I met a man who had climbed all seven of the world's greatest summits, but also just traversed all seven seas. This chance meeting at the airport, with a man who achieved extraordinary feats, reinforced the limitless potential for finding flow in pursuing ever-greater challenges.

In that moment, I thought of all that can be done in a lifetime: all the mountains to climb, seas to cross, countries to visit, experiences to have. There is no end to it. There is always more.

Finding your flow is like that. Every new goal is its own summit, complete with adventure and challenge, failure and success. But every adventure makes you something more than you were before—more experienced, more refined—a better person. Of course, it's the journey that is most important—not the destination. Once you get to one destination—you begin anew toward a new summit.

The fact is: there is always a new summit, a new mountain to climb. Fortunately, we don't have to do it all in one day or week. We can do this incrementally—here a little and there a little, continuously over time.

In his book *Atomic Habits* James Clear explains the power of incremental improvements—that if you improve just 1 percent each day over the course of a year you will improve by thirty-seven-fold. But the inverse is also true: doing something slightly worse over that same time can take you off your game. I call this the Law of Accelerated Deviation, meaning: the more you do or don't do something, the effects are exponential—for better or for worse.

Understanding this was the genius of the famed British head of cycling Sir Dave Brailsford. Aware of Britain's dismal seventy-six-year cycling history, Brailsford put into practice his theory of marginal gains by breaking down everything possible about the sport and improving it by just 1 percent. This included small aerodynamic refinements, team truck cleanliness, handwashing, food preparations, sleeping protocols...all of which contributed to what he called the *Podium Principles*: strategy, human performance, and continuous improvement. Through Brailsford's efforts, his British team won seven out of ten gold medals in track cycling in the 2008 Olympics and repeated that success in London four years later. His team has since won three of the last four Tour de France competitions.

As I often tell clients: *You are either getting better or worse—there is no neutral.*

When I was fourteen years old and pondering how to get into better shape while learning to play tennis, I resisted a running regimen. But not wanting to be a complete failure by not trying, I set a goal of running down the driveway and to the end of the road (just to the stop sign). The next night I repeated it, but this time I took a right at the stop sign and ran down to the bottom of the hill—then turned around and came back home. I felt a little pride in this small improvement.

This process continued each night and went something like this: Night Three: Ran down street, took a right, went downhill, crossed the bridge and continued for another five minutes. Night Four: Ran down street, took a right, went downhill, crossed the bridge and continued for another ten minutes... Night Seven: Ran down the street, took a right, went downhill, crossed the bridge and continued until I met the next stop sign at the highway. Night Eight: Ran down street, took a right, went downhill, crossed the bridge and continued until I met the next stop sign. I then crossed the highway 15 and ran up the hill. It veered left so I followed it, proceeded down a hill and into fog near a marshy field. The fog was refreshing and a new experience. Now I felt like I was having an adventure. Night Nine: All of the above steps, but this time I continued through the foggy field up to the next stop sign, took a right, and continued around the golf course. I continued until I came to the Loose Line bridge. I couldn't believe how far out I was. I turned around and ran all the way home. I had run fifty-one minutes—about 6.5 miles. I was drenched, exhausted, and amazingly satisfied.

Incrementally, with small victories along the way, I went from only a few hundred feet to more than six miles, each night fueling and inspiring the next!

Buried deep in this experience is a true principle: While most of us are overwhelmed by the changes we wish to make, by **taking the simplest and easiest first steps** (even if that means driving to the gym and touching the door handle before driving home), that slight action initiates a momentum of action with huge long-term implications. That dark night in 1981 has since led to hundreds of these late-night adventures that still continue to this day—inviting friends to join to simultaneously work on my interpersonal flow.

Lifelong Learning & the Greatest Coach You'll Ever Have

At this point in the book, I hope you're experiencing a simple yet profound shift—from passive learning to self-directed empowerment. Think back to a time when you first discovered something that sparked great interest—a moment when you felt that tingling excitement in your gut, eager to explore something you were passionate about. That was the moment you shifted from passive learner to active seeker of knowledge. You were inspired to hunt down a video, article, or book, or perhaps even reach out to an expert in your area of passion. You followed your own vision and took ownership of your learning and growth—because it was about you, your destiny, and only you could find it!

The true power in our quest for flow emerges when we actively discover the ideas, knowledge, and skills that resonate with our deepest passions, values, and purpose. Each of us must learn to be our own teacher, coach, and cheerleader as we follow that inner voice calling us toward a path to find our personal flow.

While research and expert guidance help illuminate the principles and best practices that support flow, the journey to mastery is deeply personal. The "how" is unique to you—driven by your experiences, challenges, and self-discovery. It's up to you to sort through your Flow Assets and Liabilities and decide What's Important Now—to identify the current "One Thing" that, if mastered, would move the needle on everything.

Building a Life That Flows

Rather than settling for mediocrity (rife with distractions and trivial pursuits), let's embrace the challenge of making every moment more flow-like, infusing targeted strategies to elevate our daily experiences. Why not see what you are made of, shoot for living the exceptional life, however you define it?. Given your unique genetic code, personal, family and cultural history; with your own distinct traits, qualities, and dispositions—even the culmination of all your ancestors—you are the first of your kind on this world stage, at this time. Why not see what great things might flow from you?

Flow is a way of looking at your life and asking: "Am I making the most of every moment, working on my next 'One Thing,' influencing and leading myself and others toward their full potential, and becoming the person I most want to become?"

As we break down our days, we are quick to find how much time is spent on common tasks; nevertheless, we can still find flow in every part of our day—even the average moments—with the right knowledge, skills and tools.

Regardless of the activity, *flow is about being focused and absorbed in the moment whatever it contains.* Any moment, big or small, can flow with intent, purpose and joy.

The Hourglass of Your Life

Envisioning our lives as an hourglass not only illustrates the fleeting nature of time but also emphasizes the importance of consciously preparing for and reflecting on each moment to maximize our flow—each grain of sand representing a moment in time. As each moment approaches the center (this moment), it then falls atop all previous moments, which represent your personal history. If you are wise, you prepare for your key moments of performance, enter them with intent, and exit them having extracted the lessons from each. Armed with new knowledge, you prepare for the next key moment, and so on—optimized by the many Flow Assets you've acquired along the way—working on your next "One Thing," then your next, then again, as you get even better at removing the noise and interference by building greater capacity. This represents the top half of the hourglass.

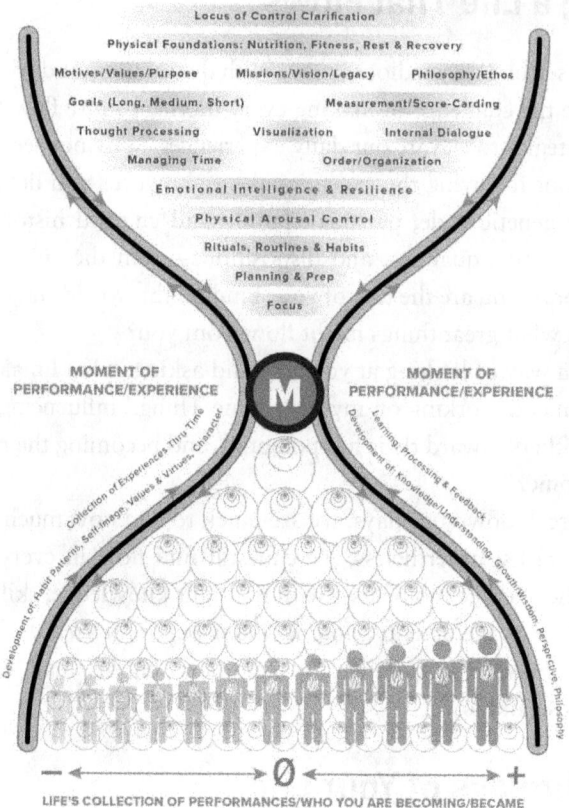

This hourglass-shaped *Preparation and Processing of Experience Model* turns the Attentional Leadership® framework on its head when rotating it ninety degrees counterclockwise.

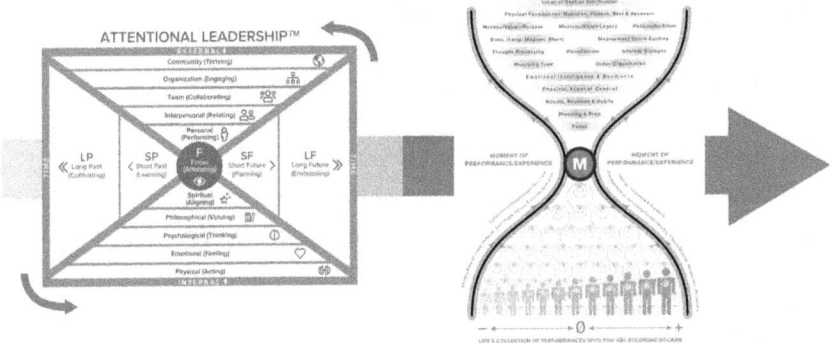

It offers yet another perspective for understanding life as you transact with it moment to moment. Here you can see how so many Flow Assets come together to support your focus during any Moment of Performance. But to what effect does your sand collect?

Leaving Your Legacy

Will you maximize your moments and discover your purpose and potential while making a net contribution—leaving a legacy while helping others do the same?

Ultimately, finding your flow is for the purpose of having a positive influence—to be a net contributor, not consumer—leaving the world and those in it better off for your existence.

Net consumers are self-focused and indulgent folks who seek their own advantage at the expense of others and society. These people take more than they give and produce greater chaos and disorder than flow.

By contrast net contributors not only discover their own flow and greatness, but also bring out the best in others, leaving a legacy of order, love, and a net positive (+) contribution. They recognize that finding their flow is not just for their benefit but for the people around them—making them net producers of goodness and value. If this idea intrigues you, let me recommend "How Will You Measure Your Life" by Clayton Christensen[139]—the former Harvard Business School professor and spiritual leader who wrote clearly and poignantly on this subject.

When measuring and identifying one's contributions made through consistent self-improvement in the service of something larger than yourself—such a legacy is bound to emerge—a flow-finder who helps other people, teams, organizations—even societies do the same.

Living a Life in Crescendo

One of my dearest friends reminded me that at the origin of the word *Sin* lies the notion of *missing the mark*—failing to learn the laws and principles that govern success and happiness in this life and the next.

Imagine what it might feel like to get to the end of your mortal journey only to be reminded daily—for eternity—that you left this world with your talents misused, with your music and contributions still in you. Perhaps this is the truest meaning of hell. In contrast, imagine intentionally chipping away at your imperfections, like a rough stone rolling, moving ever closer to your refined self, with full focus and a commitment to discover your innate gifts and talents—using them for your benefit and that of others. Perhaps this has something to do with eternal joy.

What is the reward of living your life in crescendo—where every month and year gives rise to another toward a higher level where new challenges arrive, offering new opportunities for knowledge and growth? You experience not only the joy of discovering what you are made of—but the opportunity to leave a legacy that inspires others—even beyond your own children and their children's children—to be an example—where emerging generations are inspired and believe in themselves because of your story. In reading a recent biography, I came across such a man, David Goggins.

Exceeding God's Expectations

Having known a few Navy SEALs during my career, I'm impressed by their capacity to engage in "missions impossible." What's also striking is their balance between their warrior ethos and their humility. As special as they are, who they become has often less to do with God-given talent and more to do with their compelling commitment and passion to serve a cause greater than themselves for which they are willing to do what most people are not.

In his book *Can't Hurt Me*, David Goggins tells his amazing story—transforming himself from a three-hundred-pound rat exterminator who washed out of the Air Force to becoming a Navy SEAL (after failing twice). His journey of pushing himself, iterating toward success (riddled with failure and learning along the way), led him to becoming not only a SEAL, but also an ultra-marathoner—(perhaps the first person to ever run a hundred miles with no previous training (an exceedingly painful experience with "exquisite" suffering), a world-record holder for the most pull-ups in a twenty-four-hour period, and the first person to become a SEAL and complete Army Ranger school.

In the *Epilogue* he foretells his post-death interview with God. He describes hearing God tell him how much he exceeded His expectations, that despite his upbringing, challenges in school, physical limitations (even a hole in his heart), family struggles, and his assertion that "no talent is required" suggests that we should give up making excuses why we can't achieve our greatest aspirations and goals. Goggin's is the epitome of internalizing Secrets 1, 2, and 3. He's always looking for his next "One Thing," he iterates through until its mastery, and he takes what he learns to serve and lead others—discovering his full purpose and potential and finding his flow in the process.

What an amazing sentiment—to exceed God's expectations—to be an example of what is possible when serious attention is given with intention toward worthy and challenging goals.

As you seek to find your own flow—even exceed your own expectations—study the lives of great people, those who have overcome extreme obstacles and challenges to do great things—seemingly impossible things. Their stories all point to the same simple truth: If you are willing and committed to moving forward, iterating toward new ceilings of failure, pushing through to the next level and the willingness to do it again and again—the next more challenging than the last—*that you can, not just find your flow, but discover what God intended you to become in the service of others.*

This is the Beginning...

EPILOGUE

Inspired is the person who envisions the future yet
engages the moment, and does so with the end in mind.

Humble is the person who strives for truth, whose beliefs
follow truth, whose thoughts follow their beliefs, whose feelings follow their
thoughts, and whose actions align them all.

Immersed is the person who optimizes their arena—aligning with others in the
teams, organizations and communities they serve.

Wise is the person who measures progress, analyzes outcomes, and learns
from every experience—who cultivates their best, harvests their worst, and
challenges every assumption along the way.

Mindful is the person who can see the forest and the tree—
placing their attention with intention deliberately on their
WIN—attending to that "One Thing" towards mastery.

Persistent is the person who, through struggle and strife,
victory and defeat—discovers new truths, and knowledge and progresses
toward the measure of their creation.

Dedicated is the person who, as a rough stone rolling, ever engaged on an
upward slope—seeks to unveil their music within.

Content is the person who does these things—in the arenas
and on the stages for which they have been called—in the service of others—
for something larger than self—their legacy affirmed.

Endnotes

1. Mandino, O. (1983) *The Greatest Salesman In The World*. Bantam Books
2. Campbell, J. (1988). *The Hero with a Thousand Faces*. Fontana Press.
3. Roosevelt, T. (2014). *Citizenship in a Republic*. CreateSpace Independent Publishing Platform.
4. Loehr, J. E., & Schwartz, T. (2003). *The power of full engagement: Managing energy, not time, is the key to high performance and personal renewal*. Free Press.
5. Wu, J., Xie, M., Lai, Y., Mao, Y., & Harmat, L. (2021). Flow as a Key Predictor of Subjective Well-Being Among Chinese University Students: A Chain Mediating Model. *Frontiers in Psychology*, 12, 743906. https://doi.org/10.3389/fpsyg.2021.743906
6. Collins, A., Sarkisian, N., & Winner, E. (2008). Flow and Happiness in Later Life: An Investigation into the Role of Daily and Weekly Flow Experiences. *Journal of Happiness Studies*, 10, 703–719. https://doi.org/10.1007/s10902-008-9116-3
7. Swann, C., Jackman, P. C., Schweickle, M. J., & Vella, S. A. (2019). Optimal experiences in exercise: A qualitative investigation of flow and clutch states. *Psychology of Sport and Exercise*, 40, 87–98. https://doi.org/10.1016/j.psychsport.2018.09.007
8. Benmira, S., & Agboola, M. (2021). Evolution of leadership theory. *BMJ Leader*, 5(1). https://doi.org/10.1136/leader-2020-000296
9. Fenske, M. J., & Raymond, J. E. (2006). Affective Influences of Selective Attention. *Current Directions in Psychological Science*, 15(6), 312–316. https://doi.org/10.1111/j.1467-8721.2006.00459.x
10. Jackson, S. A. (1992). *Elite athletes in flow: The psychology of optimal experience* [Unpublished doctoral dissertation,]. University of North Carolina.
11. Csikszentmihalyi, M., & Csikszentmihalyi, I. (1988). *Optimal experience*. Cambridge University Press.
12. Crimmins, E. M. (2015). Lifespan and Healthspan: Past, Present, and Promise. *The Gerontologist*, 55(6), 901–911. https://doi.org/10.1093/geront/gnv130
13. Wilson, R. A. (2010). Aesthetics and a Sense of Wonder. *Exchange: The Early Childhood Leaders' Magazine Since 1978*.
14. Gröpel, P., & Mesagno, C. (2019). Choking interventions in sports: A systematic review. *International Review of Sport and Exercise Psychology*, 12(1), 176–201. https://doi.org/10.1080/1750984X.2017.1408134
15. Lewis, B. P., & Linder, D. E. (1997). Thinking about Choking? Attentional Processes and Paradoxical Performance. *Personality and Social Psychology Bulletin*, 23(9), 937–944. https://doi.org/10.1177/0146167297239003
16. Redford, R. (Director). (2000, November 3). *The Legend of Bagger Vance* [Drama, Fantasy, Sport]. Twentieth Century Fox, Dreamworks Pictures, Epsilon Motion Pictures.
17. Hesse, H. (1982). *Siddhartha* (H. Rosner, Trans.; 18th.PRINTING edition). Bantam.
18. Sarantakes, N. E. (2023). The Olympics and the Cold War: A Historiography. *Journal of Cold War Studies*, 25(4), 127–158. https://doi.org/10.1162/jcws_a_01173
19. Pagnini, F., Manzey, D., Rosnet, E., Ferravante, D., White, O., & Smith, N. (2023). Human behavior and performance in deep space exploration: Next challenges and research gaps. *NPJ Microgravity*, 9, 27. https://doi.org/10.1038/s41526-023-00270-7
20. Thornton, S. (2009). *Seven Days in the Art World* (1st edition). W. W. Norton & Company.
21. Frankl, V. E. (1992). *Man's search for meaning*. Beacon Press.
22. Mandela, N. (1995). *Long Walk to Freedom: The Autobiography of Nelson Mandela*. Back Bay Books.
23. Mundell, C. E. (2000). *The role of perceived skill, perceived challenge, and flow in the experience of positive and negative affect*. George Mason University.
24. Csikszentmihalyi, M. (1997). *Finding flow: The psychology of engagement with everyday life*. Basic Books.
25. Norsworthy, C., Dimmock, J. A., Nicholas, J., Krause, A., & Jackson, B. (2023). Psychological Flow Training: Feasibility and Preliminary Efficacy of an Educational Intervention on Flow. *International Journal of Applied Positive Psychology*, 1–24. https://doi.org/10.1007/s41042-023-00098-2
26. Massimini, F., & Carli, M. (1988). The systematic assessment of flow in daily experience. In M. Csikszentmihalyi & I. S. Csikszentmihalyi (Eds.), *Optimal Experience: Psychological studies of flow in consciousness* (pp. 266–278). Cambridge University Press.
27. Csikszentmihalyi, M. (1985). Reflection on enjoyment. *Perspectives in Biology and Medicine*, 28(4), 489–497.
28. Csikszentmihalyi, M. (1997). *Finding flow: The psychology of engagement with everyday life*. Basic Books.
29. *Diagnostic and Statistical Manual of Mental Disorders*. (n.d.). DSM Library.

Retrieved May 24, 2024, from https://dsm.psychiatryonline.org/doi/book/10.1176/appi.books.9780890425787

30. Seligman, M. E. P. (2006). *Learned Optimism: How to Change Your Mind and Your Life* (Reprint edition). Vintage.

31. Asgharipoor, N., Asgharnejad Farid, A., Arshadi, H., & Sahebi, A. (2012). A Comparative Study on the Effectiveness of Positive Psychotherapy and Group Cognitive-Behavioral Therapy for the Patients Suffering from Major Depressive Disorder. *Iranian Journal of Psychiatry and Behavioral Sciences*, 6(2), 33–41.

32. Stiller, B. (Director). (2013, December 25). *The Secret Life of Walter Mitty* [Adventure, Comedy, Drama]. Twentieth Century Fox, TSG Entertainment, Samuel Goldwyn Films.

33. Buckingham, M., & Coffman, C. (1999b). *First, break all the rules: What the world's greatest managers do differently*. Simon & Schuster.

34. Commons, M. L., Trudeau, E. J., Stein, S. A., Richards, F. A., & Krause, S. R. (1998). Hierarchical complexity of tasks shows the existence of developmental stages. *Developmental Review*, 18, 237–278.; Dawson, T. L., Commons, M. L., & Wilson, M. (2002). The shape of development. *European Journal of Developmental Psychology*, 2(2), 163–195.

35. Docter, P., & Carmen, R. D. (Directors). (2015, June 19). *Inside Out* [Animation, Adventure, Comedy]. Pixar Animation Studios, Walt Disney Pictures.

36. Jackson, S. A., & Csikszentmihalyi, M. (1999). *Flow in sports*.

37. Orlick, T. (1990). *In pursuit of excellence*. Leisure Press.

38. Mangold, J. (Director). (2019, November 15). *Ford v Ferrari* [Action, Biography, Drama]. Chernin Entertainment, TSG Entertainment, Turnpike Films.

39. Koch, R. (1999). *The 80/20 Principle: The Secret to Achieving More with Less* (Reprint edition). Crown Currency.

40. Christensen, J., & King, P. (2016). *Access for All: A New Generation's Challenges on the California Coast*. UCLA. https://www.ioes.ucla.edu/wp-content/uploads/UCLA-Beach-Surveys-Summary-Statistics.pdf

41. Collins, J. (2001). *Good to Great: Why Some Companies Make the Leap and Others Don't* (1st edition). Harper Business.

42. Martin, K. (2017). The Saga of the Bird-Brained Bombers. *NIST*. https://www.nist.gov/blogs/taking-measure/saga-bird-brained-bombers

43. Epton, T., Currie, S., & Armitage, C. J. (2017). Unique effects of setting goals on behavior change: Systematic review and meta-analysis. *Journal of Consulting and Clinical Psychology*, 85(12), 1182–1198. https://doi.org/10.1037/ccp0000260

44. Locke, E. A., & Latham, G. P. (1990). *A theory of goal setting and task performance*. Prentice-Hall.

45. Burton, D., Naylor, S., & Holliday, B. (1993). Goal setting in sport. *Handbook of Research on Sport Psychology*, 467–491.

46. MacLeod, A. K., Coates, E., & Hetherton, J. (2008). Increasing well-being through teaching goal-setting and planning skills: Results of a brief intervention. *Journal of Happiness Studies*, 9(2), 185–196. https://doi.org/10.1007/s10902-007-9057-2

47. Kennedy, D. R., & Porter, A. L. (2022). The Illusion of Urgency. *American Journal of Pharmaceutical Education*, 86(7), 8914. https://doi.org/10.5688/ajpe8914

48. Covey, S. R. (1990). *The 7 Habits of Highly Effective People* (1st edition). Free Press.

49. G, D. (2022, March 14). *20+ Little-Known Time Management Statistics For 2022*. TechJury. https://techjury.net/blog/time-management-statistics/

50. King, A. C., Winett, R. A., & Lovett, S. B. (1986). Enhancing coping behaviors in at-risk populations: The effects of time-management instruction and social support in women from dual-earner families. *Behavior Therapy*, 17(1), 57–66. https://doi.org/10.1016/S0005-7894(86)80114-9

51. Barling, J., Cheung, D., & Kelloway, E. K. (1996). Time management and achievement striving interact to predict car sales performance. *Journal of Applied Psychology*, 81(6), 821-826.

52. Geyser, I. (n.d.). *The Relationship Between Time Management Behaviour, Flow, Happiness and Life Satisfaction in the Hospitality Training Environment* [M.Com., University of Johannesburg (South Africa)]. Retrieved April 16, 2022, from https://www.proquest.com/docview/2572696578/abstract/CE169599F2F94929PQ/1

53. Hazell, J., Cotterill, S. T., & Hill, D. M. (2014). An exploration of pre-performance routines, self-efficacy, anxiety and performance in semi-professional soccer. *European Journal of Sport Science*, 14(6), 603–610. https://doi.org/10.1080/17461391.2014.888484

54. Crews, D. J., & Boutcher, S. H. (1986). Effects of structured preshot behaviors on beginning golf performance. *Perceptual and Motor Skills*, 62, 291–294.

55. Karakas, F. (2009). Spirituality and

Performance in Organizations: A Literature Review. *Journal of Business Ethics, 94*(1), 89–106. https://doi.org/10.1007/s10551-009-0251-5

56. Dal Corso, L., Carlo, A., Carluccio, F., Colledani, D., & Falco, A. (2020). Employee burnout and positive dimensions of well-being: A latent workplace spirituality profile analysis. *PloS One, 15*(11), 0242267.
57. Benefiel, M., Fry, L. W., & Geigle, D. (2014). Spirituality and religion in the workplace: History, theory, and research. *Psychology of Religion and Spirituality, 6*(3), 175.
58. Day, N. E. (2005). Religion in the Workplace: Correlates and Consequences of Individual Behavior. *Journal of Management, Spirituality & Religion, 2*(1), 104–135. https://doi.org/10.1080/14766080509518568
59. Johnson, H. (2004). Taboo No More. *Training.*
60. Covey, S. R. (2012). *Principle-Centered Leadership* (Unabridged edition). Franklin Covey on Brilliance Audio.
61. Youssef, C. M., & Luthans, F. (2007). Positive organizational behavior in the workplace: The impact of hope, optimism, and resilience. *Journal of Management, 33*(5), 774–800.
62. Lopez, S. J. (2013, March 8). *Want More Productive Workers—Give Them Hope.* CNBC. https://www.cnbc.com/id/100537689
63. Javanmard, H. (2012). The impact of spirituality on work performance. *Indian Journal of Science and Technology, 5*(1), 1961–1966.
64. Nature by Ralph Waldo Emerson | Essay. (n.d.). *Ralph Waldo Emerson.* Retrieved May 24, 2024, from https://emersoncentral.com/texts/nature-addresses-lectures/nature2/chapter1-nature/
65. Fagen, A., Acharya, N., & Kaufman, G. E. (2014). Positive Reinforcement Training for a Trunk Wash in Nepal's Working Elephants: Demonstrating Alternatives to Traditional Elephant Training Techniques. *Journal of Applied Animal Welfare Science: JAAWS, 17*(2), 83–97. https://doi.org/10.1080/10888705.2014.856258
66. Cassidy, S., & Eachus, P. (2000). Learning style, academic belief systems, self-report student proficiency and academic achievement in higher education. *Educational Psychology, 20*(3), 307–322.
67. Schäfer, C. (2013). How Individual Beliefs Impact Individual Performance. *Human Resource Management Research, 3*(3), 71 81.
68. Nelson, L. R., & Furst, M. L. (1972). An objective study of the effects of expectation on competitive performance. *The Journal of Psychology: Interdisciplinary and Applied, 81*(1), 69–72. https://doi.org/10.1080/00223980.1972.9923790
69. SITNFlash. (2016, September 14). More Than Just a Sugar Pill: Why the placebo effect is real. *Science in the News.* https://sitn.hms.harvard.edu/flash/2016/just-sugar-pill-placebo-effect-real/
70. Rosenthal, R., & Jacobson, L. (1968). *Pygmalion in the classroom.* https://doi.org/10.2307/1162010
71. Ericsson, A., & Pool, R. (2017). *Peak: Secrets from the new science of expertise* (First Mariner Books edition). Mariner Books/Houghton Mifflin Harcourt.
72. Franklin, B. (2019). *The Autobiography of Benjamin Franklin.* CreateSpace Independent Publishing Platform.
73. Ertosun, O. G., & Adiguzel, Z. (2018). Leadership, personal values and organizational culture. In *Strategic Design and Innovative Thinking in Business Operations* (pp. 51–74). Springer.
74. Poulton, C. D. P. (2016). *The impact of value systems on the development of effective leadership.* [Thesis]. https://researchspace.ukzn.ac.za/handle/10413/12962
75. *Founders Online: From Thomas Jefferson to Thomas Jefferson Smith, 21 February 1 ....* (n.d.). University of Virginia Press. Retrieved September 16, 2022, from http://founders.archives.gov/documents/Jefferson/98-01-02-4987
76. Washington, G., & Toner, J. M. (Joseph M. (with University of Michigan). (1888). *Washington's rules of civility and decent behavior in company and conversation.* Washington, W. H. Morrison. http://archive.org/details/washingtonsrule00washgoog
77. Pausch, R., & Zaslow, J. (2008). *The last lecture* (First Edition). Hyperion.
78. Turnipseed, D. L. (2002). Are good soldiers good?: Exploring the link between organization citizenship behavior and personal ethics. *Journal of Business Research, 55*(1), 1–15.
79. Wu, C. F. (2002). The relationship of ethical decision-making to business ethics and performance in Taiwan. *Journal of Business Ethics, 35*(3), 163–176.
80. Burns, D. D. (1999a). *Feeling good: The new mood therapy* (Rev. and updated). Avon.
81. Brown, T. C., & Latham, G. P. (2006). The effect of training in verbal self-guidance on performance effectiveness in a MBA program. *Canadian Journal of Behavioural Science / Revue Canadienne Des Sciences Du Comportement, 38*(1), 1–11. https://doi.org/10.1037/h0087266

82. Hamilton, R. A., Scott, D., & MacDougall, M. P. (2007). Assessing the effectiveness of self-talk interventions on endurance performance. *Journal of Applied Sport Psychology, 19*(2), 226–239.
83. Walter, N., Nikoleizig, L., & Alfermann, D. (2019). Effects of self-talk training on competitive anxiety, self-efficacy, volitional skills, and performance: An intervention study with junior sub-elite athletes. *Sports, 7*(6), 148.
84. Theodorakis, Y., Weinberg, R., Natsis, P., Douma, I., & Kazakas, P. (2000). The effects of motivational versus instructional self-talk on improving motor performance. *The Sport Psychologist, 14*(3), 253–271.
85. Dickens, C. (2020). *A Christmas Carol* (Public Domain Edition). CreateSpace Independent Publishing Platform.
86. Cook, D. A., & Artino Jr, A. R. (2016). Motivation to learn: An overview of contemporary theories. *Medical Education, 50*(10), 997–1014. https://doi.org/10.1111/medu.13074
87. Goleman, D. (2005). *Emotional Intelligence: Why It Can Matter More Than IQ* (10th Anniversary edition). Bantam.
88. Trotta, J. (2018, December 10). *Emotional Intelligence—What Do the Numbers Mean?* LinkedIn. https://www.linkedin.com/pulse/emotional-intelligence-what-do-numbers-mean-joanne-trotta/
89. Stein, S. J., & Book, H. E. (2011). *The EQ Edge: Emotional Intelligence and Your Success* (3rd edition). Jossey-Bass.
90. Comaford, C. (2017, October 15). *The Secret to Controlling Your Emotions – Before They Control You*. Forbes. https://www.forbes.com/sites/christinecomaford/2017/10/15/the-secret-to-controlling-your-emotions-before-they-control-you/?sh=13140aaf37de
91. Côté, S., Gyurak, A., & Levenson, R. W. (2010). The ability to regulate emotion is associated with greater well-being, income, and socioeconomic status. *Emotion, 10*(6), 923.
92. *Working with People Who Aren't Self-Aware*. (n.d.). Retrieved August 3, 2022, from https://hbr.org/2018/10/working-with-people-who-arent-self-aware
93. DiMaria, C. H., Peroni, C., & Sarracino, F. (2020). Happiness matters: Productivity gains from subjective well-being. *Journal of Happiness Studies, 21*(1), 139–160.
94. Cena, H., & Calder, P. C. (2020). Defining a Healthy Diet: Evidence for the Role of Contemporary Dietary Patterns in Health and Disease. *Nutrients, 12*(2), 334. https://doi.org/10.3390/nu12020334
95. Pfeffer, J., & Sutton, R. I. (2000). *The Knowing-doing Gap: How Smart Companies Turn Knowledge into Action*. Harvard Business Press.
96. *How Nutrition Helps Teens' School Performance | Banner Health.* (2023a, November 13). https://www.bannerhealth.com/healthcareblog/teach-me/how-the-right-food-choices-can-help-teens-succeed-at-school
97. Bulatseskul, G. (2017, January 5). Nutrition and Productivity: How Foods Can Affect Your Performance. *Healthy Blog.* https://foodtolive.com/healthy-blog/nutrition-productivity-foods-can-affect-performance/
98. Merrill, R. M., Aldana, S. G., Pope, J. E., Anderson, D. R., Coberley, C. R., & Whitmer, and the H. R. S. S., R. William. (2012). Presenteeism According to Healthy Behaviors, Physical Health, and Work Environment. *Population Health Management, 15*(5), 293–301. https://doi.org/10.1089/pop.2012.0003
99. *How Exercise Is Good for Your Brain*. (n.d.). Cleveland Clinic. Retrieved May 28, 2024, from https://health.clevelandclinic.org/exercise-and-brain-health
100. *How Exercise Improves Cognitive Function and Overall Brain Health.* (2019, August 1). Urology of Virginia. http://www.urologyofva.net/articles/category/healthy-living/3330548/08/01/2019/how-exercise-improves-cognitive-function-and-overall-brain-health
101. *The Influence of Exercise on Cognitive Abilities—PMC*. (n.d.). Retrieved May 7, 2022, from https://www.ncbi.nlm.nih.gov/pmc/articles/PMC3951958/
102. Newsom, R. (2022, April 19). *Sleep & Job Performance: Can Sleep Deprivation Hurt Your Work?* Sleep Foundation. http://www.sleepfoundation.org/sleep-hygiene/good-sleep-and-job-performance
103. Selye, H. (1956). *The stress of life* (pp. xvi, 324). McGraw-Hill.
104. Wallace, R. K., & Benson, H. (1972). The physiology of meditation. *Scientific American, 226*, 85–90.
105. *Stress Management: Breathing Exercises for Relaxation*. (2020). Michigan Medicine. https://www.uofmhealth.org/health-library/uz2255
106. Ma, X., Yue, Z. Q., Gong, Z. Q., Zhang, H., Duan, N. Y., Shi, Y. T., Wei, G. X., & Li, Y. F. (n.d.). The Effect of Diaphragmatic Breathing on Attention, Negative Affect and Stress in Healthy Adults—PMC. *Frontiers in Psychology, 8*(874). Retrieved May 7, 2022, from https://www.ncbi.nlm.nih.gov/pmc/articles/PMC5455070/

107. Dirzyte, A., & Patapas, A. (2022). Positive Organizational Practices, Life Satisfaction, and Psychological Capital in the Public and Private Sectors. *Sustainability, 14*(1), Article 1. https://doi.org/10.3390/su14010488
108. Christensen, M., Dawson, J., & Nielsen, K. (2021). The Role of Adequate Resources, Community and Supportive Leadership in Creating Engaged Academics. *International Journal of Environmental Research and Public Health, 18*(5), 2776. https://doi.org/10.3390/ijerph18052776
109. *The JD-R Model: Analyzing and Improving Employee Well-Being*. (2017). Mindtools. https://www.mindtools.com/pages/article/job-demands-resources-model.htm
110. Chen, J. C., & Silverthorne, C. (2008). The impact of locus of control on job stress, job performance and job satisfaction in Taiwan. *Leadership & Organization Development Journal*.
111. Mastroianni, K., & Storberg-Walker, J. (2014). Do work relationships matter? Characteristics of workplace interactions that enhance or detract from employee perceptions of well-being and health behaviors. *Health Psychology and Behavioral Medicine, 2*(1), 798–819. https://doi.org/10.1080/21642850.2014.933343
112. Umberson, D., & Montez, J. K. (2010). Social Relationships and Health: A Flashpoint for Health Policy. *Journal of Health and Social Behavior, 51*(Suppl), S54–S66. https://doi.org/10.1177/0022146510383501
113. Mann, A., & Darby, R. (2014, August 5). *Should Managers Focus on Performance or Engagement?* Gallup. http://news.gallup.com/businessjournal/174197/managers-focus-performance-engagement.aspx
114. Morgan, K. (2020). Why your in-office friendships still matter. *BBC*. http://www.bbc.com/worklife/article/20200925-why-your-in-office-friendships-still-matter
115. Varshney, D., & Varshney, N. K. (2017). Measuring the impact of trust on job performance and self-efficacy in a project: Evidence from Saudi Arabia. *Journal of Applied Business Research (JABR), 33*(5), 941–950.
116. Daly, R. (2020). *22 Statistics that Reveal the Truth About Teams*. AIIR Consulting. https://aiirconsulting.com/22-statistics-that-reveal-the-truth-about-teams/
117. Sedgwick, P., & Greenwood, N. (2015). Understanding the Hawthorne effect. *Bmj, 351*.
118. Heinz, K. (2019, October 2). *42 Shocking Company Culture Statistics You Need to Know*. Built In. https://builtin.com/company-culture/company-culture-statistics
119. *Employers Rank Organizational Fit Most Important in Evaluating Potential New Hires*. (2016). Graduate Management Admission Council. http://www.gmac.com/market-intelligence-and-research/research-insights/employment-outlook/employers-rank-organizational-fit-most-important-evaluating-new-hires
120. *Aligning Personal and Corporate Values - 2030.Builders*. (n.d.) Retrieved August 3, 2022, from https://2030.builders/articles/aligning-personal-and-corporate-values/.
121. Herway, J. (2017, December 7). *How to Create a Culture of Psychological Safety*. Gallup. http://www.gallup.com/workplace/236198/create-culture-psychological-safety.aspx
122. Heinz, K. (2019, October 2). *42 Shocking Company Culture Statistics You Need to Know*. Built In. https://builtin.com/company-culture/company-culture-statistics
123. Theodori, G. L. (2001). Examining the Effects of Community Satisfaction and Attachment on Individual Well-Being*. *Rural Sociology, 66*(4), 618–628. https://doi.org/10.1111/j.1549-0831.2001.tb00087.x
124. Parker, K., Horowitz, J. M., Brown, A., Fry, R., Cohn, D., & Igielnik, R. (2018, May 22). 5. Americans' satisfaction with and attachment to their communities. *Pew Research Center's Social & Demographic Trends Project*. https://www.pewresearch.org/social-trends/2018/05/22/americans-satisfaction-with-and-attachment-to-their-communities/
125. Helm, B. W. (2017). *Communities of respect: Grounding responsibility, authority, and dignity*. Oxford University Press. https://global.oup.com/academic/product/communities-of-respect-9780198801863?cc=us&lang=en&
126. Jones, R., Heim, D., Hunter, S., & Ellaway, A. (2014). The relative influence of neighbourhood incivilities, cognitive social capital, club membership and individual characteristics on positive mental health. *Health & Place, 28*, 187–193. https://doi.org/10.1016/j.healthplace.2014.04.006
127. Marmot, M., & Bell, R. (2012). Fair society, healthy lives. *Public Health, 126* Suppl 1, S4–S10. https://doi.org/10.1016/j.puhe.2012.05.014
128. Scotland, P. H. (n.d.). *Communities*. Retrieved August 6, 2022, from http://www.healthscotland.scot/health-inequalities/impact-of-social-and-physical-environments/communities
129. The Art of Giving Feedback: 10 Tips for Busy Managers. (2019, July 25). *Toggl Blog*.

https://toggl.com/blog/giving-feedback-10-tips-for-managers
130. Gavett, G. (n.d.). The Power of Reflection at Work. *Harvard Business Review*. Retrieved August 6, 2022, from https://hbr.org/2014/05/the-power-of-reflection-at-work
131. Grant Halvorson, H. (2010, September 7). *Yesterday Influences Your Performance Today in Surprising Ways*. Psychology Today. https://www.psychologytoday.com/us/blog/the-science-success/201009/yesterday-influences-your-performance-today-in-surprising-ways
132. Waitley, D. E. (1983). *The psychology of winning*. Nightingale-Conant Corporation.
133. Bandura, A. (1977). Self-efficacy: Toward a unifying theory of behavioral change. *Psychological Review*, 84(2), 191–215.
134. Robinson, T. (n.d.). *How Reframing Your Failures Will Actually Bring Success*. Lifehack. https://www.lifehack.org/articles/productivity/how-reframing-your-failures-will-actually-bring-success.html
135. Furnham, A., & Argyle, M. (1998). *The psychology of money* (pp. xii, 332). Taylor & Frances/Routledge.
136. Kelly, S., & Dean, M. L. (2017). *Endurance: A year in space, a lifetime of discovery* (First edition). Alfred A. Knopf.
137. Orlick, T. (1990). *In pursuit of excellence*. Leisure Press.
138. Ericsson, A., & Pool, R. (2017). *Peak: Secrets from the new science of expertise* (First Mariner Books edition). Mariner Books/Houghton Mifflin Harcourt.
139. Christensen, C. M., Allworth, J., & Dillon, K. (2012). *How Will You Measure Your Life?* Harper Business.

References

Aligning Personal and Corporate Values—2030.Builders. (n.d.). Retrieved August 3, 2022, from https://2030.builders/articles/aligning-personal-and-corporate-values/

Asgharipoor, N., Asgharnejad Farid, A., Arshadi, H., & Sahebi, A. (2012). A Comparative Study on the Effectiveness of Positive Psychotherapy and Group Cognitive-Behavioral Therapy for the Patients Suffering From Major Depressive Disorder. *Iranian Journal of Psychiatry and Behavioral Sciences, 6*(2), 33–41.

Bandura, A. (1977). Self-efficacy: Toward a unifying theory of behavioral change. *Psychological Review, 84*(2), 191–215.

Barling, J., Cheung, D., & Kelloway, E. K. (1996). Time management and achievement striving interact to predict car sales performance. *Journal of Applied Psychology, 81*(6), 821-826.

Benefiel, M., Fry, L. W., & Geigle, D. (2014). Spirituality and religion in the workplace: History, theory, and research. *Psychology of Religion and Spirituality, 6*(3), 175.

Benmira, S., & Agboola, M. (2021). Evolution of leadership theory. *BMJ Leader, 5*(1). https://doi.org/10.1136/leader-2020-000296

Buckingham, M., & Coffman, C. (1999). *First, break all the rules: What the world's greatest managers do differently*. Simon & Schuster.

Bulatseskul, G. (2017, January 5). Nutrition and Productivity: How Foods Can Affect Your Performance. Healthy Blog. https://foodtolive.com/healthy-blog/nutrition-productivity-foods-can-affect-performance/

Burns, D. D. (1999). *Feeling good: The new mood therapy* (Rev. and updated). Avon.

Burton, D., Naylor, S., & Holliday, B. (1993). Goal setting in sport. *Handbook of Research on Sport Psychology*, 467–491.

Campbell, J. (1988). *The Hero with a Thousand Faces*. Fontana Press.

Cassidy, S., & Eachus, P. (2000). Learning style, academic belief systems, self-report student proficiency and academic achievement in higher education. *Educational Psychology, 20*(3), 307–322.

Cena, H., & Calder, P. C. (2020). Defining a Healthy Diet: Evidence for the Role of Contemporary Dietary Patterns in Health and Disease. *Nutrients, 12*(2), 334. https://doi.org/10.3390/nu12020334

Chen, J. C., & Silverthorne, C. (2008). The impact of locus of control on job stress, job performance and job satisfaction in Taiwan. *Leadership & Organization Development Journal*.

Christensen, C. M., Allworth, J., & Dillon, K. (2012). *How Will You Measure Your Life?* Harper Business.

Christensen, J., & King, P. (2016). *Access for All: A New Generation's Challenges on the California Coast*. UCLA. https://www.ioes.ucla.edu/wp-content/uploads/UCLA-Beach-Surveys-Summary-Statistics.pdf

Christensen, M., Dawson, J., & Nielsen, K. (2021). The Role of Adequate Resources, Community and Supportive Leadership in Creating Engaged Academics. *International Journal of Environmental Research and Public Health, 18*(5), 2776. https://doi.org/10.3390/ijerph18052776

Cleveland Clinic. "How Exercise Is Good for Your Brain." Accessed May 29, 2024. https://health.clevelandclinic.org/exercise-and-brain-health.

Collins, A., Sarkisian, N., & Winner, E. (2008). Flow and Happiness in Later Life: An Investigation into the Role of Daily and Weekly Flow Experiences. *Journal of Happiness Studies, 10*, 703–719. https://doi.org/10.1007/s10902-008-9116-3

Collins, J. (2001). *Good to Great: Why Some Companies Make the Leap and Others Don't* (1st edition). Harper Business.

Comaford, C. (2017, October 15). *The Secret To Controlling Your Emotions – Before They Control You*. Forbes. https://www.forbes.com/sites/christinecomaford/2017/10/15/the-secret-to-controlling-your-emotions-before-they-control-you/?sh=13140aaf37de

Commons, M. L., Trudeau, E. J., Stein, S. A., Richards, F. A., & Krause, S. R. (1998). Hierarchical complexity of tasks shows the existence of developmental stages. *Developmental Review, 18*, 237–278.

Cook, D. A., & Artino Jr, A. R. (2016). Motivation to learn: An overview of contemporary theories. *Medical Education, 50*(10), 997–1014. https://doi.org/10.1111/medu.13074

Côté, S., Gyurak, A., & Levenson, R. W. (2010). The ability to regulate emotion is associated with greater well-being, income, and socioeconomic status. *Emotion, 10*(6), 923.

Covey, S. R. (1990). *The 7 Habits of Highly Effective People* (1st edition). Free Press.

Covey, S. R. (2012). *Principle-Centered Leadership* (Unabridged edition). Franklin Covey on Brilliance Audio

Crews, D. J., & Boutcher, S. H. (1986). Effects on structured preshot behaviors on beginning golf performance. *Perceptual and Motor Skills, 62*, 291–294.

Crimmins, E. M. (2015). Lifespan and Healthspan: Past, Present, and Promise. *The Gerontologist, 55*(6), 901–911. https://doi.org/10.1093/geront/gnv130

Csikszentmihalyi, M. (1997). *Finding flow: The psychology of engagement with everyday life*. Basic Books.

Csikszentmihalyi, M. (1985). Reflection on enjoyment. *Perspectives in Biology and Medicine, 28*(4), 489–497.
Csikszentmihalyi, M., & Csikszentmihalyi, I. (1988). *Optimal experience*. Cambridge University Press.
Dal Corso, L., Carlo, A., Carluccio, F., Colledani, D., & Falco, A. (2020). Employee burnout and positive dimensions of well-being: A latent workplace spirituality profile analysis. *PloS One, 15*(11), 0242267.
Daly, R. (2020). *22 Statistics that Reveal the Truth About Teams*. AIIR Consulting. https://aiirconsulting.com/22-statistics-that-reveal-the-truth-about-teams/
Dawson, T. L., Commons, M. L., & Wilson, M. (2002). The shape of development. *European Journal of Developmental Psychology, 2*(2), 163–195.
Day, N. E. (2005). Religion in the Workplace: Correlates and Consequences of Individual Behavior. *Journal of Management, Spirituality & Religion, 2*(1), 104–135. https://doi.org/10.1080/14766080509518568
Dickens, C. (2020). *A Christmas Carol* (Public Domain Edition). CreateSpace Independent Publishing Platform.
DiMaria, C. H., Peroni, C., & Sarracino, F. (2020). Happiness matters: Productivity gains from subjective well-being. *Journal of Happiness Studies, 21*(1), 139–160.
Diagnostic and Statistical Manual of Mental Disorders. (n.d.). DSM Library. Retrieved May 24, 2024, from https://dsm.psychiatryonline.org/doi/book/10.1176/appi.books.9780890425787
Dirzyte, A., & Patapas, A. (2022). Positive Organizational Practices, Life Satisfaction, and Psychological Capital in the Public and Private Sectors. *Sustainability, 14*(1), Article 1. https://doi.org/10.3390/su14010488
Docter, P., & Carmen, R. D. (Directors). (2015, June 19). *Inside Out* [Animation, Adventure,
Employers Rank Organizational Fit Most Important in Evaluating Potential New Hires. (2016). Graduate Management Admission Council. http://www.gmac.com/market-intelligence-and-research/research-insights/employment-outlook/employers-rank-organizational-fit-most-important-evaluating-new-hires
Epton, T., Currie, S., & Armitage, C. J. (2017). Unique effects of setting goals on behavior change: Systematic review and meta-analysis. *Journal of Consulting and Clinical Psychology, 85*(12), 1182–1198. https://doi.org/10.1037/ccp0000260
Ericsson, A., & Pool, R. (2017). *Peak: Secrets from the new science of expertise* (First Mariner Books edition). Mariner Books/Houghton Mifflin Harcourt.
Ertosun, O. G., & Adiguzel, Z. (2018). Leadership, personal values and organizational culture. In *Strategic Design and Innovative Thinking in Business Operations* (pp. 51–74). Springer.
Fagen, A., Acharya, N., & Kaufman, G. E. (2014). Positive Reinforcement Training for a Trunk Wash in Nepal's Working Elephants: Demonstrating Alternatives to Traditional Elephant Training Techniques. *Journal of Applied Animal Welfare Science: JAAWS, 17*(2), 83–97. https://doi.org/10.1080/10888705.2014.856258
Founders Online: From Thomas Jefferson to Thomas Jefferson Smith, 21 February 1 .... (n.d.). University of Virginia Press. Retrieved September 16, 2022, from http://founders.archives.gov/documents/Jefferson/98-01-02-4987
Frankl, V. E. (1992). *Man's search for meaning*. Beacon Press.
Franklin, B. (2019). *The Autobiography of Benjamin Franklin*. CreateSpace Independent Publishing Platform.
Furnham, A., & Argyle, M. (1998). *The psychology of money* (pp. xii, 332). Taylor & Frances/Routledge.
G, D. (2022, March 14). *20+ Little-Known Time Management Statistics For 2022*. TechJury. https://techjury.net/blog/time-management-statistics/
Gavett, G. (n.d.). The Power of Reflection at Work. *Harvard Business Review*. Retrieved August 6, 2022, from https://hbr.org/2014/05/the-power-of-reflection-at-work
Geyser, I. (n.d.). The Relationship Between Time Management Behaviour, Flow, Happiness and Life Satisfaction in the Hospitality Training Environment [M.Com., University of Johannesburg (South Africa)]. Retrieved April 16, 2022, from https://www.proquest.com/docview/2572696578/abstract/CE169599F2F94929PQ/1
Goleman, D. (2005). *Emotional Intelligence: Why It Can Matter More Than IQ* (10th Anniversary edition). Bantam.
Grant Halvorson, H. (2010, September 7). *Yesterday Influences Your Performance Today in Surprising Ways*. Psychology Today. https://www.psychologytoday.com/us/blog/the-science-success/201009/yesterday-influences-your-performance-today-in-surprising-ways
Gröpel, P., & Mesagno, C. (2019). Choking interventions in sports: A systematic review. *International Review of Sport and Exercise Psychology, 12*(1), 176–201. https://doi.org/10.1080/1750984X.2017.1408934
Hamilton, R. A., Scott, D., & MacDougall, M. P. (2007). Assessing the effectiveness of self-talk interventions on endurance performance. *Journal of Applied Sport Psychology, 19*(2), 226–239.
Hazell, J., Cotterill, S. T., & Hill, D. M. (2014). An exploration of pre-performance routines, self-efficacy, anxiety and performance in semi-professional soccer. *European Journal of Sport Science, 14*(6), 603–610. https://doi.org/10.1080/17461391.2014.888484

Heinz, K. (2019, October 2). *42 Shocking Company Culture Statistics You Need to Know*. Built In. https://builtin.com/company-culture/company-culture-statistics

Helm, B. W. (2017). *Communities of respect: Grounding responsibility, authority, and dignity*. Oxford University Press. https://global.oup.com/academic/product/communities-of-respect-9780198801863?cc=u s&lang=en&

Herway, J. (2017, December 7). *How to Create a Culture of Psychological Safety*. Gallup. http://www.gallup.com/workplace/236198/create-culture-psychological-safety.

Hesse, H. (1982). *Siddhartha* (H. Rosner, Trans.; 18th.PRINTING edition). Bantam.

How Exercise Improves Cognitive Function and Overall Brain Health. (2019, August 1). Urology of Virginia. http://www.urologyofva.net/articles/category/healthy-living/3330548/08/01/2019/how-exercise-improves-cognitive-function-and-overall-brain-health

How Nutrition Helps Teens' School Performance | Banner Health. (2023a, November 13). https://www.bannerhealth.com/healthcareblog/teach-me/how-the-right-food-choices-can-help-teens-succeed-at-school

Jackson, S. A. (1992). *Elite athletes in flow: The psychology of optimal experience* [Unpublished doctoral dissertation,]. University of North Carolina.

Jackson, S. A., & Csikszentmihalyi, M. (1999). *Flow in sports*.

Javanmard, H. (2012). The impact of spirituality on work performance. *Indian Journal of Science and Technology, 5*(1), 1961–1966.

Johnson, H. (2004). Taboo No More. *Training*.

Jones, R., Heim, D., Hunter, S., & Ellaway, A. (2014). The relative influence of neighbourhood incivilities, cognitive social capital, club membership and individual characteristics on positive mental health. *Health & Place, 28*, 187–193. https://doi.org/10.1016/j.healthplace.2014.04.006

Karakas, F. (2009). Spirituality and Performance in Organizations: A Literature Review. *Journal of Business Ethics, 94*(1), 89–106. https://doi.org/10.1007/s10551-009-0251-5

Kelly, S., & Dean, M. L. (2017). *Endurance: A year in space, a lifetime of discovery* (First edition). Alfred A. Knopf.

Kennedy, D. R., & Porter, A. L. (2022). The Illusion of Urgency. *American Journal of Pharmaceutical Education, 86*(7), 8914. https://doi.org/10.5688/ajpe8914

King, A. C., Winett, R. A., & Lovett, S. B. (1986). Enhancing coping behaviors in at-risk populations: The effects of time-management instruction and social support in women from dual-earner families. *Behavior Therapy, 17*(1), 57–66.

Koch, R. (1999). *The 80/20 Principle: The Secret to Achieving More with Less* (Reprint edition). Crown Currency.

Lewis, B. P., & Linder, D. E. (1997). Thinking about Choking? Attentional Processes and Paradoxical Performance. *Personality and Social Psychology Bulletin, 23*(9), 937–944. https://doi.org/10.1177/0146167297239003

Locke, E. A., & Latham, G. P. (1990). *A theory of goal setting and task performance*. Prentice-Hall.

Loehr, J. E., & Schwartz, T. (2003). *The power of full engagement: Managing energy, not time, is the key to high performance and personal renewal*. Free Press.

Lopez, S. J. (2013, March 8). *Want More Productive Workers—Give Them Hope*. CNBC. https://www.cnbc.com/id/100537689

Ma, X., Yue, Z. Q., Gong, Z. Q., Zhang, H., Duan, N. Y., Shi, Y. T., Wei, G. X., & Li, Y. F. (n.d.). The Effect of Diaphragmatic Breathing on Attention, Negative Affect and Stress in Healthy Adults—PMC. *Frontiers in Psychology, 8*(874). Retrieved May 7, 2022, from https://www.ncbi.nlm.nih.gov/pmc/articles/PMC5455070/

MacLeod, A. K., Coates, E., & Hetherton, J. (2008). Increasing well-being through teaching goal-setting and planning skills: Results of a brief intervention. *Journal of Happiness Studies, 9*(2), 185–196. https://doi.org/10.1007/s10902-007-9057-2

Mandela, N. (1995). *Long Walk to Freedom: The Autobiography of Nelson Mandela*. Back Bay Books.

Mandino, O. (1983). *The Greatest Salesman In The World*. Bantam Books.

Mangold, J. (Director). (2019, November 15). *Ford v Ferrari* [Action, Biography, Drama]. Chernin Entertainment, TSG Entertainment, Turnpike Films.

Mann, A., & Darby, R. (2014, August 5). *Should Managers Focus on Performance or Engagement?* Gallup. http://news.gallup.com/businessjournal/174197/managers-focus-performance-engagement.aspx

Marmot, M., & Bell, R. (2012). Fair society, healthy lives. *Public Health, 126 Suppl 1*, S4–S10. https://doi.org/10.1016/j.puhe.2012.05.014

Martin, K. (2017). *The Saga of the Bird-Brained Bombers*. NIST. https://www.nist.gov/blogs/taking-measure/saga-bird-brained-bombers

Massimini, F., & Carli, M. (1988). The systematic assessment of flow in daily experience. In M. Csikszentmihalyi & I. S. Csikszentmihalyi (Eds.), *Optimal Experience: Psychological studies of flow in consciousness* (pp. 266–278). Cambridge University Press.

Mastroianni, K., & Storberg-Walker, J. (2014). Do work relationships matter? Characteristics of workplace interactions that enhance or detract from employee perceptions of well-being and health behaviors. *Health Psychology and Behavioral Medicine*, 2(1), 798–819. https://doi.org/10.1080/21642850.2014.933493

Merrill, R. M., Aldana, S. G., Pope, J. E., Anderson, D. R., Coberley, C. R., & Whitmer, and the H. R. S. S., R. William. (2012). Presenteeism According to Healthy Behaviors, Physical Health, and Work Environment. *Population Health Management*, 15(5), 293–301. https://doi.org/10.1089/pop.2012.0003

Morgan, K. (2020). Why your in-office friendships still matter. *BBC*. http://www.bbc.com/worklife/article/20200925-why-your-in-office-friendships-still-matter

Mundell, C. E. (2000). *The role of perceived skill, perceived challenge, and flow in the experience of positive and negative affect*. George Mason University.

Nature by Ralph Waldo Emerson | Essay. (n.d.). *Ralph Waldo Emerson*. Retrieved May 24, 2024, from https://emersoncentral.com/texts/nature-addresses-lectures/nature2/chapter1-nature/

Nelson, L. R., & Furst, M. L. (1972). An objective study of the effects of expectation on competitive performance. *The Journal of Psychology: Interdisciplinary and Applied*, 81(1), 69–72. https://doi.org/10.1080/00223980.1972.9923790

Newsom, R. (2022, April 19). *Sleep & Job Performance: Can Sleep Deprivation Hurt Your Work?* Sleep Foundation. http://www.sleepfoundation.org/sleep-hygiene/good-sleep-and-job-performance

Norsworthy, C., Dimmock, J. A., Nicholas, J., Krause, A., & Jackson, B. (2023). Psychological Flow Training: Feasibility and Preliminary Efficacy of an Educational Intervention on Flow. *International Journal of Applied Positive Psychology*, 1–24. https://doi.org/10.1007/s41042-023-00098-2

Orlick, T. (1990). *In pursuit of excellence*. Leisure Press.

Pagnini, F., Manzey, D., Rosnet, E., Ferravante, D., White, O., & Smith, N. (2023). Human behavior and performance in deep space exploration: Next challenges and research gaps. *NPJ Microgravity*, 9, 27. https://doi.org/10.1038/s41526-023-00270-7

Parker, K., Horowitz, J. M., Brown, A., Fry, R., Cohn, D., & Igielnik, R. (2018, May 22). 5. Americans' satisfaction with and attachment to their communities. *Pew Research Center's Social & Demographic Trends Project*. https://www.pewresearch.org/social-trends/2018/05/22/americans-satisfaction-with-and-attachment-to-their-communities/

Pausch, R., & Zaslow, J. (2008). *The last lecture* (First Edition). Hyperion.

Pfeffer, J., & Sutton, R. I. (2000). *The Knowing-doing Gap: How Smart Companies Turn Knowledge into Action*. Harvard Business Press.

Poulton, C. D. P. (2016). *The impact of value systems on the development of effective leadership*. [Thesis]. https://researchspace.ukzn.ac.za/handle/10413/12962

Redford, R. (Director). (2000, November 3). *The Legend of Bagger Vance* [Drama, Fantasy, Sport]. Twentieth Century Fox, Dreamworks Pictures, Epsilon Motion Pictures.

Robinson, T. (n.d.). *How Reframing Your Failures Will Actually Bring Success*. Lifehack. https://www.lifehack.org/articles/productivity/how-reframing-your-failures-will-actually-bring-success.html

Roosevelt, T. (2014). *Citizenship in a Republic*. CreateSpace Independent Publishing Platform.

Rosenthal, R., & Jacobson, L. (1968). *Pygmalion in the classroom*. https://doi.org/10.2307/1162010

Sarantakes, N. E. (2023). The Olympics and the Cold War: A Historiography. *Journal of Cold War Studies*, 25(4), 127–158. https://doi.org/10.1162/jcws_a_01173

Schäfer, C. (2013). How Individual Beliefs Impact Individual Performance. *Human Resource Management Research*, 3(3), 71 81.

Scotland, P. H. (n.d.). *Communities*. Retrieved August 6, 2022, from http://www.healthscotland.scot/health-inequalities/impact-of-social-and-physical-environments/communities

Sedgwick, P., & Greenwood, N. (2015). Understanding the Hawthorne effect. *Bmj*, 351.

Seligman, M. E. P. (2006). *Learned Optimism: How to Change Your Mind and Your Life* (Reprint edition). Vintage.

Selye, H. (1956). *The stress of life* (pp. xvi, 324). McGraw-Hill.

SITNFlash. (2016, September 14). More Than Just a Sugar Pill: Why the placebo effect is real. *Science in the News*. https://sitn.hms.harvard.edu/flash/2016/just-sugar-pill-placebo-effect-real/

Stein, S. J., & Book, H. E. (2011). *The EQ Edge: Emotional Intelligence and Your Success* (3rd edition). Jossey-Bass.

Stiller, B. (Director). (2013, December 25). *The Secret Life of Walter Mitty* [Adventure, Comedy, Drama]. Twentieth Century Fox, TSG Entertainment, Samuel Goldwyn Films.

Stress Management: Breathing Exercises for Relaxation. (2020). Michigan Medicine. https://www.uofmhealth.org/health-library/uz2255

Swann, C., Jackman, P. C., Schweickle, M. J., & Vella, S. A. (2019). Optimal experiences in exercise: A qualitative investigation of flow and clutch states. *Psychology of Sport and Exercise*, 40, 87–98. https://doi.org/10.1016/j.psychsport.2018.09.007

The Art of Giving Feedback: 10 Tips for Busy Managers. (2019, July 25). *Toggl Blog*. https://toggl.com/blog/giving-feedback-10-tips-for-managers

The Influence of Exercise on Cognitive Abilities—PMC. (n.d.). Retrieved May 7, 2022, from https://www.ncbi.nlm.nih.gov/pmc/articles/PMC3951958/

The JD-R Model: Analyzing and Improving Employee Well-Being. (2017). Mindtools. https://www.mindtools.com/pages/article/job-demands-resources-model.htm

Theodorakis, Y., Weinberg, R., Natsis, P., Douma, I., & Kazakas, P. (2000). The effects of motivational versus instructional self-talk on improving motor performance. *The Sport Psychologist, 14*(3), 253–271.

Theodori, G. L. (2001). Examining the Effects of Community Satisfaction and Attachment on Individual Well-Being*. *Rural Sociology, 66*(4), 618–628. https://doi.org/10.1111/j.1549-0831.2001.tb00087.x

Thornton, S. (2009). *Seven Days in the Art World* (1st edition). W. W. Norton & Company.

Trotta, J. (2018, December 10). *Emotional Intelligence—What Do the Numbers Mean?* LinkedIn. https://www.linkedin.com/pulse/emotional-intelligence-what-do-numbers-mean-joanne-trotta/

Turnipseed, D. L. (2002). Are good soldiers good?: Exploring the link between organization citizenship behavior and personal ethics. *Journal of Business Research, 55*(1), 1–15.

Umberson, D., & Montez, J. K. (2010). Social Relationships and Health: A Flashpoint for Health Policy. *Journal of Health and Social Behavior, 51*(Suppl), S54–S66. https://doi.org/10.1177/0022146510383501

Varshney, D., & Varshney, N. K. (2017). Measuring the impact of trust on job performance and self-efficacy in a project: Evidence from Saudi Arabia. *Journal of Applied Business Research (JABR), 33*(5), 941–950.

Waitley, D. E. (1983). *The psychology of winning*. Nightingale-Conant Corporation.

Wallace, R. K., & Benson, H. (1972). The physiology of meditation. *Scientific American, 226*, 85–90.

Walter, N., Nikoleizig, L., & Alfermann, D. (2019). Effects of self-talk training on competitive anxiety, self-efficacy, volitional skills, and performance: An intervention study with junior sub-elite athletes. *Sports, 7*(6), 148.

Washington, G., & Toner, J. M. (Joseph M. (with University of Michigan). (1888). *Washington's rules of civility and decent behavior in company and conversation*. Washington, W. H. Morrison. http://archive.org/details/washingtonsrule00washgoog

Working with People Who Aren't Self-Aware. (n.d.). Retrieved August 3, 2022, from https://hbr.org/2018/10/working-with-people-who-arent-self-aware

Wu, C. F. (2002). The relationship of ethical decision-making to business ethics and performance in Taiwan. *Journal of Business Ethics, 35*(3), 163–176.

Wu, J., Xie, M., Lai, Y., Mao, Y., & Harmat, L. (2021). Flow as a Key Predictor of Subjective Well-Being Among Chinese University Students: A Chain Mediating Model. *Frontiers in Psychology, 12*, 743906. https://doi.org/10.3389/fpsyg.2021.743906

Youssef, C. M., & Luthans, F. (2007). Positive organizational behavior in the workplace: The impact of hope, optimism, and resilience. *Journal of Management, 33*(5), 774–800.

Afterword

Finding Your Music Within

Having worked with thousands of elite performers, leaders, and everyday professionals, I've observed a universal thread that unites all seekers of greatness—a profound aspiration to discover that singular melody that resonates within.

Discovering that melody requires us to embrace a grand paradox: that while all of us must take the path and pay the price of greatness—your melody cannot be copied from another. We must find and unearth it within ourselves.

For more than three decades I have known Bruce as an athlete and a professional, and we have continued our discussions over the years and explored the finer elements, features, and depths of human performance. Our deep discussions have been varied and complex. But Bruce has done something in this book that few have accomplished: drawing out of the depths of complexity something of greater elegance and simplicity.

Resting atop the iceberg of performance, flow, and human achievement there are three essential summits:

- The discernment that, amidst the myriad of dimensions, factors, principles, tools, and practices, there are any number of ways to optimize performance, yet there are a precious few that make the biggest difference at any given moment (The First Secret).
- The courage to embrace your "One Thing" and to pursue its mastery with a willingness to Fail Faster and Better toward mastery (The Second Secret).

- The wisdom to understand that the principles and processes that enhance the self are equally transformative when applied to relationships, teams, organizations, communities, and beyond (The Third Secret).

The First Secret is revealed through the "Five Alignments™ Framework" and the 1080° Sweep™ Assessment to pinpoint your current WINs. The Second Secret is understood through the "Five Elements of Iteration," paving your path to mastery. The Third Secret reveals the "Five Dimensions of Influence," illustrating the scalability of awareness, mastery, and transformation.

This book offers a beautiful gateway into the essential practices of peak performers and leaders who seek to make the most of their given talents through the disciplines, professions, and arenas where their music is composed and melodies played.

You, the reader, have everything you need to get started—to leverage your attention by placing it on your first WIN, then your second, and so on to discover the very best in yourself, and along the way, bring out the best in others.

A bounty of research, literature, and resources have laid the groundwork for your journey. It's all "out there" ready for you to draw from and use. Let these three secrets guide you in unveiling your inner symphony and empower you to leave that indelible imprint on the world that only you can make. Godspeed in this—what we call The Hero's Journey.

—Dr. Jim Loehr

Acknowledgements

This book stands on the shoulders of many giants in the field. I am grateful for the community of thought leaders, researches and practitioners whose groundbreaking work has paved the way for my own explorations and applications of Flow, Performance, and Positive Psychology in pursuit of elevating the human condition.

While the list is too lengthy to give everyone their due credit, I must highlight a few for their unique contributions to this work: Dr. R. Christopher Barden, for lighting the fire since 1983 and ever since; Dr. Jim Loehr, the theoretical and practical beacon—always a step ahead—always there to support; Dr. Steve Wilkinson, a second father, whose late-night discussions and beatings on the court helped refine my approach to learning and growth; Dr. Stephen R. Covey, whose mentorship elevated my thinking and confidence; Dr. Stephen M.R. Covey, who elevates Flow through Trust; Dr. Barbara Mink and my dissertation committee, for the freedom to explore Flow and find my own voice; Dr. Mihaly Csikszentmihalyi, the father of Flow, who encouraged my quest for practical application; Dr. Len Zaichkowski, who kicked off my academic journey; Alan Fine, who taught me that eliminating "Interference" outweighs acquiring new "Knowledge"; Dr. Nate Zinsser, for his inspirational work at USMA (West Point) and willingness to discuss big ideas; Dr. Kevin Mullaney, for our ongoing dialogues at and outside the US Naval Academy; Robert Nelson, for his mentorship in applying these concepts to organizational strategy; Dr. Keith Henschen, my first doctoral advisor; Dr. Terry Orlick, and his passion for helping children find their Flow; Dr. Martin Seligman, who inspired the "other side" of psychology; Dr. Ken Ravizza, who challenged me to find a "Flow Formula"; and Dr. Laura Crawshaw, who reminded me that "a good dissertation is a done dissertation." Oh, and to Carter Bloch, for throwing that strawberry out the window and igniting my quest and career.

I extend my sincere thanks to each of these mentors, colleagues, and friends. Your relentless pursuit of knowledge, innovation, and application continues to illuminate the path for future generations.

I must also express my profound appreciation to my editorial team for bringing this manuscript to life. Thank you Ken Shelton, Editor Extraordinaire, whose keen eye and thoughtful suggestions have inspired this work over many years. Many thanks to Zach Kristensen, MJ Fievre, Annie Oswald—including editors, proofreaders, and support staff—for getting the ball over the goal line.

Special thanks to Wendy Brown, whose support has been indispensable throughout this journey. No greater collaborator and supporter have I ever known.

In every sense, this book has been a collaborative endeavor. To all who have walked this path with me I thank you.

Most importantly, a heartfelt thanks to my family for their patience and understanding, and to all my friends who supported me through this journey.

Appendix A
Big Ideas to Remember

Principles Govern Everything—including your arena, craft, and work. If you align yourself to them, build greater capacity by abiding by their precepts, they will help you eliminate the interference and obstacles getting in the way of your best self.

Life Is Made of Moments. Moments are all we have. Here they come, now they are here, and then they are gone. When you optimize your moments (788,400 of them if you are lucky), life takes care of itself.

Flow Is Universal (Practically). You can find flow in just about any activity, anywhere, at just about any time—if you know how to tap into it.

What You Know (the Game Itself) Is Only as Good as Who You've Become. Whatever your life endeavor, there is the technical side of the game itself, which is unique and distinct (i.e., tennis, medicine, aviation, etc.). And then there are the Internal, External, and Time Flow Factors that influence every arena. Seek to improve on both sides of the equation.

Awareness Is More Than Half the Battle. Remember, broad focus = more light. Narrow focus = depth of field. These are trade-offs. You need to find a balance between looking broadly to identify your next WIN and staying focused on the game itself.

Phases of Learning (UI, CI, CC, UC). We begin all learning not knowing what we don't know (Unconscious Incompetence) and then become aware of what we don't know (Conscious Incompetence). We then can close the gap by intentional learning and practice (Conscious Competence), and then as we master our knowledge and skills can do them without thinking (Unconscious Competence).

Know Your Current Flow Assets and Flow Liabilities. Flow Liabilities = noise and interference. Flow Assets = greater focus and full engagement. Turning Flow Liabilities into Flow Assets has the greatest ROI.

There Is No Universal Flow Formula—Only Your Personal Flow Formula. By taking stock of your own Flow Assets and Liabilities (both internal and external), you can identify your own unique Personal Flow Formula specific to you and your situation.

Know What's Important Now (WIN) and Choose Your "One Thing." Of all the things you could improve, just "One Thing" can move the needle on everything (Secret #1). What's your "One Thing"? From a developmental perspective consider your "One Thing" from both the "what" and "who" perspective. What's the one technical skill that would up your current game? What's the one leadership skill that would help you deliver on it?

Look Broadly, Choose Wisely & Dig Deeply (Five Steps of the FOCUS Planning Process). Moving your needle requires that you shift from broad awareness to narrow focus, through multiple layers of depth—opening and closing the aperture as you move from abstract themes to concrete actions. The FOCUS Planning Process will help you do this.

Leverage Strategic Focus to Deliver Performance Focus. Strategic Focus is all about taking regular strategic pit stops to look under your own hood. By identifying your current Flow Assets and Flow Liabilities you can leverage your time off the field in order to build capacity to optimize your Performance Focus on the field.

The Five Alignments. Between the core dimensions (Internal, External, and Time) and the fifteen sub-dimensions there are Five Alignments. When there is nothing getting in the way of your designed Future (Alignment One); when you are fully engaged from the spiritual to the physical (Alignment Two); when all of your physical and social contexts are compelling you to thrive (Alignment Three); and when you have optimized your experiences in the Past (Alignment Four)—these together give you unhindered focus in the moment (Alignment Five).

Fail Faster and Better (The Five Elements). After identifying your "One Thing" place it at the center of your attention. Define the Inputs (time, energy, and resources) you are willing to invest; clarify exactly what you are going to do (the Process); observe the Outcomes you are getting, and utilize Feedback loops to assess your progress. If you are not getting what you want, modify your Inputs and Process (even the Outcomes, Feedback, and the Goal itself if necessary) *until* you get the results you want (Secret 2).

Think Like a Scientist (The Five Correlations). Understanding the relationship between what you are "doing" and what you are "getting" is critical. There are five to remember: 1. Doing anything to get anything (pure experimentation to see what happens); 2. Doing something more to get something more (more practice = more skill); 3. Doing something more to get something less (more exercise = lower stress); 4. Doing something less to get something more (less social media = more time with family); 5. Doing something less to get something less (less negative self-talk = less stress). Know that you can find success with any of these correlations.

You Are Either Getting Better or Getting Worse. Life is rarely static. If you are not intentional about your craft, knowledge and skills fall away. If you are a continuous learner and constantly look for new knowledge and innovative ways to do things, you can maintain a positive slope.

You Are Your Own Best Coach. While you should continue to learn from the experts and science of your craft, remember that you are and will always be your own best coach. Take continuous strategic stops to plan strategically in order to perform optimally.

There Is No Finish Line. Now that you have the skills to lead yourself more intentionally toward your best self, I hope that you see this as a lifelong process—recognizing that there is always another WIN—another "One Thing"—that this is a process of self-progression—here and beyond.

See Flow as a System. Every dimension and factor is interconnected. Influencing one influences others—for positive or negative effect. Attentional Leadership moves from two dimensions to three dimensions to showcase systemic connections.

Serve and Lead Yourself in Order to Serve and Lead Others. Although finding your flow is a very personal and very self-focused process, I hope you realize this great paradox: That all of this work on yourself is ultimately designed for you to be in the service of others, and that the principles that govern you are the principles that govern them, the team, the organization, the community and beyond. Attentional Leadership is knowing "Where," "When," and "How Long" to place your attention with intention on What's Important Now (WIN)—even that "One Thing" that moves everything. Attention = influence.

Appendix B
Attentional Leadership Resources

Welcome to Your Next Step in Attentional Leadership!

You've taken the first step by completing *The 3 Secrets of Attentional Leadership*®, discovering the importance of focusing on your WINS (What's Important Now), and unlocking your flow. But your journey doesn't end here—it's time to turn insight into action, moving from "knowing" to "doing." This is where your real growth begins.

As your guide on the path to Attentional Leadership®, we're excited to welcome you as the newest member of our community. To support your success, we've created an exclusive webpage just for emerging attentional leaders like you. It's packed with everything you need to continue your journey, amplify your leadership, and expand your influence.

What's waiting for you:
- **Tools and Resources:** Practical guides and downloadable content to help you apply Attentional Leadership principles in real life.
- **Courses:** Step-by-step programs to take your learning to the next level.
- **Community:** Connect with like-minded individuals who are committed to mastering focus and flow.

Ready to elevate your leadership?

Scan the QR code now to unlock the full power of Attentional Leadership!

About the Author

Dr. Bruce H. Jackson has dedicated his career to the development of individuals, teams, organizations, and communities that seek to maximize influence, leadership, and change.

Bruce is the founder of the Attentional Leadership® Institute —a strategy, training, assessment, and coaching firm dedicated to helping individuals, teams, and organizations achieve peak performance.

Formerly a consultant/educator/coach serving Korn Ferry/Hay Group, the Center for the Advancement of Leadership, InsideOut Development, Learning Strategies Corporation, BlueEQ, and others, Bruce works with global associations, Fortune 500 companies, colleges/universities, and non-profit institutions to develop and implement principles of performance, leadership, and change—for professionals, students, and public servants alike. On the side of philanthropy, Dr. Jackson directs the C. Charles Jackson Foundation and Charlie Life & Leadership Academy—advancing leadership centers, programs, training, and research throughout the world to develop a new generation of emerging and influential leaders.

Bruce earned his doctorate in Human and Organizational Systems from Fielding Graduate University, where his research led to the development of Attentional Leadership Theory™ (ALT)—a holistic and multi-dimensional approach to address strategic change.

Bruce earned master's degrees in counseling psychology (Boston University), Business Administration (University of Minnesota, Carlson School of Management), Organizational Development (Fielding Graduate University), and Public Administration (Harvard University, John F. Kennedy School of Government)—all of which provided a broad and deep understanding of human capacity building, leadership development, and organization effectiveness within diverse industries and arenas.

Bruce, his wife Marta, and their three children currently live in Highland, Utah.